MW01025898

Compendium of Theology

Compendium of Theology

BY THOMAS AQUINAS

Translated by Richard J. Regan

OXFORD
UNIVERSITY PRESS

2009

OXFORD
UNIVERSITY PRESS

Oxford University Press, Inc., publishes works that further
Oxford University's objective of excellence
in research, scholarship, and education.

Oxford New York
Auckland Cape Town Dar es Salaam Hong Kong Karachi
Kuala Lumpur Madrid Melbourne Mexico City Nairobi
New Delhi Shanghai Taipei Toronto

With offices in
Argentina Austria Brazil Chile Czech Republic France Greece
Guatemala Hungary Italy Japan Poland Portugal Singapore
South Korea Switzerland Thailand Turkey Ukraine Vietnam

Copyright © 2009 by Oxford University Press, Inc.

Published by Oxford University Press, Inc.
198 Madison Avenue, New York, New York 10016

www.oup.com

Oxford is a registered trademark of Oxford University Press

All rights reserved. No part of this publication may be reproduced,
stored in a retrieval system, or transmitted, in any form or by any means,
electronic, mechanical, photocopying, recording, or otherwise,
without the prior permission of Oxford University Press.

Library of Congress Cataloging-in-Publication Data
Thomas, Aquinas, Saint, 1225?–1274.
[Compendium theologiae. English]
Compendium of theology / by Thomas Aquinas ; translated by Richard J. Regan.
p. cm.
Includes indexes.
ISBN 978-0-19-538530-4; 978-0-19-538531-1 (pbk.)
1. Theology, Doctrinal—Early works to 1800.
2. Catholic Church—Doctrines—Early works to 1800.
I. Regan, Richard J. II. Title.
BX1749.T36 2009
230'.2—dc22   2009002155

Printed in the United States of America
on acid-free paper

To Brother Reginald

Preface

The *Compendium of Theology* (CT) is probably the least well known and least studied of Thomas Aquinas's general works. This is unfortunate, since the main book of the CT on faith summarily analyzes philosophical and theological dimensions of Christian belief in a nonacademic way easily accessible to an educated adult. In my opinion, the CT explores two central theological areas with extraordinary clarity and cogency: (1) the unity and diversity of the Trinity (CT I, 37–67) and (2) the unity and diversity of the incarnate Word (CT I, 207–212). Moreover, CT II, 9, contains Thomas's most expansive explanation of the beatific vision. Some material, of course, is highly speculative and less relevant (e.g., the detailed descriptions of the resurrected bodies of the just [CT I, 168], and of the last judgment [CT I, 244–45]).

The Latin text of the CT on which this translation is based is the Leonine edition: Thomas Aquinas, *Opera Omnia*, vol. 42 (Rome: Dominican Friars of San Tommaso, 1979). The text frequently indicates that the matter under consideration is related to prior sections. For the convenience of the reader, I have taken the liberty of inserting into the text the exact citation in square brackets. I have also incorporated the Scriptural references into the running text. I have followed the Hebrew numbering of the Psalms. The citations of Aristotle in the notes follow the usual Bekker notation. The numbered subdivisions are mine, not the Leonine text's.

For English translation of technical Latin theological terms (e.g., *suppositum*), I consulted the *Index Thomisticus* and E. A. Livingston, ed., *The Oxford Dictionary of the Christian Church*, 3rd ed. (Oxford: Oxford University Press, 1997). I translate some technical philosophical terms in nontraditional but,

I hope, not idiosyncratic ways. For example, I translate *esse* in a participial context as *existing* rather than *being* in order to emphasize the word's active rather than static or factual sense in the usage of Thomas. And I translate *actus* and *potentia* as *actuality* and *potentiality* in the context where *actus* signifies a thing or power, not a specific act, and *potentia* in the same context as *potentiality*.

Hackett Publishing Company has graciously granted me permission to adapt material from *A Summary of Philosophy* (Indianapolis: Hackett Publishing Co., 2003) for the Introduction and Glossary in this work. I am also grateful to W. Norris Clarke and Brian Davies, Professors of Fordham University, for their advice.

—Richard J. Regan
Bronx, New York

Contents

THE EFFECTS PRODUCED BY GOD

1. Creation and Diversity

2. Christ's Incarnation

Biblical Abbreviations

Acts	Acts of the Apostles
Col.	Colossians
Cor.	Corinthians
Eccl.	Ecclesiastes
Eph.	Ephesians
Ex.	Exodus
Ez.	Ezekiel
Gal.	Galatians
Gen.	Genesis
Hab.	Habakkuk
Heb.	Hebrews
Is.	Isaiah
Jas.	James
Jer.	Jeremiah
Jo.	John
Lam.	Lamentations
Lk.	Luke
Mic.	Micah
Mk.	Mark
Mt.	Matthew
Num.	Numbers
Pet.	Peter
Phil.	Philippians
Prov.	Proverbs

Ps.	Psalm
Rev.	Revelation
Rom.	Romans
Sam.	Samuel
Sir.	Sirach
Thess.	Thessalonians
Tim.	Timothy
Wis.	Wisdom
Zech.	Zechariah

Other Abbreviations

A., a.	article
CCL	*Corpus Christianorum, series latina*
chap.	chapter
comm.	comment
CS	Thomas Aquinas, *Commentary on the Sentences*
CSEL	*Corpus scriptorum ecclesiasticorum latinorum*
CT	Thomas Aquinas, *Compendium of Theology*
d.	distinction
Dion.	*Dionysiaca*
fund.	foundation
hom.	homily
n.	note or number
PG	J. P. Migne, *Patrologia graeca*
PL	J. P. Migne, *Patrologia latina*
Q., q.	question
SCG	Thomas Aquinas, *Summa contra gentiles*
ST	Thomas Aquinas, *Summa theologiae*
tr.	treatise
v.	verse

Compendium of Theology

Introduction

Christian writers such as John the Evangelist, the Apostle Paul of Tarsus, the Apostolic Fathers, and the Fathers of the Church expressed theological reflections on God and his plan of salvation for the human race. Early Church Councils struggled to find fitting words to express the mysteries of the incarnation and the Trinity. And ascetical writers, usually monks, focused on the interior life but generally perceived no need to study the physical world except as an instrument of spiritual or moral instruction.

Augustine of Hippo (A.D. 354–430) was the foremost Western Church Father, and medieval Western theologians regarded his explanation and exposition of Christian doctrine as authoritative and quasi-normative. Augustine's theology reflected the contemporarily dominant Neo-Platonist philosophical tradition.[1] Some aspects of Neo-Platonism were unacceptable to Christian thinkers. For example, the Neo-Platonist theory of emanation, the theory that the material world originated necessarily by a series of hierarchically descendent radiations from an infinite source, is clearly contrary to the Judeo-Christian tenet of creation. But there were other elements of Neo-Platonism that were attractive to Christian thinkers. The infinite perfection of the One of Neo-Platonism is compatible with the infinite perfection of the Christian God. The ideal forms of Neo-Platonism, if interpreted as ideas in the mind of God regarding the natures of the things he creates, ground the intelligibility of the world and his providence. And the Neo-Platonist emphasis on the superiority of spirit over matter resonated with Christian doctrine.

In the twelfth and thirteenth centuries of our era, the texts of the major works of Aristotle were reintroduced into Western Europe.[2] Aristotle's works,

apart from those on logic and rhetoric, had been lost to the West since the col-
lapse of the Roman Empire, although medieval thinkers knew citations of the
works by Latin authors. In the twelfth century, James of Venice translated the
Physics, the *De anima,* and the *Metaphysics* into Latin. In the thirteenth century,
Robert Grosseteste produced the first complete translation of the *Nicomachean
Ethics,* and William of Moerbeke revised the translations of James and newly
translated other works of Aristotle. In short, by the last quarter of the thirteenth
century, the basic corpus of Aristotle's philosophical works was readily available
to Latin-literate scholars of the universities of Western Europe. The Arabic commentaries on Aristotle by Avicenna (A.D. 980–1030) and Averroes (A.D. 1126–1198)
had also been translated into Latin by the middle of the thirteenth century.[3]

The Aristotelian approach to philosophy was attractive from many perspec-
tives.[4] Aristotle's explanation of intellection, rooted in sense perception and not
merely occasioned by it, seemed to correspond more closely to human experience. Where the Neo-Platonists regarded material things as ephemeral and
unintelligible apart from the ideal forms of which they were obscure reflections, Aristotle regarded material things as unqualifiedly real and intelligible by
reason of their own proper forms. Aristotle was thereby able to study material
things, including the human composite of matter and spirit, in terms of four
causes (efficient, final, formal, and material) and foster physical sciences, albeit
not physical sciences in the modern sense. (*See* Glossary, s.v. *Cause, Science
[Aristotelian].*) Where Neo-Platonists argued to the existence of the One from
internal data (ideas), Aristotle argued to the existence of the Prime Mover from
external data (motion and change).

Access to the texts of Aristotle's major works and the commentaries by Avicenna and Averroes invited and challenged Christian thinkers to find new ways to
understand the world, the human person, and Christian revelation. Reconciling
Aristotle with the tenets of the Christian faith posed serious problems. Aristotle
seemed to hold that the world always and necessarily existed, but the Christian
church teaches that God freely created the world, and that it had a beginning
and might have not existed. Aristotle's Prime Mover was a self-absorbed intelligence that had no providential design for the world or its human inhabitants, but
the Christian church teaches that God is an intelligence that has a providential
design for the world and each human being. Aristotle did not explicitly affirm
the personal immortality of the human soul, and he considered proper human
behavior exclusively as a prerequisite for happiness in this life, but the Christian
church teaches unequivocally that each individual soul is immortal, and that
proper behavior in this world is a prerequisite for blessedness in the next.

The nearly simultaneous availability of Averroes' commentaries in Latin
compounded these problems,[5] since Western thinkers considered Averroes the

authoritative interpreter of Aristotle. One might argue that Aristotle supposed rather than affirmed that the world is eternal and necessarily exists,[6] but Averroes explicitly affirmed that the world is such. One might interpret Aristotle to hold that the individual human is intellectual and so immortal,[7] but Averroes categorically denied that the individual human soul was intellectual by its own power and held that it perished with the dissolution of the human being. And Averroes asserted not only that philosophical reason and religious faith are different ways of thinking, but that the way of reason, that is, the way of philosophy, is superior to the way of faith, that is, the way of theology. (Needless to say, the latter position in particular aroused opposition from contemporary Muslim theologians.)

An important institutional change accompanied the infusion of Aristotelian thought into the culture of Western Europe in the twelfth and thirteenth centuries. Beginning at Bologna in the eleventh century, universities arose to provide scholarly and professional education.[8] Hitherto, the only centers of learning were the cathedral and monastic schools. With the rise of universities, the focus of formal learning went beyond basics (grammar, rhetoric, logic, and various mathematical skills) to higher disciplines (science, philosophy, and theology). Prominent among the new universities, especially in theology, was the University of Paris, which developed from the cathedral school of Notre Dame in the last quarter of the twelfth century. Like other universities, the University of Paris was a self-governing corporation of students and masters (i.e., professors). It was composed of four faculties: arts, medicine, law, and theology. In addition to the arts of writing and speech (grammar, rhetoric, and logic), and the mathematical arts (arithmetic, geometry, astronomy, and music), the arts faculty taught Aristotelian scientific and philosophical subjects (biology, physics, psychology, ethics, and metaphysics).

Another important institutional change was the foundation of the religious orders of the Dominican and Franciscan friars in the thirteenth century. Unlike monks, the friars were engaged in external apostolic ministries, and the Dominican Thomas Aquinas (A.D. 1224/1225–1274) and the Franciscan Bonaventure (A.D. 1217?–1274) were among the leading masters of the University of Paris faculty of theology. This is in contrast with the preceding two centuries, in which the leading Christian thinkers, Anselm (A.D. 1033–1109) and Bernard of Clairvaux (A.D. 1090–1153, were products of the monasteries.

The theology faculty of the University of Paris was the most distinguished in medieval Christendom and, in addition to Bonaventure and Aquinas himself, boasted such masters as Alexander of Hales (A.D. 1170/1185–1245) and Albert the Great (A.D. 1200?–1280). The lecture format in theology typically consisted of a bachelor's commentary on the *Sentences* of Peter Lombard (A.D. 1100?–1160) or a master's commentary on the Bible But the public disputation provided the discipline's cutting edge. In these disputations, students and masters would defend theses before all comers. Those defending theses would recapitulate objections, state and explain the defenders' contrary position, and reply specifically to the objections. The ST and the SCG adopted this basic question-and-answer format.

Some masters of the arts faculty of the University of Paris enthusiastically embraced a radical Aristotelianism regarding the world and especially the human soul similar to that of Averroes. Prominent among these masters were Siger of Brabant (A.D. 1240?–1281/1284) and John of Jandun (A.D. 1286?–1328). Since radical Aristotelian views about the world and the human soul are clearly in conflict with central tenets of Christian belief, masters who openly taught such views risked condemnation by church officials. Whether for this practical reason or for theoretical reasons, radical Aristotelians like Siger and John seemed to resort to what orthodox adversaries called a theory of double truth. Such a theory would involve maintaining that a proposition can be true from the perspective or reason and philosophy and simultaneously false from the perspective of faith and theology. Although Aquinas taught in the theology faculty, he strenuously contested positions of the philosophical arts faculty that he regarded as contrary to faith or reason.

Earlier medieval Christians sought Christian wisdom principally by meditating on Scripture. Twelfth and thirteenth-century theologians sought to supplement such wisdom with another kind. And so there arose speculative theologians like Albert, Bonaventure, and Aquinas. The contrast between the concerns of Bernard of Clairvaux and the speculative theologians illustrates the shift of intellectual focus. Bernard sought to gain Christian wisdom by seeking the ways of God to human beings in the mysteries of faith. The speculative theologians sought to gain Christian wisdom by seeking to trace the ways of human beings to God by the use of the natural gift of human reason. This was a watershed in the intellectual history of Western Christianity.

When the thirteenth-century Christian scholars read the works of Aristotle, they were introduced to a new way of looking at the physical world, the human constitution, and the possibilities of reason for the study of theology and ethics. But unlike the radical Aristotelians, they proceeded cautiously and critically, since Aristotle's assumptions or tenets about the eternity of matter and motion and Averroes' commentary were incompatible with the Judeo-Christian idea of creation. Most of all, they could not accept the position of Averroes that there is only one, collective human intellect (potential), which would entail denial of individual, personal immortality.

They could, of course, argue from Scripture that one or another tenet of Aristotelian thought or Arabic commentary was contrary to Christian faith. But

Aristotle and the commentators claimed to have demonstrated their position by reason, and so Christian thinkers needed to use reason to refute the assumptions or tenets they deemed erroneous. Christian thinkers also needed to demonstrate that their beliefs, however inaccessible to reason, were not contrary to reason. And to do these things, they had to learn how to philosophize and theologize speculatively, that is, to know what reason could prove or help to explain, and what reason could not.

Thomas Aquinas and the CT

As indicated, Thomas Aquinas was a Dominican friar who lived and flourished in the second and third quarters of the thirteenth century of our era. Born near Naples in 1224/1225, he studied with Albert at Paris and Cologne, became a master at the University of Paris in 1256 and taught there until sometime before 1260. He then taught Dominicans at Orvieto preparing for pastoral ministry and was assigned in 1265 to organize a house of studies for young Dominicans at Rome. He was assigned to the University of Paris in 1268 and taught there until 1272. He then established another house of studies at Naples and taught there for a year. Instructed to attend the Council of Lyons, he died en route at Fossanova in 1274.

In addition to major works (the *Commentary on the Sentences* of Peter Lombard, the SCG, and the ST), commentaries on Aristotle and the Bible, and treatises on disputed questions, Aquinas wrote the CT, a work less studied by scholars but one deserving to be better known. The prologue of the CT (I, 1) makes clear that the object of the work is to present a summary exposition of Christian doctrine. Modeling the work on the *Enchiridion* of Augustine of Hippo, Aquinas planned to explain the theological virtues of faith, hope, and charity in three successive parts (books). He completed only the first book and nine chapters of the second. He explains faith in relation to articles of the Creed, principally the Nicene-Constantinopolitan Creed but also the so-called Apostles' Creed, and he began to explain hope in relation to the petitions of the Our Father. We can reasonably assume that he would have explained charity principally in relation to the Ten Commandments, since his Lenten sermons at Naples (A.D. 1273) were organized around the Creed, the Our Father, and the Ten Commandments.

The CT is a resumé of Christian doctrine, and Aquinas says that it is an abridgment imitating the abasement of Christ when he became a human being (CT I, 1). In the course of summarizing Christian theology, he also advances explicitly philosophical arguments about God, the world, and the human constitution, that is, arguments based on reason rather than Scripture or church authority, as preambles of faith. The purpose of the CT is very different from the purpose of the *Commentary on the Sentences,* the SCG, the ST, and the treatises on disputed questions. The *Commentary on the Sentences,* the SCG, and the treatises on disputed questions aim to engage professionals and to convince them of the truth of Aquinas' positions. The ST is a summary of theology probably for prospective Dominican preachers. The *Commentary on the Sentences,* the SCG, and ST adopt the dominant style of medieval theological academic debate. In contrast, the CT aims to provide a manual for literate, nonacademic lay Christians. As a result, there are in the CT no explicit citations of Averroes or Avicenna, and only seven of Aristotle. The thought of Aristotle, of course, is implicit in many of Thomas's arguments (e.g., the arguments based of the distinction between actuality and potentiality). And Aquinas implicitly refutes the positions of Averroes and Avicenna when he states his own contrary positions (e.g., when he argues that each human being has a potential and an active intellect). Even Augustine, the preeminent theologian of the Western church in the Middles Ages, is infrequently cited.

The format of the CT reflects its nonacademic purpose. Aquinas typically states at the beginning of each chapter the topic or thesis under consideration, makes distinctions he considers necessary, and presents his arguments without supporting citations. Only rarely does he raise and answer objections (e.g., CT I, 52–52, 91–92, 132–33, 161). By contrast, the SCG and the ST state questions, pose objections, answer the questions, and respond successively to the objections.

Date of Composition

It is difficult to assign an exact date to the composition of the CT. Modern scholars have reached no conclusion that enjoys general agreement. The suggested dates range from A.D. 1259 to 1273. On the one hand, the incomplete state of the work suggests the top end of the scale (1272–1273). On the other hand, internal criticism indicates a stylistic affinity between the book of faith and the SCG, which supports dating the work between 1265 and 1267. J. Perrier has sensibly proposed that the two books on faith and hope were composed at different times.[9] As Perrier notes, the tone of the two books is very different, and the book on hope, unlike the book on faith, shows a strong affinity to the development followed in the Lenten sermons at Naples. In this hypothesis, Aquinas broke off composition of the CT after he completed the book on faith, probably in the period between 1265 and 1267, and resumed composition of the unfinished book on hope at Naples between 1272 and 1273. Sickness and death then prevented completion of the book on hope and any composition of the book on charity.

The Book on Faith: God

The book on faith has a two-fold object: the unity of the divine essence, the Trinity of persons, and God's effects in creatures (CT I, 3–184), and the humanity of Christ (CT I, 185–246). The first section of the book treats of God as one (CT I, 3–35) and triune (CT I, 37–67). The chapters on God as one treat of the Godhead as such, essentially a philosophy of God, in connection with the first article of the Creed: "We believe in one God." The treatment parallels that of ST I, QQ. 2–4, 7–11, 13–14, 19, 25, but the themes are often less developed. For example, the CT presents only two ways of proving God's existence, namely, from the movement and alteration of material things (CT I, 1) and from their contingent existence, namely, that they can (by reason of substantial change) exist and not exist (CT I, 6), whereas the ST offers five (ST I, Q. 2, A. 3). The CT does not even mention Anselm's so-called ontological argument (cf. ST I, Q. 2, A. 1). And he devotes only two articles (CT I, 4 and 25) to predication about God.

The argument for the existence of God from the contingent existence of material things is particularly interesting for the light it may shed on interpretation of the third way of the ST. The latter argument, although evidently arguing from the fact that material things can exist and not exist, uses temporal references that seem to assume or imply that the material world could not be eternal. The argument in the CT from the fact that material things can exist and not exist, on the other hand, has no temporal reference. According to the latter argument, contingently existing things (i.e., things that can come to be and pass away) can neither severally nor collectively explain their existence. Therefore, something intrinsically necessary (i.e., something that cannot come to be from something else and pass away) needs to exist, and ultimately something absolutely necessary (i.e., something intrinsically necessary whose existence does not depend on anything else). The argument in SCG I, 15, is similar.

Perhaps the arguments in the CT and the SCG, on the one hand, and the argument in the ST, on the other, are reconcilable. When Aquinas says in the argument in the ST that contingent things (i.e., substantially changeable things) at one time did not exist, he may mean only that something intrinsically necessary needs to cause the contingent things to come to be. And when he says that, if every existing material thing is contingent, there was a time when there was nothing, he may mean only that nothing at all would have existed to cause contingent things to come to be.

Indeed, if one interprets the third way in the ST as a different argument from the one in the CT and the SCG, an argument resting on a claim that contingent (i.e., material) things could not have always existed, an incongruous consequence follows. Since Aquinas maintains in the ST itself (ST I, Q. 46, A. 2) that reason cannot disprove the possibility that the world always existed, such an interpretation of the third way would evidently imply that he held contradictory positions about the possibility of an eternal world. Moreover, most commentators agree that the argument from the contingent existence of material things in the CT and the SCG is stronger than an argument predicated on the impossibility of eternal matter, and many would consider the latter invalid. If the commentators are right, then we need to ask why Aquinas would opt for the weaker argument in the third way.

Aquinas' treatment of the Trinity follows the traditional exposition of Augustine (*On the Trinity*). Aquinas explains the five properties or notions proper to the persons: (1) not generated or proceeding from another person, which belongs only to the Father; (2) generating, which also belongs only to the Father; (3) generated, which belongs only to the Son; (4) active procession, which belongs to both the Father and the Son; and (5) passive generation, which belongs only to the Holy Spirit. There are four relations: (1) of the Father to the Son; (2) of the Son to the Father; (3) of the Father and the Son to the Holy Spirit; and (4) of the Holy Spirit to the Father and the Son. There are three persons: the Father, the Son, and the Holy Spirit. There are two processions: the generation of the Son by the Father and the procession of the Holy Spirit from the Father and the Son. And there is one God. (A popular witticism summed up the count as "five notions, four relations, three persons, two processions, one God—and no proof!")

Philosophical reason, in Aquinas' view, can prove that God exists, and that there is only one God, and can predicate true things about him analogously. Moreover, theological reason can demonstrate how and why the Trinity does not contradict reason. But the Trinity itself remains an object of faith totally inaccessible to unaided human reason.

The Book on Faith: Creation and God's Effects in Creatures

After considering God in himself, Aquinas turns to God's causal activity and its effects. CT I, 68–74, 95–103, deals with creation and the diversity of creatures (cf. ST I, QQ. 44–47). CT I, 75–94, deals with intellectual substances, especially the human soul and its intellectual process (cf. ST I, 75–88, 90). CT I, 104–108, deals with the final end of intellectual creatures and with the beatific vision (cf. ST I, QQ. 1–5). CT I, 109–122, treats of God's goodness and the goodness of creatures (cf. ST, QQ. 5, 6, 48, 49). CT I, 123–43, deals with God's providence (cf. ST I, Q. 8, A. 13; Q. 14, A.13; Q. 19, A. 9; Q. 22) and his governance of the world (cf. ST I, QQ. 103–105, 108). Among other things, these chapters consider God's knowledge of future contingent things (CT I, 134), miracles (CT I, 136), and moral evil (CT I, 142). There is also a description of the hierarchy of angels (CT I, 126). Most of this analysis of creation and God's effects in creatures is essentially philosophical, although evidently relevant to Christian faith.

On the human soul, contrary to Averroes, Aquinas holds that each possesses its own active and potential intellect (CT I, 85–88), and that each soul is spiritual and immortal (CT I, 84). But contrary to Augustine, who holds that the human soul is a complete substance,[10] Aquinas holds that each soul is the form of the body in the proper sense, that is, the ultimate source of all the vital activities of human beings (CT I, 89), and that there are no other souls, namely vegetative and sensory souls, in the human composite (CT I, 90). In short, the individual human soul, like other substantial forms, is only part, albeit the determinative part, of each human composite, but unlike other substantial forms, the soul cannot perish because it is spiritual.

Many of Aquinas's contemporaries, especially those hostile to Aristotle, thought it theologically and philosophically impossible for the spiritual soul to be the form of the material body. (Even Albert, who usually followed Aristotle, held that the spiritual soul was not the form of the body in the proper sense, although the soul perfected and actualized the body.[11]) If the human soul is the form of the body, they argued, then the soul would be incomplete without a body and so incapable of existing apart from the body. But Aquinas thought that analysis of experience justified his conclusions that the substance of human beings is a composite of body and soul, *and* that the soul engages in intellectual activities intrinsically independent of matter. However paradoxical it may be that something intrinsically subsistent can be part of something else, and that a part of something could be something intrinsically subsistent, he did not hesitate to follow where the evidence of experience and the analysis of reason led him. Moreover, his position supplies a rationale for Christian belief in the resurrection of the body, since the soul united to the glorified body will again be a human composite.

The rest of the section on creation and creatures, indeed the rest of the book on faith in the second part on the humanity of Christ, is devoted to created things in explicit relation to salvation history. That is to say, Thomas moves from considering the created natural order with incidental reference to the supernatural order to considering the created supernatural order itself. CT I, 144–47, considers the role of grace in God's special providence for human beings and the remission of their sins (cf. ST I-II, QQ. 109–114). CT I, 148, argues that the whole created universe is for the sake of human beings, and CT I, 149–50, considers the ultimate end of human beings (cf. ST I-II, QQ. 1–5).

CT I, 151–63, considers the resurrection of the body, which is an article of Christian faith. Thomas does so in considerable detail. The discussion is, of course, highly speculative, since such an eventuality lacks any similitude in the empirical world, but Thomas is at least aware of some of the conceptual problems connected with the idea of a resurrection of long dead bodies. Whether his analysis is satisfactory is another matter. In connection with the final resurrection, CT I, 164–66, considers the beatific vision enjoyed by the just (cf. ST I-II, Q. 5); CT I, 167–69, the glorified body of the just; and CT I, 170–71, the renewal of material creation. CT I, 172–180, 183–84, discusses the punishment of hell in detail, and the need of purgatory (cf. ST I-II, Q. 87, and *De malo*, Q. 7, A. 10 and A. 11). CT I, 241–46, imaginatively speculates about the last judgment (cf. ST III, Q. 59).

The Book on Faith: The Humanity of Christ

The first part of the book on faith deals with God in himself, both one and triune, and his created effects, especially human beings. The second part deals with the humanity of Christ and closely follows successive articles of the Creed. CT I, 185, links the topics to articles of the Creed. CT I, 186–97, describes Adam's state of original justice (cf. ST I, Q. 94–97), Eve's sin, his sin, and his sin's consequences for his descendants (cf. ST I–II, QQ. 81–83). CT I, 198–219, considers the incarnation (cf. ST III, QQ. 1–19, 31–32), and CT I, 220, 202–8, specifically considers Christological errors condemned by early church Councils: those of Photinus, Nestorius, Arius, Apollinaris, Eutyches, and Mani. CT I, 220, explains the articles of the Creed about Christ's conception and birth. CT I, 221–26, treats of Mary's motherhood of Christ, her virginity, and her holiness (cf. ST III, QQ. 27–32). CT I, 227–40, treats of Christ's passion, death, and resurrection (cf. ST III, QQ. 46–56). CT I, 241–46, concludes with a description of the last judgment (cf. ST III, Q. 59). The last chapter (CT I, 246) summarily distinguishes all the articles of faith.

The Book on Hope

Book II begins to develop Aquinas's explanation of the theological virtue of hope in the context of the Lord's Prayer. The virtue is necessary for salvation

and expressed in petitions (CT II, 1–4). CT II, 5, explains the communal sig-
nificance of the word *Our* in the address to the Father. CT II, 6 and 7, explains
God's power to grant our petitions and the objects for which Christians can and
should hope. The last complete chapters, CT II, 8 and 9, deal with the first two
petitions of the Our Father: "Hallowed be thy name, thy kingdom come."

In chapter 9, Aquinas gives his most expansive explication of the beatific
vision. Happiness in the life hereafter consists of the vision of God (cf. ST I-II,
Q. 3, A. 8), a vision human beings are incapable of achieving by their natural
power. The vision of God, however, is not superimposed on the natural end of
human beings like a tower on a skyscraper. Rather, human beings have only
one end in the concrete order of salvation: incomplete happiness in this life
as human beings advance in intellectual and moral virtue, and complete happiness in the next life as they rest content in the vision of God. Indeed, since
human beings naturally desire to know complete truth, they *naturally* desire
to know God as he is in himself. Therefore, they cannot be completely happy
without the vision of God, although no finite intellect can behold him without
his assistance.

Chapter 9 is very long (504 lines in the Leonine text). It takes up again
themes about the end of human beings and the beatific vision already developed in CT II, 104–108, 149, 164–66, without the least allusion to the fact that
the topics have already been considered, albeit less comprehensively. This re-
inforces the argument that Book II was not written immediately after Book I.
The different perspective of Book II, however, may explain the repetition of the
themes. The book on faith set out the destiny of human beings in the context
of God's overall plan, and the book on hope explains the concrete state of Christian hope and it's dimensions.

An early copyist (MS. C¹ of the late thirteenth or early fourteenth century)
noted in a margin of CT II, 9, in what is line 35 in the Leonine text, a doubt
about the authenticity of the text (cf. Leonine edition, pp. 6–7). In addition to
the repetition of themes from Book I, the different style of II, 9, could have
attracted the attention of the copyist. For example, the expression *the result is*
(*consequens est*) appears 11 times in the first 200 lines of CT II, 9, but never
in CT II, 1–8. But the expression or its Latin equivalent (*fit*) belongs to Tho-
mist vocabulary (e.g., it appears seven times in CT I, 185–212), and the first
witnesses, including C¹, present the full text of CT II, 9, and the few lines of
CT II, 10. Therefore, despite the repletion of themes and the difference in
style in CT II, 9, the Leonine editors judge that there is no reason to doubt the
chapter's authenticity.

The remaining petitions of the Our Father would have offered Aquinas
an opportunity to touch on themes in the ST not yet considered in the CT.

Comment on the third petition, *Thy will be done,* etc., could have involved consideration of God's will and predestination (cf. ST I, QQ. 19–23). Comment on the fourth petition, *Give us this day our daily bread,* could have involved consideration of excessive solicitude about temporal affairs (cf. ST II-II, Q. 55, AA. 6 and 7). Comment on the fifth petition, *Forgive us our trespasses,* etc., could have involved consideration of God's justice and mercy (cf. ST I, Q. 21). Comment on the sixth petition, *Lead us not into temptation,* could have involved consideration of human sin (cf. ST I-II, QQ. 72–81). And comment on the seventh petition, *Deliver us from evil,* could have involved consideration of the devil (cf. ST I, Q. 114; ST I-II, Q. 80). But, regrettably, we can only speculate about what Aquinas would have done. On Thomas's treatment of the Our Father in the 1273 Lenten sermons, see Nicholas Ayo, *The Lord's Prayer: A Survey Theological and Literary* (Lanham, Md.: Rowman and Littlefield, 2002).

PART I

Faith

The Aim of the Work

The eternal Father's Word, comprehending all things in his immensity, in order to recall human beings weakened by sin to the height of divine glory, willed to become small by taking on our smallness, not by laying aside his majesty. He compressed the teaching on human salvation in a brief summary for the sake of those who are busy. He did this in order that no one would be excused from grasping the teaching of the heavenly word, something that he had extensively and lucidly transmitted in the various books of sacred Scripture for those devoted to learning.

For human salvation consists of knowing the truth, lest various errors confuse the human intellect; of intending our proper end, lest the human intellect defect from true happiness[1] by striving for improper ends; and of observing righteousness, lest diverse sins make the human intellect become unclean. And the Word included the knowledge of truth necessary for human salvation in a few short articles of faith. Hence, Paul says in Rom. 9:28: "The Lord will render summary sentence on the earth"; and in Rom. 10:8: "It is indeed the word of faith that we preach." The Word directed human intention by a short prayer, in which he taught us how to pray and showed us for what our aim and hope should strive. In a precept of charity, he summed up human righteousness, which consists of observing the law, since "love is the fullness of the law" (Rom. 13:10). And so Paul taught that the total perfection of the present life consists of faith, hope, and charity, as summary headings regarding our salvation, saying in 1 Cor. 13:13: "But now faith, hope, and charity abide." And so these three things are the ones by which we worship God, as the blessed Augustine says.[2]

Therefore, we direct our whole attention in the present work about these three things to transmitting to you, dearest son Reginald, a summary instruction on the Christian religion, instruction that you can always keep in mind. And we shall first treat of faith, second of hope, and third of charity, since this both retains the order of Paul and is required by right reason. For there cannot be right love unless the proper end of hope should be established, and we cannot establish the proper end of hope if one should lack knowledge of the truth. First, therefore, faith, by which you may know the truth, is necessary. Second, hope, by which your intention may be focused on the proper end, is necessary. Third, charity, by which your affection may be completely ordered, is necessary.

◄§ 2 §►

The Order of the Things to Be Said about Faith

And faith is a foretaste of the knowledge that will make us blessed in the future. And so also Paul says in Heb. 11:1 that faith is "the substance of things to be hoped for," as if causing the things to be hoped for (i.e., future blessedness) to subsist in us already in an inchoative way. Moreover, the Lord taught that the knowledge making us blessed consists of two objects, namely, the divinity of the Trinity and the humanity of Christ. And so, speaking to the Father, he says in Jo. 17:3: "This is the eternal life, that they may know you, the true God," etc. Therefore, the whole knowledge of faith involves these two things, namely, the divinity of the Trinity and the humanity of Christ. Nor is it strange that the humanity of Christ is an object of faith, since it is the way by which we can attain the divinity. Therefore, we need to know the way in our pilgrimage by which we can attain the end, and there would not be enough thanks to God in heaven were we not to know the way by which we have been saved. This is why the Lord said to his disciples in Jo. 14:4: "And you know where I am going, and you know the way."

And we need to know three things about the divinity: first, the unity of essence; second, the Trinity of persons; and third, the effects of divinity.

THE UNITY OF THE DIVINE ESSENCE

◄↭ 3 ↭►

God Exists

Regarding the unity of the divine essence, we first need to hold that God exists, and reason perceives this. For we see that everything moved is moved by something else: lower things by higher things (e.g., elements by heavenly bodies); weaker elements by stronger elements; and even lower heavenly bodies by higher heavenly bodies. An infinite series of moved causes of motion[3] is impossible. For everything moved by something is an instrument, as it were, of the first cause of motion. Therefore, every moved cause will be an instrumental cause if there should be no first cause of motion. But there is necessarily no first cause of motion if there should be an infinite regress of things that cause motion and are being moved. Therefore, all the infinite things causing motion and being moved will be instrumental causes. But it is ridiculous, even to the uneducated, to hold that instruments are moved without a chief efficient cause. For example, this is as if, regarding the construction of an arch or a bed, one should posit a saw or an axe without a carpenter at work. Therefore, there needs to be a first cause of motion that is supreme over everything, and we call this first cause of motion God.

◄↭ 4 ↭►

God Is Immovable

And the foregoing argument makes evident that God is altogether immovable, since he is the first cause of motion. Therefore, if he were to be moved, he himself would need to be moved either by himself or by something else. He cannot be moved by something else, since there would then need to be another cause of motion prior to him, and this is contrary to the nature of the first cause of motion. And if he moves himself, this might happen in one of two ways: either he causes the motion and is moved in the same respect, or he causes the motion by part of himself and is moved in another respect.

The first alternative is impossible. For everything moved, as such, is potential, and everything causing motion is actual. Therefore, if he were to be causing motion and to be moved in the same respect, he would necessarily be actual and potential in the same respect, which is impossible. The second alternative is also impossible. For, if there were to be one thing causing motion and something else undergoing motion, he would be the first cause of motion by the part of himself causing the motion, not by himself as such. But what is of itself the first cause of motion is prior to what is not. Therefore, he cannot be the first cause of motion if causing motion belongs to him by reason of part of himself. Therefore, the first cause of motion needs to be altogether immovable.

We can also consider this conclusion from things that are moved and cause motion. For every kind of motion seems to come from something immovable, namely, something that is not moved in that way. For example, we see that alterations, and coming to be and passing away, in lower material things are traceable to a heavenly body as the first cause of the motions. But a heavenly body is not moved at all in this way, since it cannot come to be or pass away, or be altered. Therefore, the first source of every motion needs to be immovable.

◄ξ 5 ξ►

God Is Eternal

And it is further evident from the foregoing that God is eternal. For everything that begins to exist or ceases to exist undergoes this by movement or change. But we have shown that God is altogether immovable. Therefore, he is eternal.

◄ξ 6 ξ►

God Necessarily Exists of Himself

And the foregoing shows that God necessarily exists. Everything that can exist or not exist is mutable, but God is altogether immutable, as I have shown [I, 4]. Therefore, it is impossible that God exist or not exist. And every existing thing that cannot not exist exists necessarily, since to exist necessarily and to be unable not to exist mean the same thing. Therefore, God exists necessarily.

Second, everything that can exist or not exist needs something else that causes it to exist, since such a kind of thing, as such, is open to both. And what causes something to exist is prior to it. Therefore, there is something prior to what can exist or not exist. But there is nothing prior to God. Therefore, such a thing cannot exist or not exist but necessarily exists. But there are some necessary things that have a cause of their necessary existence, a cause that needs to be prior to them. Therefore, God, who is the first of all things, does not have a cause of his necessary existence. And so God necessarily exists of himself.

◄ 7 ►

God Always Exists

The foregoing makes clear that God always exists. For everything that necessarily exists always exists, since what is unable not to exist, cannot not exist, and so such a thing always exists. But God necessarily exists, as I have shown [I, 6]. Therefore, God always exists.

Second, nothing begins to exist or ceases to exist except by movement or change. But God is altogether immutable, as I have shown [I, 4]. Therefore, he cannot have begun to exist or cease to exist.

Third, anything that did not always exist needs something to cause its being if it should begin to exist, since nothing brings itself from potentiality to actuality or from nonexisting to existing. But nothing can cause God's being. For he is the first being, since a cause is prior to its effect. Therefore, God necessarily always existed.

Fourth, what does not belong to something from an external cause belongs to it of itself. But existing does not belong to God from an external cause, since such a cause would be prior to him. Therefore, God has existing of himself. But things that exist of themselves, always and necessarily exist. Therefore, God always exists.

◄ 8 ►

There Is No Succession in God

And the foregoing makes clear that there is no succession in God. Rather, his existing is at once whole. For there is succession only in things that are in some way subject to motion, since temporal succession is the result of the prior and posterior things in motion. But God is in no way subject to motion, as I have shown [I, 4]. Therefore, there is no succession in him. Rather, his existing is at once whole.

Second, if something's existing is not at once whole, it necessarily could lose something and gain something, since it loses the thing that departs and can gain the thing expected in the future. But God neither loses nor gains anything, since he is immovable. Therefore, his existing is at once whole.

These two arguments make clear that God is eternal in the proper sense. For something that always exists, and whose existing is at once whole, is eternal in the proper sense. Just so, Boethius says: "Eternity is the all-at-once and complete possession of unending life."[4]

◄ 9 ►

God Is Simple

The foregoing also makes clear that the first cause of motion is necessarily simple. For, in every composition, there need to be two things related to each other as potentiality to actuality. But in the first cause of motion, if it is altogether immovable, there cannot be potentiality with actuality, for a thing is movable because it has potentiality. Therefore, the first cause of motion cannot be composite.

Second, there needs to be something prior to anything composite, since components are by nature prior to the composite. Therefore, the first of all beings cannot be composite. We also see in the order of existing things that simple things are superior to composite things. For example, the elements are by nature prior to mixed material substances, and fire, which is the subtlest element, is prior to other elements.[5] And heavenly bodies, which are constituted in greater simplicity because they are free of every contrariety, are prior to all the elements. Therefore, we conclude that the first of beings needs to be altogether simple.

◄ 10 ►

God Is His Essence

And it further follows that God is his essence. For the essence of each thing is what its definition signifies. And what the definition signifies is the same as the thing defined, unless by accident, namely, inasmuch as something besides the definition may belong to the thing defined. For example, white may belong to a human being besides whatever consitutes a rational and mortal animal. And so rational and mortal animal is the same as human being but not the same as a white human being insofar as the human being is white. Therefore, in whatever thing there are not two elements, one of which is intrinsic and the other accidental, the thing's essence is necessarily altogether identical with it. But there are not two elements, one intrinsic and the other accidental, in God, since he is simple, as I have shown [I, 9]. Therefore, his essence is necessarily altogether identical with himself.

Second, in whatever things the essence is not altogether identical with the thing to which the essence belongs, there is something by way of potentiality and something by way of actuality. For the essence is related as a form to the thing to which the essence belongs (e.g., humanity to human beings). But in God, there is pure actuality, not potentiality and actuality. Therefore, he is his essence.

◄੨ 11 ੭►

God's Essence Is Simply His Existing

It is further necessary that God's essence is nothing but his existing. In whatever thing the essence is one thing, and the existing another thing, it is necessary that the thing exists by one thing and is a kind of thing by the other thing. For we say of anything that it exists by its act of existing, but we say what something is by its essence. And so also the definition signifying the essence shows what the thing is. But there is not in God one thing by which he exists and another thing by which he is a kind of thing, since there is no composition in him, as I have shown [I, 9]. Therefore, his essence and his existing do not differ in him.

Second, I have shown that God is pure actuality without admixture of any potentiality [I, 9]. Therefore, his essence is necessarily his ultimate actuality, since every actuality that does not yet have its ultimate actuality is potential regarding it. But the ultimate actuality is existence itself. For inasmuch as every motion is a transition from potentiality to actuality, that toward which every motion tends needs to be the ultimate actuality. And inasmuch as natural motion tends toward what is naturally desired, this object needs to be the ultimate actuality that all things desire, which is existence itself. Therefore, the divine essence, which is pure and ultimate actuality, necessarily is existence itself.

◄੨ 12 ੭►

God Is Not in a Genus

And the foregoing makes clear that God is not in a genus as a species of it. Since a specific difference added to a genus constitutes a species, the essence of any species has something added to a genus. But existing itself, which is the essence of God, contains in itself nothing added to something else. Therefore, God is not the species of any genus.

Second, since a genus contains specific differences potentially, there is actuality mixed with potentiality in all the things constituted of a genus and specific differences. But I have shown that there is in God pure actuality without admixture of potentiality [I, 9]. Therefore, his essence is not constituted of a genus and a specific difference, and so he is not in a genus.

◄₹ 13 ₷►

God Is Not a Genus

And we need further to show that God also cannot be a genus. For we consider by a genus what a thing is, not that the thing exists, since specific differences constitute things in their own kind of existing. But what God is, is existence itself. Therefore, he cannot be in a genus.

Second, specific differences divide every genus. But it does not belong to existing itself to take on specific differences, since differences partake of a genus only incidentally, insofar as the species constituted by the differences partake of a genus. And there cannot be a specific difference that does not partake of existing, since nonbeing is not the specific difference of anything. Therefore, God cannot be a genus predicated of many species.

◄₹ 14 ₷►

God Is Not a Species Predicated of Many Things

Nor can we predicate God as a species of many individual things, since some things outside a specific essence differentiate different individual things that are the same in a specific essence. For example, human beings are the same in their humanity, but they are distinguished from one another by what is added to the nature of humanity. But this cannot happen in God, since he is his essence, as I have shown [I, 10]. Therefore, God cannot be a species predicated of many individuals.

Second, many individuals of the same species differ by their existing and are the same only in their specific essence. Therefore, whenever there are many individuals in a species, an individual thing's existing and its specific essence need to be different. But existing and essence are the same in God, as I have shown [I, 11]. Therefore, we cannot predicate God as a species of many things.

◅≀ 15 ≀►

There Is Necessarily Only One God

Hence, it is also clear that there is necessarily only one God, since, if there should be many gods, we would be speaking of gods either equivocally or univocally. If we should use the term equivocally, this use is not relevant to the proposition under consideration, since nothing prevents others from calling something a god that we call a stone. And if we should use the term univocally, the many gods would need to be generically or specifically the same, and I have shown that God cannot be a genus or species containing many things in it [I, 13–14]. Therefore, there cannot be many gods.

Second, that by which a common essence is individuated cannot belong to many things, and so, although there can be many human beings, a particular human being can be only one thing. Therefore, if an essence should be individuated by itself and not by something else, it cannot belong to many things. But the divine essence is individuated by itself, since the essence and what exists are the same in God. For I have shown that God is his essence [I, 10]. Therefore, there can be only one God.

Third, there are two ways in which a form can be multiplied: one by specific differences (e.g., a general form like color into different specific colors); the other by the subjects in which the form inheres (e.g., whiteness in different white things). Therefore, every form that cannot be multiplied by specific differences, if it should not exist in a subject, cannot be multiplied. For example, whiteness, if it were to subsist apart from a substance, would be unique. But the divine essence is his very existing, and it does not belong to existing to take on specific differences, as I have shown [I, 13]. Therefore, inasmuch as divine existing itself is an intrinsically subsisting form, as it were, since God is his existing, there can be only one divine essence. Therefore, there cannot be many gods.

◅≀ 16 ≀►

God Cannot Be a Material Substance

And it is further clear that God himself cannot be a material substance. For we find a composition in every material substance, since every material substance is something having parts. Therefore, what is altogether simple cannot be a material substance.

Second, material substances cause motion only by being moved, as is evident in all such things to those who study them. Therefore, the first cause of motion, if it is altogether immovable, cannot be a material substance.

◄≀ 17 ≀►

God Cannot Be the Form of a Material Substance

Nor can God be the form of, or a power in, a material substance. For, inasmuch as every material substance can be moved, things in a material substance are necessarily moved, at least by accident, when a material substance is moved. But the first cause of motion cannot be moved intrinsically or accidentally, since it is necessarily altogether immovable, as I have shown [I, 4]. Therefore, it cannot be the form or power in a material substance.

Second, a cause of motion, in order to be such, needs to have mastery over the thing to be moved. For example, we see that the more the power of a cause of motion surpasses the power of a movable thing, the swifter is the motion. Therefore, the first of all the causes of motion most of all needs to be the master of the things moved. But this could not be so if the first cause of motion were fettered in any way to a movable thing, as would need to be the case if it were the form or power of a movable thing. Therefore, the first cause of motion is neither a material substance nor the power or form in a material substance. This is why Anaxagoras posited a Mind separate from matter to command and move all things.[6]

◄≀ 18 ≀►

God Is Essentially Infinite

Hence, we can also consider that God is infinite. He is not infinite privatively, as the capacity of quantity to be acted upon is infinite, namely, as we predicate infinite of what is by reason of its kind of thing naturally constituted to have a limit but does not. Rather, God is infinite negatively, as we predicate infinite of what is in no way limited. For an actuality is limited only by the potentiality that receives it. For example, forms are limited by the potentiality of matter. Therefore, the first cause of motion is necessarily infinite if it is actuality without admixture of potentiality and is not the form or power in a material substance.

The very order found in things shows this, since the higher things are in the hierarchy of beings, the greater they are in their own way of being. For higher elements are greater in quantity as well as simplicity. And their generation demonstrates this, since fire is generated from air, air from water, and water from earth, in increased proportion. And it is obviously clear that a heavenly body surpasses the whole quantity of the elements. Therefore, what is the first of all beings and can have nothing else prior to it is necessarily of infinite magnitude in its own way.

Nor is it strange if we should hold that what is simple and lacks corporeal magnitude is infinite, and that it in its immeasurability surpasses every magnitude of a material substance. For our intellect, which is immaterial and simple, surpasses the quantity of all material substances by the power of its thought and includes all things. Therefore, what is the first of all things, including all of them in its universal immeasurability, surpasses them much more.

◄҂ 19 ѕ►

God Is Infinitely Powerful

Hence, it is clear that God is infinitely powerful. For power results from the essence of a thing, since each thing can act according to the way in which it exists. Therefore, if God is essentially infinite, his power is necessarily infinite.

This is also apparent if one should diligently look at the order of things. For each thing has receptive or passive power insofar as the thing is potential, and active power insofar as the thing is actual. Therefore, what is only potential, namely, prime matter, has infinite receptive power but shares in no active power. And the more form something has over prime matter, the more the thing abounds in active power. And so fire is the most active of all the elements. Therefore, God, who is pure actuality without admixture of potentiality, infinitely abounds in active power over all things.

◄҂ 20 ѕ►

The Infinite in God Does Not Signify Imperfection

And although the infinite found in quantities is imperfect, calling God infinite shows the greatest perfection in him. For the infinite in quantities belongs to matter insofar as matter is deprived of limit. But imperfection befalls something insofar as matter is deprived of form, and every perfection results from form. Therefore, inasmuch as God is infinite because he is pure form or actuality, without admixture of matter or any potentiality, his infinity belongs to the greatest perfection of himself.

We can also consider this from other things. It is true that, in one and the same thing brought from being imperfect to being perfect, the imperfect thing is prior in time to the perfect thing (e.g., one is a boy before becoming a man). Still, everything imperfect necessarily derives its origin from something perfect (e.g., a boy originates only from a man, and seed only from an animal or a plant). Therefore, what is by nature prior to all things, causing motion in all things, needs to be more perfect than all of them.

◄? 21 ?►

Every Kind of Perfection in Things Is in God and in Him More Eminently

From the foregoing, it is also apparent that all the perfections found in any things are necessarily in God originally and superabundantly. For everything that brings something to perfection has in itself beforehand the perfection that it brings into something else. For example, teachers already possess the learning they transmit to others. Therefore, if God, as the first cause of motion, brings all other things to their perfections, all the perfections of things need to preexist superabundantly in him.

Second, everything having a particular perfection if it should lack another is generically or specifically limited, since form, which is a thing's perfection, situates each thing in a genus and a species. But nothing constituted in a genus and a species can belong to an infinite essence, since the ultimate specific difference that posits something in a species limits its essence. And so also we call the concept denoting species a definition or limit. Therefore, if the divine essence is infinite, it cannot have only the perfection of a particular genus or species and be deprived of other perfections. Rather, it is necessary that the perfections of all genera and species exist in it.

◄? 22 ?►

All Perfections Are One in God

And if we should combine all the things that I have said hitherto, it is clear that all the perfections in God are really one thing. For I have shown before that God is simple [I, 9], and where there is simplicity, there can be no distinction of the perfections that are present. Therefore, if the perfections of all things are in God, they cannot be different things in him. Therefore, we conclude that all the perfections are one thing in him.

And this becomes manifest to one who reflects on cognitive powers. For a higher cognitive power knows by one and the same thing all the things that lower cognitive powers know by different things. For example, the intellect by one simple power judges all the things that sight, hearing, and the other senses perceive. The like is apparent in the sciences. There are many lower sciences regarding different kinds of things, which are their objects, but one science, which is superior to the others, is disposed toward all things, and we call this science first philosophy. The same is evident in governmental powers. For all the power dispersed in different offices under a king's control is included in royal power, since it is one and the same power. So also the perfections multiplied in lower things by the diversity of the things are necessarily united in the pinnacle of things, namely, God.

◄₹ 23 s►

There Is No Accident in God

The foregoing makes clear that there can be no accident in God. For, if all the perfections are one in him, and existing, power, action, and all such things belong to perfection, all the things in him are necessarily the same as his essence. Therefore, none of the things in him is an accident.

Second, nothing to the perfection of which something can be added can be infinite in perfection. But if there is something of which some perfection is an accident, a perfection necessarily can be added to the thing's essence, since every accident is added to an essence. Therefore, the perfection in its essence is not infinite. But I have shown that God by his essence is infinitely perfect [I, 19]. Therefore, there can be no accidental perfection in him. Rather, everything in him is his substance.

Third, we easily reach this conclusion from his supreme simplicity, since he is pure actuality and the first thing among beings. For there is a mode of composition of an accident in relation to the subject in which the accident inheres. And the subject cannot be pure actuality, since the accident is a form of the subject, and what exists intrinsically is always prior to what exists accidentally.

And from all these considerations as to the aforementioned things, we can hold that nothing in God is predicated as an accident.

◄₹ 24 s►

Many Names Do Not Take Away the Simplicity in God

And the foregoing makes clear why we predicate many names of God, although he in himself is altogether simple. For our intellect, since it is inadequate to grasp his essence in itself, rises to know him from the things in our midst, in which we observe diverse perfections, the root and source of all of which is one perfection in God, as I have shown [I, 19]. And inasmuch as we can name some-thing only insofar as we understand it, since names are the signs of things understood, we can name God only from the perfections found in other things, the source of which is in him. Because such things have many perfections, we necessarily assign many names to God.

But if we were to behold his essence in itself, many names would not be required. Rather, our knowledge of him would be simple, just like his essence, and we await this on the day of our glory, as Zech. 14:9 says: "On that day, there will be one Lord and one name of him."

◄⅔ 25 ⅗►

We Predicate Different Names of God,
but They Are Not Synonyms

And from these things, we can consider three things, the first of which is that different names, although they signify the same reality in God, are not syno-nyms. For in order for certain names to be synonyms they need to signify the same thing and represent the same intellectual concept. But where different considerations (i.e., understandings that the intellect has about a thing) signify the same thing, the names are not synonyms. They are not because they do not have completely the same meaning, since names directly signify intellectual concepts that are the likenesses of things. And so different names predicated of God, since they signify different understandings that our intellect has about God, are not synonyms, although they signify entirely the same thing.

◄⅔ 26 ⅗►

Definitions of the Names Cannot Define
What Is in God

The second consideration is that, since our intellect does not completely grasp the divine essence by any of the concepts that the different names predicated of God signify, definitions of the names cannot define what is in God. For example, the definition of power cannot be the definition of divine power, and similarly in the case of other names. And this is evidenced in another way. For every definition is by genus and specific difference, and, in the strict sense, what is defined is a species. But I have shown that the divine essence is not contained in a genus or a species [I, 13–14]. And so the divine essence cannot be defined.

◄₹ 27 ₷►

We Do Not Predicate Names of God and Other Things Altogether Univocally or Altogether Equivocally

The third consideration is that we do not predicate names of God and other things altogether univocally or altogether equivocally. The names cannot be predicated univocally. For the definition of what is predicated of a creature is not the definition of what is predicated of God, but names predicated univocally should have the same definition. Similarly, the names cannot be predicated altogether equivocally. For in the case of names equivocal by chance we apply the same name to one thing having no relation to another thing, and so we cannot through one thing reason about the other thing.

But we attribute the names predicated of God and other things to God by an order that he has to the things, regarding which our intellect considers what the names signify. And so we can also reason about God through other things. Therefore, the names are not predicated of God and other things altogether equivocally, as in the case of names equivocal by chance. Therefore, we predicate the names by analogy (i.e., by their proportion to one thing). For we attribute to God such names signifying the perfections of other things because we relate the other things to God as the first source. And it is clear from this that, regarding application of the names to God, we primarily predicate such names of creatures, since the intellect thereby ascends from creatures to God. Nevertheless, it is clear, regarding the thing signified by the names, that we primarily predicate the names of God, from whom the perfections descend to other things.

◄₹ 28 ₷►

God Is Intelligent

And further, it is necessary to show that God is intelligent. For I have shown that all the perfections of any beings preexist in him superabundantly [I, 21]. But of all the perfections of beings, understanding itself seems to be preeminent, since intellectual things are more powerful than all the others. Therefore, God is necessarily intelligent.

Second, I have shown before that God is pure actuality without admixture of potentiality [I, 9]. But matter is potential being. Therefore, God is altogether free from matter. But freedom from matter causes the ability to understand, and the fact that material forms become actually intelligible by being abstracted from matter and material conditions indicates this. Therefore, God is intelligent.

Third, I have shown that God is the first cause of motion [I, 3]. But this seems to belong to the intellect, since the intellect seems to use all other things as instruments, as it were, to produce motion. And so also human beings by their intellects use animals, plants, and nonliving things as instruments, as it were. Therefore, God, who is the first cause of change, is necessarily intelligent.

29

Understanding in God Is Actual, Not Potential or Habitual

And since there is in God only something actual and nothing potential, as I have shown [I, 4], God necessarily is intelligent only actually, not potentially or habitually. And it is clear from this that he in understanding undergoes no succession or alteration. For an intellect, when it understands many things successively, necessarily understands another thing potentially when it understands one thing actually. Therefore, if God understands nothing potentially, he understands without succession. And so it follows that he understands at once whatever he understands, since there is no succession of things that are simultaneous. And it also follows that he newly understands nothing, since an intellect newly understanding was something previously understood potentially.

So also it is clear that his intellect is not discursive, so as to come from one thing to knowledge of something else, as our intellect experiences in reasoning. For example, there is such a discursive process in our intellect from something known to knowledge of something that we were not actually considering before. And these things cannot happen in the divine intellect.

30

God Does Not Understand by Any Other Form than His Essence

The foregoing also makes clear that God does not understand by a form other than his essence. For every intellect that understands by any form other than itself is related to the intelligible form as potentiality to actuality, since the intelligible form is the perfection of the intellect that moves it to understand actually. Therefore, if there is pure actuality and nothing potential in God, he necessarily understands by his essence, not by another form. And so it follows that he directly and chiefly understands himself. For the essence of a thing does not properly and directly lead to knowing anything except that of which it is the essence. For example, we properly know human being by the definition of human being, and horse by the definition of horse. Therefore, if God understands by his essence, what he directly and chiefly understands is necessarily himself. And since he is his essence, it follows that his intellect, the means by which he understands, and the object understood, are altogether the same in him.

◄╡ 31 ╞►

God Is His Understanding

God is also necessarily his understanding. For understanding as actual consideration is the second actuality, since the intellect or habitual knowledge is the first actuality. Therefore, every intellect that is not its understanding is related to its understanding as potentiality to actuality. For in the order of potentialities and actualities, when speaking about one and the same thing, what is prior is always potential in relation to what follows, and the ultimate thing perfects. (The converse is true in the case of different things, since the thing causing motion and active is related to the thing moved and acted upon as efficient cause to potentiality.) But in God, since he is pure actuality, there is nothing that is related to anything else as potentiality to actuality. Therefore, God is necessarily his understanding.

Second, intellect is related to understanding in the same way that essence is related to existing. But God understands by his essence, and his essence is his existing. Therefore, his intellect is his understanding. And so we posit no composition in him because of the fact that he understands, since intellect, understanding, and intelligible form are not different things in him, and they are the same as his essence.

◄╡ 32 ╞►

God Necessarily Has Volition

And it is further clear that God necessarily has volition. For he understands himself, the perfect good, as is clear from what I have said [I, 30]. But one necessarily loves the understood good and does so by the will. Therefore, God necessarily has volition.

Second, I have shown that God is the first cause of motion through his intellect [I, 28]. But the intellect causes motion only through appetite, and the appetite that accompanies the intellect is the will. Therefore, God necessarily has volition.

◄¿ 33 ѕ►

God's Will Is Necessarily the Same as His Intellect

And it is clear that God's will is the same as his intellect. For the understood good, since it is the object of the will, moves the will and is the actuality and perfection of the will. But there is in God no distinction between causing movement and being moved, actuality and potentiality, or perfection and the perfectible, as is clear from what I said before [I, 9–10]. Therefore, the divine will is necessarily the very good understood. But the understood good is the divine intellect and the divine essence. Therefore, the will of God is the same as his intellect and his essence.

Second, the intellect and the will are more excellent than other perfections of things, and the fact that we find intellect and will in more excellent things indicates this. But the perfections of all things are one thing in God (i.e., his essence), as I have shown before [I, 22]. Therefore, intellect and will in God are the same as his essence.

◄¿ 34 ѕ►

God's Will Is His Willing Itself

Hence, it is also clear that the divine will is God's willing itself. For I have shown that the will in God is the same as the good willed by him [I, 33]. But this could not be so unless his willing were the same as his will, since willing belongs to the will by reason of the thing willed. Therefore, God's will is his willing.

Second, God's will is the same as his intellect and his essence. But God's intellect is his understanding, and his essence is his existing. And so it is clear that God's will is not repugnant to his simplicity.

◄¿ 35 ѕ►

An Article of Faith Includes All the Aforementioned Things

From all the things that I said before, we can conclude that God is one, simple, perfect, infinite, intelligent, and willing.[7] And all of these are included in the Creed in a brief article in which we profess our belief "in one God almighty."[8]

For the name *God* [Lat.: *deus*] seems to be so called from the Greek name *theos*, which is derived from *theaste* (i.e., to see or contemplate).[9] And so it is manifest in the very name of God that he is intelligent and, consequently, willing. In call- ing him one, we exclude plurality of gods and every kind of composition, since only something simple is absolutely one. In calling him almighty, we show that he has infinite power, from which nothing can be taken away. And that he is infinite and perfect is included in the latter, since a thing's power results from the perfection of its essence.

◄ 36 ►

Philosophers Hold All of These Things

Indeed, many pagan philosophers also acutely considered the things about God related in the foregoing chapters, although some of them erred about these things. And those who spoke the truth about these things could barely arrive at it after long and diligent inquiry. There are other things about God at which they could not arrive, things communicated to us in the teaching of the Chris- tian religion, things about which Christian faith instructs us beyond human understanding. And this is that, although God is one and simple, as I have shown [I, 9 and 15], there is God the Father, God the Son, and God the Holy Spirit, and these three are one God, not three gods. And we intend to consider this as much as it is possible for us.

THE TRINITY OF PERSONS

◄ 37 ►

How We Posit the Word in God

And we should understand from the things previously mentioned that God understands and loves himself [I, 21 and 32], and that understanding and will- ing in him are the same as his existing [I, 31 and 34]. Therefore, since God understands himself, and every understood thing is in one who understands, God is necessarily in himself as a thing understood in one who understands. And an understood thing, as it is in the one who understands, is a word of the intellect. For we signify by an external word what we internally understand in the intellect, since words are the signs of things understood, as Aristotle says.[10] Therefore, we need to posit God's word in him.

◆≀ 38 ≀◆

We Call the Word in God a Conception

And even in ordinary discourse, we call what is contained in the intellect as an internal word a conception of the intellect. For we say that anything formed in the womb of a living animal by a life-giving power is physically conceived, with the male the active party, and the female in which the conception takes place the passive party. And so the thing conceived belongs to the nature of both, and has specifically the same form, as it were. And what the intellect understands is formed in the intellect, with the intelligible thing the active thing, as it were, and with the intellect the passive thing, as it were. And the very object understood by the intellect, existing within the intellect, has the same form as both the intelligible thing moving the intellect (the thing of which the understood object is a likeness) and as the intellect being acted upon (insofar as the object has intelligible existing). And so we deservedly call what is understood by the intellect a conception of the intellect.

◆≀ 39 ≀◆

How the Word Is Related to the Father

And in this matter, we should consider a difference. For what is conceived in the intellect, since it is a likeness of the thing understood, representing the thing's form, seems to be an offspring of the thing. Therefore, when the intellect understands something other than itself, the understood thing is like a father of the word conceived in the intellect, and the intellect more resembles a mother, whose property is that conception takes place in her. But when the intellect understands itself, the word conceived is related to the one understanding as an offspring is to a father. Therefore, when we speak of the word insofar as God understands himself, we need to relate the word to God, to whom the word belongs, as a son to a father.

◆≀ 40 ≀◆

How We Understand Generation in God

Hence, we are taught in the rule of the Catholic faith to profess the Father and the Son, when we say: "I believe in God the Father and his Son." And lest anyone on hearing the names *Father* and *Son* suppose the carnal generation by which, among ourselves, we speak of fathers and sons, John the Evangelist, to whom heavenly secrets were revealed, substituted *Word* for *Son*. This was so that we acknowledge that the generation is intelligible generation.

◄? 41 ?►

The Word (i.e., the Son) Has the Same Existing and Essence as God the Father

And we should consider that in us natural existing is one thing, and understanding another. Therefore, the word conceived in our intellect, a word that has only intelligible existing, necessarily is of a different nature and essence than our intellect, which has natural existing. But existing and understanding in God are the same thing. Therefore, the Word of God, which is in God, and whose Word he is as to intelligible existing, has the same existing as God, whose Word he is. And so he necessarily has the same essence and nature as God, and all the things predicated of God belong to the Word of God.

◄? 42 ?►

The Catholic Faith Teaches These Things

And so we are taught in the rule of the Catholic faith that the Son is "of the same substance as the Father," which excludes two things. First, it excludes understanding the Father and the Son by the carnal generation that cutting off the substance of a son from a father causes, with the consequence that the Son would necessarily not be of the same substance as the Father. Second, it also excludes understanding the Father and the Son by intelligible generation as we conceive a word in our mind, as if the word comes accidentally to the intellect and does not belong to its essence.

◄? 43 ?►

In God, the Word Does Not Differ by Time, Form, or Nature from the Father

And things essentially the same cannot differ by time, form, or nature. Therefore, the Word, since it is consubstantial with the Father, necessarily cannot differ from the Father in any of the said ways. The Word cannot differ from the Father by time. For, regarding the Word in God, we hold that God understands himself by intelligibly conceiving his Word. Therefore, it is necessarily the case that, if the Word of God did not exist at some time, God would not have then understood himself. But God, whensoever he existed, always understood himself, since his understanding is his existing. Therefore, his Word also always existed. And so we say in the rule of the Catholic faith that the Son of God is "eternally begotten of the Father."

It is also impossible that the Word of God differ from God by form, as if something lessened, since God knows himself no less than what he is. But the Word has perfect form because that of which the Word is such is perfectly understood. Therefore, the Word of God is necessarily altogether perfect by the form of divinity.

But we find that some things that come from other things do not acquire the perfect form of those things. This happens in one way in nonunivocal generations (e.g., the sun generates an animal, not a sun). Therefore, in order to exclude such imperfection from divine generation, we profess that the Son is begotten "God from God."

It happens in a second way that something generated or coming from something falls short of the thing from which it comes because of lack of purity. Such is the case when, from something in itself simple and pure, something falling short of the first form comes about by application to extraneous matter. For example: a house in matter results from the house in a builder's mind; color results from light received on the surface of a material substance; a mixed material substance results from fire added to other elements; and a shadow results from a ray of light against a dark material substance. Therefore, to exclude this from divine generation, the Creed adds: "Light from light."

Third, something coming from something does not acquire the latter's form because of lack of truth, namely, in that it receives only a likeness, not truly the nature, of the latter. Examples of this are the image of a human being in a mirror, a picture, or a sculpture, or the likeness of a thing in our intellect or one of our senses, since we call the image of a human being the likeness of a human being, not a true human being. As Aristotle says[11]: "The form of a stone, not the stone, is in the soul." Therefore, in order to exclude this from divine generation, the Creed adds: "True God from true God."

The Word also cannot differ by nature from God, whose Word it is, since it is natural to God to understand himself. For every intellect has some things that it by nature understands (e.g., our intellect by nature understands first principles). Therefore, much more does God, whose understanding is his existing, by nature understand himself. Therefore, his Word is from him by nature, not as things that come about in ways other than natural origin, as, for example, artifacts, which we are said to make, come from us. But we are said to beget things that by nature come from us (e.g., a son). Therefore, lest we think that the Word of God comes from God by the power of his will and not by nature, the Creed adds: "Begotten, not made."

◄✕ 44 ✕►

Conclusion from the Foregoing

All the aforementioned conditions of divine generation belong to the fact that the Son is of the same substance as the Father, as the foregoing things make clear. Therefore, the Creed afterward adds as a summary of all of them: "Of the same substance as the Father."

◄✕ 45 ✕►

God Is in Himself as Beloved Object in the Lover

And as the understood object, inasmuch as it is such, is in the one who understands, so also the beloved object, inasmuch as it is such, is in the one who loves. For the beloved object by an internal movement somehow moves the lover. And so, since a cause of movement is in contact with the thing moved, the beloved object is necessarily intrinsic to the lover. But as God understands himself, so he necessarily loves himself, since the understood good as such is loveable. Therefore, God is in himself as beloved object in the lover.

◄✕ 46 ✕►

We Call Love in God the Spirit

And although the understood thing is in the one who understands, and the loved thing in the one who loves, we need to consider the different nature of what it is to be such in each way. For, inasmuch as understanding comes about by an assimilation of the one who understands to what is understood, the understood thing is necessarily in one who understands, insofar as the thing's likeness exists in such a one.

But loving comes about by the beloved object moving the lover, since the beloved object draws the lover to itself. Therefore, loving is completed in the attraction of the lover to the beloved object, not in the likeness of the beloved object in the one who loves, as understanding is completed in the likeness of the understood thing being in the one who understands.

The transmission of likeness is chiefly accomplished by univocal genera-tion, regarding which we call the begetter in living things a father, and the begotten a son, and the spirit in living things causes the first movement. There-fore, in God, by what we call the Son, who is the Word of God, we express the way in which God is in himself as an understood thing is in the one who understands. Just so, by positing in God the Spirit, who is God's love, we ex-press the way in which God is in himself as the beloved object in the lover. And so the rule of the Catholic faith obliges us to believe in the Spirit.

◄≀ 47 ≀►

The Spirit in God Is Holy

And we should consider that, since the loved good has the nature of end, and the end renders the movement of the will good or evil, the love in which the highest good (i.e., God) is loved must have an eminent goodness. And we call this goodness by the name *holiness,* whether called holy as pure, in the sense of the Greeks, since there is in God the purest goodness free of every kind of defect, or called holy meaning firm, in the sense of the Latins, since there is immutable goodness in God.

And so we also call holy all the things ordered to God (e.g., the temple, ves-sels of the temple, and all the things dedicated to divine worship). Therefore, we appropriately call the Spirit, who implants in us the love by which God loves himself, the Holy Spirit. And so also the rule of the Catholic faith calls the aforementioned Spirit holy, when we say: "I believe in the Holy Spirit."

◄≀ 48 ≀►

Love in God Does Not Signify an Accident

And as God's understanding is his existing, so also is his loving. Therefore, God loves himself by his essence, not by something coming in addition to his essence. Therefore, since he loves himself because he is in himself as the be-loved in the lover, God the beloved is not in God the lover in an accidental way, as beloved objects are in us accidentally when we love. Rather, God is substan-tially in himself as the beloved object in the lover. Therefore, the Holy Spirit, who imparts divine love in us, is something subsistent in the divine essence just like the Father and the Son, not something accidental in God. And so the rule of the Catholic faith shows that we should equally adore and glorify him along with the Father and the Son.

The Holy Spirit Proceeds from the Father and the Son

We should also consider that understanding itself proceeds from the power of
the intellect to understand. But insofar as the intellect actually understands, what
is understood is in the intellect. Therefore, the fact that the understood thing
is in one who understands comes from the intellectual power of the one who
understands, and the understood thing is the word of one who understands, as
I have said before [I, 37]. Likewise, insofar as the beloved object is actually loved,
it is in the lover. But the fact that something is actually loved proceeds both
from the lover's power to love and from a loveable good that is actually understood. Therefore, the fact that the beloved object is in the lover comes from two
sources, namely the love's source and the understood intelligible thing that is
the word conceived about the loveable object. The Word in God understanding
and loving himself is the Son, and the one to whom the Word belongs is the
Father of the Word, as is clear from what I have said before [I, 39]. Therefore,
the Holy Spirit, who belongs to love insofar as God is in himself as the beloved
object in the lover, necessarily proceeds from the Father and the Son. And so the
Creed says: "Who proceeds from the Father and the Son."

In God, the Trinity of Persons Is Not Repugnant
to the Unity of Essence

And to conclude from all of the foregoing, we need to hold that there is a Trinity
in the divinity that is nonetheless not repugnant to the unity and simplicity of
the divine essence. For one ought to concede both that God exists in his nature,
and that he is understood and loved by himself. But this happens in God and
us in different ways.

For the human being in its nature is a substance, and the human being's
understanding and loving are not. Therefore, human beings are subsistent
things insofar as we consider them in their nature, but they are intellectual
representations of subsistent things, not subsisting things, insofar as they exist
in their intellect. And the same is true insofar as they exist in their selves as
beloved objects in lovers. Therefore, we can consider three things regarding a
human being: the human being that exists in its nature; the human being that
exists in the intellect; and the human being that exists in love. But these three

are not one thing, since the understanding of a human being is not the existing of the human being. Nor is the loving of a human being the existing of the human being. And of these three things, only the human being that exists in its nature is a subsistent thing.

But existing, understanding, and loving are identical in God. Therefore, God in his natural existing, God in his intellect, and God in his love are one and the same thing, and yet each of them is subsistent. Latins are accustomed to call subsistent things in an intellectual nature persons, and Greeks to call such things hypostases. Therefore, Latins speak of three persons in God, and Greeks of three hypostases, namely, the Father, the Son, and the Holy Spirit.

◄¿ 51 s►

How Positing Number in God Seems to Be Contradictory

But the aforementioned things seem to give rise to a contradiction. For if we posit a Trinity in God, we shall need to posit a difference in God that distinguishes the three persons from one another, since every plurality results from a division. And so there will not be the highest simplicity in God. For if the three are one in something and differ in something else, there must be composition in the three, and this is contrary to what I have said before [I, 19]. Moreover, if there is necessarily only one God, as I have shown before [I, 15], and no single thing arises and comes from itself, it seems impossible that there should be God begotten or God proceeding. Therefore, it is false to posit in God the names of Father, Son, and the Spirit proceeding from them.

◄¿ 52 s►

The Rational Explanation: The Differences in God
Are Only by Relations

We need to derive the principle for resolving this difficulty from the fact that things arise or proceed from other things in different ways in different things according to their different natures. For example, in nonliving things, since they do not move themselves, and only external things can move them, something externally altered or changed, as it were, arises from another thing (e.g., fire from fire, and air from air). But in living things, which have the property of moving themselves, something (e.g., the fetus of an animal and the fruit of a plant) is generated in the thing generating it.

And in living things, one should consider the different way of procession by different powers and activities of the powers. For example, there are some powers in living things whose activities reach only material substances insofar as they are material, as is evident about the powers of the vegetative soul (i.e., nutrition, growth, and reproduction). And by this kind of powers of the soul, only a corporeally distinct material thing comes to be, but a thing comes to be in living things somehow joined to the thing from which it comes to be.

And there are in living things some powers whose activities, although they do not transcend material substances, extend to the forms of material substances by receiving the forms apart from matter. This is true of all the powers of the sensory soul. For a sense receives a form apart from matter, as Aristotle says.[12] And such powers, although they receive the forms of things somehow immaterially, do not receive the forms apart from a bodily organ. Therefore, if there should be any procession in such powers of the soul, what comes to be will not be anything corporeal, whether corporeally distinct or corporeally joined to that from which it comes. Rather, what comes to be does so incorporeally and somehow immaterially, although not entirely without the support of a bodily organ. For the forms of imagined things, which are in the imagination in a spiritual way, not as a material substances in a material substance, come to be in animals in that way. And so also Augustine calls imaginary vision spiritual.[13]

And if, regarding activity of the imagination, something does not proceed in a material way, far more surely will this happen by activities of the soul's intellectual part, whose activity is altogether immaterial, not even needing a bodily organ in its activity. For the word comes to be by intellectual activity as something existing in the intellect of the one uttering it, indeed existing in the intellect by the power of natural activity, but distinct from the intellect by the order of its origin. The word is not contained in the intellect spatially, as it were, nor is it corporeally separate from it. And the reasoning is the same about the procession that we note regarding activity of the will, as the beloved object exists in the lover, as I have said before [I, 45].

The intellectual and sensory powers are by their nature more excellent than the powers of the vegetative soul. But nothing subsistent in the nature of the same species comes to be in human beings or other animals by the procession of the imaginative or sensory parts of the soul. Rather, this happens only by the procession produced by activity of the vegetative soul. This is so because, in all things composed of matter and form, division of matter produces multiplication of individuals in the same species. And so, in human beings and other animals, since they are composed of form and matter, the corporeal division found in the procession by activity of their vegetative soul, not in other activities of the soul, multiplies individuals in the same species. And in things not composed of matter and form, there can be only a distinction of form. But if the form by which we note the distinction should be the substance of a thing, the distinction necessarily belongs to particular subsistent things. This is not so if the form should not be the substance of a thing.

Therefore, it is common in the case of every intellect that what the intellect conceives necessarily proceeds in some way from the one who understands insofar as the knower understands. And it is by its procession distinguished in some way from the one who understands. What I have said before makes this clear [I, 37 and 49]. For example, the concept of the intellect (i.e., the intellectual representation) is distinguished from the intellect understanding. Likewise, the affection of one who loves, by which the beloved object is in the lover, necessarily proceeds from the will of the lover inasmuch as the lover is loving. But it belongs singularly to God's intellect that its concept (i.e., its intellectual representation) is necessarily his substance, since his understanding is his existing. And the same is true about the affection in God loving. Therefore, we conclude that the divine intellect's representation (i.e., God's Word) is distinguished from what produces it only by the relation of the procession of one thing from the other, not in being a substance. And the same thing is true about the affection of love in God loving, which belongs to the Holy Spirit.

Therefore, it is clear that nothing prevents the Word of God (i.e., the Son) from being substantially one with the Father and yet distinguished from him by the relation of procession, as I have shown above. And so also it is clear that the same thing neither arises nor proceeds from itself, since the Son is distinguished from the Father insofar as the Son proceeds from the Father. The reasoning is the same about the Holy Spirit by his relation to the Father and the Son.

◄§ 53 §►

The Relations That Distinguish the Father, the Son, and the Holy Spirit Are Real and Not Purely Conceptual

And the relations that distinguish the Father, the Son, and the Holy Spirit from one another are real relations and not purely conceptual. For the relations that extend to something that exists only in understanding, not to something that exists in the nature of things, are purely conceptual. For example, right and left regarding a stone are purely conceptual relations, not real ones. For such relations do not result from any real property in an existing stone but only from the conception of one who understands a stone as something on the left because it is to the left of an animal. But right and left are real relations in the animal, since such relations result from certain capacities found in particular parts of the animal. Therefore, since the aforementioned relations, by which the Father,

Son, and Holy Spirit are distinguished, really exist in God, the relations are necessarily real and not purely conceptual.

Such Relations Are Not Inhering Accidentally

Such relations also cannot be inhering accidentally. This is because the activities to which the aforementioned relations extend are the very substance of God, and also because I have shown before that there cannot be any accident in God [I, 23]. And so, if the aforementioned relations really exist in God, they are necessarily subsistent and are not inhering accidentally. And from what I have set forth before [I, 23], it is clear how what is an accident in other things can exist substantially in God.

≈ 55 ≈

The Aforementioned Relations in God Constitute
Personal Distinction

Therefore, since the distinctions in God are by subsistent, not accidental, relations, and there is personal distinction of subsistent things in any intellectual nature, the aforementioned relations in God necessarily constitute personal distinction. Therefore, the Father, the Son, and the Holy Spirit are three persons, and also three hypostases, since hypostasis means a complete subsistent thing.

≈ 56 ≈

There Cannot Be More than Three Persons in God

There cannot be more than three persons in God, since there can be multiple divine persons only by reason of the relation of a procession, not by division of the substance. And there also cannot be many persons by the relation of any kind of procession but of such a procession that the terminus is not something external. For if the terminus were something external, it would not have the divine nature, and so it would not be a divine person or hypostasis. But we can understand a procession in God that does not terminate in something external only by the activity of the intellect, as a word proceeds, or by the activity of the will, as love proceeds, as is clear from I have said before [I, 37 and 45]. Therefore, a divine person can proceed only as the Word that we call the Son, or as the Love that we call the Spirit.

Second, since God by his intellect understands all things in one intuition and also loves all things by one act of the will, there cannot be several words or several loves in God. Therefore, if the Son proceeds as Word, or the Holy Spirit as Love, there cannot be several Sons or several Holy Spirits.

Third, the perfect is that beyond which there is nothing. Therefore, what allows something of its own kind outside of itself is not absolutely perfect. And so also things absolutely perfect in their natures, such as God, the sun, the moon, and other like things, are not numerically multiple. But both the Son and the Holy Spirit are necessarily absolutely perfect, since each of them is God, as I have shown [I, 41 and 48]. Therefore, there cannot be several Sons or several Spirits.

Fourth, that by which something subsistent is this particular thing distinct from other things cannot be numerically multiple, since something individual cannot be predicated of many things. But the Son by sonship is this particular divine person subsistent in himself and distinct from other things, as, for example, Socrates is this human person by individuating sources. Therefore, as the individuating sources whereby Socrates is this human being can belong only to one thing, so also sonship in God can belong only to one thing. And the same is true about the relation of the Father and the Holy Spirit. Therefore, there cannot be several Fathers or several Sons or several Holy Spirits in God.

Fifth, things the same as to form can be numerically multiplied only by matter, as, for example, whiteness is multiple by being in many subjects. But there is no matter in God. Therefore, anything specifically and formally the same in God cannot be numerically multiple. But fatherhood, sonship, and the procession of the Holy Spirit are such. Therefore, there cannot be several Fathers or Sons or Holy Spirits.

◄ё 57 ѕ►

On the Properties, or Notions, in God, and How
Many There Are in the Father

And with such being the number of persons in God, it is necessary that there also is a definite number of properties of the persons whereby they are distinguished from one another. And three properties belong to the Father. First, there is a property by which he is distinguished only from the Son, and this is fatherhood. Second, there is a property by which he is distinguished from the other two, namely, the Son and the Holy Spirit. This consists of his being without a source, since he, unlike the Son and the Holy Spirit, is not God proceeding from another. Third, there is a property by which the Father along with the Son are distinguished from the Holy Spirit, and we call this the common origination of the Spirit by them. But we need not assign a property by which the Father differs from the Holy Spirit alone,[14] since the Father and the Son are the same source of the Holy Spirit, as I have shown [I, 49].

◄ 58 ►

What and How Many Are the Properties of the
Son and the Holy Spirit

And two properties need to belong to the Son: one by which he is distinguished from the Father, and this is sonship; a second by which, along with the Father, he is distinguished from the Holy Spirit, and this is, to repeat, the common origination of the Spirit by them. But we need not assign a property by which he is distinguished from the Holy Spirit alone,[15] since the Son and the Father are one and the same source of the Holy Spirit, as I have already said [I, 49 and 57]. Likewise, we need not assign a property by which the Holy Spirit and the Son together are distinguished from the Father. For the Father is distinguished from them by a property, namely, his being without a source, insofar as he is not anything proceeding. But because the Son and the Holy Spirit proceed by several processions, not by one, they are distinguished from the Father by two processions.

And the Holy Spirit has only one property, by which he is distinguished from the Father and the Son together, and we call this property procession. And there cannot be a property by which the Holy Spirit is distinguished from the Father alone or from the Son alone, as is clear from I said above.

Therefore, there are five properties attributed to the persons, namely, being without a source, fatherhood, sonship, common origination of the Spirit, and procession of the Spirit.

◄ 59 ►

Why We Call These Properties Notions

And we call these five things notions of the persons because they bring us to know the distinction of persons in God. Still, we cannot call them properties if we should retain in the idea of property that *proper* means what belongs only to one thing, since the common origination of the Spirit belongs to the Father and the Son. But nothing prevents us from calling even the common origination of the Spirit a property in the way in which we call something proper to some things in contrast to other things (e.g., two-footed is proper to human beings and birds in contrast to quadrupeds).

And since we distinguish the persons in God only by relations, and notions are the means by which we note the distinction of divine persons, all the notions necessarily belong in some way to the relations. But four of these notions are real relations by which the divine persons are related to one another. And the fifth, namely, being without a source, belongs to relation as the negation of one. For we trace negations back to the genus of affirmations, and privations to the genus of things possessed (e.g., nonhuman being to the genus of human being, and nonwhite to the genus of whiteness).

But we should note that some of the relations whereby the persons are related to one another have names (e.g., fatherhood and sonship, which properly signify relations). Other relations, namely, those by which the Father and Son are related to the Holy Spirit, and the Holy Spirit to them, lack names, and we use the names of origin instead of relations. For it is clear that the common origination and the procession of the Spirit signify origin, not the relations that result from the origin, and we can consider this from the relations of the Father and the Son. For generation signifies the active generation by the Father, from which the relation of fatherhood results, and being generated signifies the passive generation of the Son, from which the relation of sonship results. Likewise, therefore, a relation results from the common origination of the Spirit and also one from the procession of the Spirit, but we use the names of the acts for the names of the relations, since the relations lack names.

◀ 60 ▶

Although There Are Four Relations Subsisting in God,
There Are Only Three Persons

And we should consider that, although the subsistent relations in God are the divine persons themselves, as I have said before [I, 55], it is not necessary that there should be five or four persons by reason of the number of relations. For number results from a difference. For example, as one thing is indivisible or undivided, a plurality is divisible or divided. Therefore, for plurality of the persons, the relations need to have the power to differentiate by reason of contrariety, since there is formal distinction only by contrariety. Therefore, if we should look closely at the aforementioned relations, fatherhood and sonship have contrariety relative to each other, and so they are incompatible in the same subject. Therefore, fatherhood and sonship necessarily consist of two subsistent persons. But being without a source is not contrary to fatherhood, although it is contrary to sonship. And so fatherhood and being without a source can belong to one and the same person.

Similarly, the common origination of the Spirit is not contrary to fatherhood or sonship or being without a source. And so nothing prevents the common origination from belonging to both the person of the Father and the person of the Son. Therefore, the common origination of the Spirit is not a person subsisting apart from the person of the Father and the person of the Son. But the procession of the Spirit has contrariety relative to the common originating of him. And so, since the common origination belongs to the Father and the Son, the subsistent procession is necessarily a different person than the person of the Father and the person of the Son.

And so it is clear why we call God three-fold because of the three persons but do not call him five-fold because of the five notions. For the three persons are three subsistent things, but the five notions are not five subsistent things.

And although several notions or properties belong to the same person, only one constitutes the person. For a divine person is not so constituted as if to be of several properties, but because the relative subsistent property itself is the person. Therefore, if we were to understand several properties as intrinsically subsisting apart, there would then be several persons, not one. Therefore, we need to understand that, of several properties or notions belonging to one and the same person, the one that is prior in the order of nature constitutes the person. But we understand other properties or notions as belonging to the already constituted person. Being without a source cannot be the first notion of the Father that constitutes his person, both because negation does not constitute anything, and because affirmation is by nature prior to negation. And by the order of nature, the common origination of the Spirit presupposes fatherhood and sonship, just as the procession of Love presupposes the procession of the Word. And so the common origination of the Spirit cannot be the first notion of the Father or the first notion of the Son.

We conclude that the first notion of the Father is fatherhood, sonship is the first notion of the Son, and that the only notion of the Holy Spirit is procession. Therefore, we conclude that there are three persons constituting the persons, namely, fatherhood, sonship, and procession. And these three notions are necessarily properties. For what constitutes the person necessarily belongs to that person alone, since individuating sources cannot belong to several things. Therefore, we call the aforementioned three notions personal properties, constituting the persons, as it were, in the aforementioned way. But we call the other two notions properties or notions of the persons but not personal properties, since they do not constitute the person.

The Hypostases Do Not Remain When the Intellect
Has Subtracted the Personal Properties

And the foregoing makes clear that the hypostases do not remain when the intellect has subtracted the personal properties, since, in intellectual analysis, the subject in which a form inheres remains when the intellect has subtracted the form. For example, the surface remains when the intellect has subtracted whiteness from it, and the substance remains when the intellect has subtracted the surface, and prime matter remains when the intellect has subtracted the substantial form. But nothing remains when the intellect subtracts the subject. And the personal properties are the very persons as subsistent. Nor do they constitute the persons as if accruing to preexisting subjects, since only something relative, not anything predicated absolutely, can be separate in God. Therefore, we conclude that no hypostases remain when the intellect has subtracted the personal properties, but separate hypostases remain when the intellect has subtracted the nonpersonal notions.

How the Divine Essence Remains When the Intellect
Has Subtracted the Personal Properties

And if anyone should inquire whether, when the intellect has subtracted the personal properties, the divine essence remains, we need to say that it remains in one way but not in another. For the intellect analyzes in two ways. One way of analysis is by abstracting a form from matter, in which analysis the intellect proceeds from the more formal to the more material. For what is the first subject remains last, and the last form is abstracted first. The second way of analysis is by abstracting the universal from the particular, which analysis is disposed in a somewhat contrary order, since individuating material conditions are first abstracted in order to understand what is common.

And although there is no matter and form in God, or something universal and something particular, there is in him the common and the proper, and the existing subject for the common nature. For, according to our way of understanding, the persons are related to the divine essence as existing subjects proper to the common nature.

Therefore, in the first way of intellectual analysis, the common nature does not remain when the personal properties, which are the subsistent persons themselves, have been subtracted. In the second way, however, the common nature does.

On the Relation of the Personal Activities
to the Personal Properties

The foregoing can also make clear the kind of relation by the intellect of the personal activities to the personal properties. For the personal properties are subsistent persons, but a subsistent person in any nature acts by the power of the nature when the person communicates it. For a specific form is the source of generating something specifically the same. Therefore, since the divine personal activities pertain to communicating the divine nature, a subsistent divine person necessarily communicates the common divine nature by the power of the nature itself.

And we can conclude two things from this. One is that the generative power of the Father is the divine nature itself, since any power of acting is the source by whose power something is done. The second is that, according to our way of understanding, the personal activity, namely, generation, presupposes both the divine nature and the personal property of the Father (i.e., his very hypostasis). This is so even though such a property, insofar as it is a relation, results from the activity. And so, if we should consider that the Father is a subsistent person, we can say that he generates because he is the Father. But if we should consider what belongs to the relation, it seems, conversely, that we should say that he is the Father because he generates.

How We Need to Understand Generation Regarding
the Father and the Son

Still, we should note that it is necessary to understand the order of active generation to fatherhood in one way and to understand the order of passive generation (or being begotten) to sonship in another way. For active generation by the order of nature presupposes the person of the one generating. But passive generation (or being begotten) is by the order of nature prior to the person begotten, since the person begotten has his existing by being begotten. Therefore, according to our way of understanding, active generation presupposes fatherhood, insofar as fatherhood constitutes the person of the Father. But being begotten does not presuppose sonship, insofar as sonship constitutes the person of the Son. Rather, according to our way of understanding, being begotten is prior to sonship in both ways, namely, insofar as sonship constitutes the person of the Son, and insofar as sonship is a relation. And we should understand the like about things that pertain to the procession of the Holy Spirit.

◄ѯ 65 ѕ►

How the Notional Activities Differ Only
Conceptually from the Persons

And by the designated order between notional activities and notional properties, we mean only that the former differ from the latter according to our way of understanding, not that they are really different. For as God's understanding is God himself understanding, so also the Father's generating is the Father himself generating, although signified in a different way. Similarly, although one person has several notions, there is no composition in that person. For being without a source, since it is a negative property, can produce no composition. And the two relations in the person of the Father, namely, fatherhood and the common origination of the Spirit, are really the same thing as they are related to the person of the Father. For as fatherhood is the Father himself, so also the common origination of the Spirit in the Father is the Father, and the common origination of the Spirit in the Son is the Son. But they differ by the things to which they are related. For the Father is related to the Son by fatherhood, and to the Holy Spirit by the common origination of the Spirit. And likewise, the Son is related to the Father by sonship, and to the Holy Spirit by the common origination of the Spirit.

◄ѯ 66 ѕ►

The Relative Properties Are the Divine Essence Itself

The relative properties are also necessarily the divine essence itself, since the relative properties are the subsistent persons themselves. But a subsistent person in God cannot be anything other than the divine essence, since the divine essence is God himself, as I have shown before [I, 10]. And so we conclude that the relative properties are really the same as the divine essence.

Second, whatever is in something in addition to its essence is in it accidentally. But there cannot be any accident in God, as I have shown before [I, 23]. Therefore, the relative properties are not really anything other than the divine essence.

◄₹ 67 ₷►

The Relations Are Not Externally Attached, as
Followers of Gilbert de la Porrée Said

And we cannot say that the aforementioned properties are not in the persons but are externally related to them, as followers of Gilbert de la Porrée said.[16] For real relations need to be in related things, and this is manifest in creatures, since there are real relations in creatures as accidents in the subjects in which they inhere. But the relations whereby the persons are distinguished in God are real relations, as I have shown before [I, 53]. Therefore, the relations are necessarily in the divine persons but not as accidents. For even other things that are accidents in creatures, such as wisdom, justice, and the like, fall out of the category of accidents when transposed to God, as I have shown before [I, 23].

Second, there can be difference in God only by the relations, since all things predicated absolutely are common. Therefore, if the relations are externally related to the persons, no difference will remain in the persons. Therefore, there are relative properties in the persons, but in such a way that they are the persons and also the divine essence, as we say that wisdom and goodness are in God and are God himself and the divine essence, as I have shown before [I, 23].

THE EFFECTS PRODUCED BY GOD

1. Creation and Diversity

◄₹ 68 ₷►

The First Effect: Existing

Therefore, with the things that belong to the unity of the divine essence and the Trinity of persons considered, we still need to consider about the effects produced by God. And God's first effect in things is existence itself, which all other effects presuppose, and on which they are founded. And everything that exists in any way is necessarily from God. For in all ordered things, we find universally that something first and most perfect in an order causes things subsequent in that order (e.g., the hottest fire causes the heat in other hot material substances). For we find that imperfect things always originate from perfect things (e.g., semen from animals, and seeds from plants). But I have shown before that God is the first and most perfect being [I, 3–23]. Therefore, he necessarily causes existing in everything that possesses existing.

Second, we trace everything that possesses something by sharing, as to its source and cause, to what possesses that thing essentially (e.g., red-hot iron shares in incandescence from what is fire essentially). But I have shown before that God is his very existing [I, 11]. And so existing belongs to him by his essence, and existing belongs to other things by participation. For the essence of anything else is not its existing, since there can be only one existing that is absolute and intrinsically subsisting, as I have shown before [I, 15]. Therefore, God necessarily causes existing in everything that exists.

◄ẕ 69 ẕ►

In Creating Things, God Does Not Presuppose Matter

And this shows that God, in creating things, does not need preexisting matter out of which to make things. For no efficient cause antecedently needs for its activity what its own activity produces. For example, builders need preexisting stones and wood for their activity because they cannot produce those things by their own activity, but they produce the house by their activity and do not presuppose the house. And it is necessary that God's activity produces matter, since I have shown that everything that exists in any way has God as the cause of its existing [I, 68]. Therefore, we conclude that God, in creating, does not presuppose matter.

Second, actuality is by nature prior to potentiality, and so also the nature of being a source belongs primarily to actuality. But every source that in causing presupposes another source has the nature of being a source secondarily. Therefore, since God is the cause of things as the first actuality, but matter is the cause of things as potential being, it is improper that God, in causing, should presuppose matter.

Third, the more universal a cause is, the more universal its effect is. For particular causes appropriate the effects of universal causes to something determined, and this determination is related to a universal effect as actuality to potentiality. Therefore, every cause that makes something to be actual, given the potentiality for that actuality, is a particular cause in relation to a universal cause. But such causality does not belong to God, since he is the first cause, as I have shown before [I, 68]. Therefore, he does not need matter as a prerequisite for his activity.

Therefore, it belongs to him to bring things into existence from nothing, and this is to create. And so the Catholic faith professes that he is the creator.

◄ẑ 70 ẑ►

Creating Belongs Only to God

It is also clear that it belongs only to God to be the creator. For creating belongs to the cause that does not presuppose another, more universal cause, as I have said [I, 69]. But this belongs only to God. Therefore, only he is the creator.

Second, the more remote a potentiality is from actuality, the more necessary it is that there is a greater power that brings the potentiality to actuality. But however great the distance between potentiality and actuality, there always remains a greater distance if the very potentiality should be subtracted. Therefore, to create something out of nothing requires infinite power. But only God has infinite power, since only he has an infinite essence. Therefore, only God can create.

◄ẑ 71 ẑ►

The Diversity of Matter Does Not Cause the Diversity of Things

And from what I have hitherto shown, it is clear that the diversity of matter does not cause the diversity in things. For I have shown that the divine activity that brings things into existing does not presuppose matter [I, 69]. But matter causes the diversity of things only insofar as preexisting matter is necessary for producing things, namely, so that diverse forms are induced according to the diversity of matter. Therefore, matter does not cause the diversity in things produced by God.

Second, insofar as things have existing, so they have unity and plurality, since each thing is also one insofar as it is a being. But forms do not have existing because of matter. Rather, matter has existing because of forms. For actuality is better than potentiality, and that because of which something exists is necessarily better. Therefore, forms are not diverse because they belong to different matter. Rather, matter is diverse in order to belong to different forms.

◄ẑ 72 ẑ►

What Caused Diversity in Things

And if things are disposed toward unity and multiplicity in the way in which they are disposed toward existing, and if the whole existing of things depends on God, as I have shown [I, 68], God necessarily causes the plurality of things. And we should consider how this is so.

For every efficient cause necessarily produces its like insofar as it can. But the things produced by God could not have obtained a likeness of the divine goodness in the simplicity in the way in which it is found in him. And so what is one and simple in God was necessarily represented in created things in different ways and dissimilarly. Therefore, there was necessarily diversity in the things produced by God, so that the diversity of things imitated the divine perfection in their own way.

Second, each created thing is finite, since the essence of God alone is infinite, as I have shown before [I, 18]. But the addition of something else renders any finite thing greater. Therefore, it was better that there be diversity in created things, so that there would be many good things, than that there would be only one kind of thing produced by God. But it belongs to the best to produce the best. Therefore, it was fitting for God to have produced the diversity in things that creation allows.

◀ 73 ▶

On the Diversity of Things, and Their Rank and Order

And God necessarily established the diversity in things with a certain order, namely, that some were better than others. For it belongs to the abundance of divine goodness that he communicates the likeness of his goodness to created things as much as possible. But God not only is good in himself but also surpasses other things in goodness and brings them to goodness. Therefore, in order that the likeness of created things to God would be more perfect, it was necessary that some things were constituted better than other things, and that some things acted on other things by bringing them to perfection.

Second, the diversity of things consists chiefly of the diversity of forms. But formal diversity is by contrariety, since a genus is divided into different species by contrary specific differences, and there needs to be an order in contrariety, since one or the other of contraries is always more perfect. Therefore, God necessarily established the diversity of things with a certain order, namely, that some are better than others.

◀ 74 ▶

How Some Created Things Have More Potentiality and Less Actuality, and Other Things the Converse

And each thing is excellent and perfect inasmuch as it approaches likeness to God, and God is pure actuality without admixture of potentiality. Therefore, the highest things in the scale of beings are necessarily more actual and have less potentiality, and inferior things are necessarily more potential. And we need to consider how this is.

For God is eternal and immutable in his existing, but the things subject to coming to be and passing away, things that sometimes exist and sometimes do not, are the lowest in the scale of things, as they have less likeness of divine existing. And because existing accompanies a thing's form, these things are such things when they have their form but cease to exist when they are deprived of it. Therefore, there is necessarily something in them that can sometimes have the form and sometimes be deprived of it, and we call this thing matter. Therefore, such lowest things need to be composed of matter and form.

And the highest things in the scale of created beings most approach likeness to divine existing. Nor is there in the highest things potentiality for existing and not existing. Rather, they have obtained everlasting existing from God by creation. And since what is matter is a potentiality for the existing that is through form, those beings in which there is no potentiality for existing and not existing are not composites of matter and form but simply forms that subsist in the existing that they received from God. And such substances necessarily cannot pass away, since there is potentiality for nonexisting in all things that can pass away, but there is no such potentiality in the case of substances that are subsistent forms, as I have just said. Therefore, such substances cannot pass away.

Moreover, something passes away only by the separation of its form from itself, since existing always results from form. But the highest substances, since they are subsistent forms, cannot be separated from their forms and so cannot lose existing. Therefore, they cannot pass away.

And there are in between both of the aforementioned things some things in which, although there is no potentiality for existing and not existing, there is potentiality for place. And such things are the heavenly bodies, which are not subject to coming to be and passing away because there is no contrariety in them, and yet they are mutable as to place. And so there are in some things matter as well as movement, since motion is the actuality of something potential. Therefore, heavenly bodies have matter subject only to change of place, not to coming to be or passing away.

2. Intellectual Substances, Understanding, and the Human Soul

◄₹ 75 ₷►

There Are Intellectual Substances, Which We Call Immaterial

The aforementioned substances that we called immaterial are also necessarily intellectual. For something is intellectual because it is free of matter, and we can perceive this from the intelligible itself, since the actually intelligible and the intellect actually understanding are one and the same thing. But it is clear that something is actually intelligible because it is separate from matter, since we have intellectual knowledge even of material things only by abstracting from matter. And so there needs to be the same judgment about the intellect, namely, that immaterial things are intellectual.

Second, immaterial substances are the first and highest in the scale of beings, since actuality is by nature prior to potentiality. But the intellect is clearly superior to all other things, since the intellect uses material things as instruments, as it were. Therefore, immaterial substances are necessarily intellectual.

Third, the higher some things are in the scale of beings, the more they approach divine likeness. For we see that some things of the lowest rank (i.e., nonliving things) share in divine likeness only as to existing. Other things (i.e., plants) share in divine likeness as to existing and living. And other things (i.e., animals) also share in divine likeness as to knowing. But the highest way of knowing is by the intellect and the most God-like. Therefore, the highest creatures are intellectual, and we say that they are made in the image of God because they approach closer to the likeness of God than other creatures do.

◄¿ 76 ﺱ►

How Such Substance Are Free to Decide

And the foregoing shows that they are free to decide. For what understands, unlike nonliving things, does not act or desire without judgment. Nor is the judgment of the intellect by natural impulse, as in the case of irrational animals. Rather, the judgment of the intellect is by the intellect's own understanding, since the intellect knows the end, means to the end, and the relation of the one to the other. And so the intellect can cause the judgment whereby it desires and does something for the sake of an end. But we call what causes itself free. Therefore, every understanding thing desires and acts with free judgment, which is to be free to decide. Therefore, the highest substances are free to decide.

Second, what is not bound to a particular determined thing is free. But the appetite of an intellectual substance is not bound to a particular determined good, since that appetite follows the understanding of the intellect, which regards good in general. Therefore, the appetite of an intellectual substance, being in general disposed toward any good, is free.

◄ॐ 77 ॐ►

There Is Order and Rank in Intellectual Substances
According to the Perfection of Nature

And as these intellectual substances are superior by a rank to other substances, so also these substances necessarily differ from one another by particular ranks. For they cannot differ from one another by material difference, since they lack matter. And so, if there are several of them, a formal distinction, which constitutes a specific difference, necessarily causes the plurality. And in whatever things there is specific diversity, it is necessary to consider the rank and order in their regard. And the reason for this is that, as the addition and subtraction of units in the case of numbers change the species, so natural things are found to differ specifically by adding and subtracting specific differences. For example, something only alive differs specifically from something alive and sensory, and something alive and only sensory differs specifically from something alive, sensory, and rational. Therefore, the aforementioned immaterial substances are necessarily distinguished by particular ranks and orders.

◄ॐ 78 ॐ►

How There Are Ranks in Understanding
in Intellectual Substances

And since a thing's way of activity is according to the way of its substance, higher intellectual substances, as possessing more universal and more integrated intelligible forms and powers, necessarily understand more excellently. Moreover, lower intellectual substances are necessarily weaker in understanding and have more numerous and less universal forms.

◄ॐ 79 ॐ►

The Substance by Which Human Beings Understand Is the
Lowest in the Genus of Intellectual Substances

And since there is no infinite regress in things, as one needs to discover among the aforementioned substances the highest one, which most closely approximates God, so one needs to discover the lowest one, which most closely approximates corporeal matter.

And this can be made clear in different ways. For understanding befits human beings over other animals, since it is clear that only a human being considers universals, the relation between things, and immaterial things, all of which understanding alone perceives. And understanding cannot be an act performed by a bodily organ, as the eye exercises vision. For every instrument of cognitive power necessarily lacks the kind of things known by it. For example, the pupil of an eye by its nature lacks the colors known, since we know colors inasmuch as forms of the colors are received in the pupil, and what receives is necessarily bare of what it receives. But the intellect knows every kind of sensibly perceptible nature. Therefore, if the intellect were to know by means of a bodily organ, that organ would necessarily be bare of every sensibly perceptible nature, which is impossible.

Second, every cognitive faculty knows in the way in which the form of a known thing is present to it, since the form is the source of the faculty's knowledge. But the intellect knows things in an immaterial way, even naturally material things, by abstracting the universal form from individuating material conditions. Therefore, the form of a known thing cannot be in the intellect in a material way. Therefore, the form is not received in a bodily organ, since every bodily organ is material.

The same thing is also apparent from the fact that the senses are weakened and impaired by the most sensibly perceptible objects (e.g., hearing by loud sounds, and vision by very bright light). And this happens because the balance of the organ is weakened. On the other hand, the excellence of intelligible things strengthens the intellect, since one who understands higher intelligible things can understand other things more rather than less.

Therefore, since human beings understand, and their understanding is not by means of a bodily organ, there needs to be an immaterial substance by which they understand. For even the subsistence of something that can intrinsically have activity apart from matter does not depend on matter. Indeed, all powers and forms that cannot intrinsically subsist without matter cannot have activity apart from matter. For example, a material substance by its heat, not heat by itself, makes something hot.

Therefore, the immaterial substance by which a human being understands is the lowest in the genus of intellectual substances and the closest to matter.

◄¿ 80 ¿►

On the Difference between Intellects in Understanding

Intelligible existing is superior to sensible existing as the intellect is superior to the senses. And the lower things in the scale of beings resemble higher things as much as they can (e.g., material substances, which can come to be and pass away, resemble in some way the orderly movements of heavenly bodies). Therefore, sensibly perceptible things in their own way likewise necessarily resemble intelligible things, and so we can, howsoever, come to knowledge of intelligible things from the likeness of sensibly perceptible things. And there is in sensibly perceptible things something highest, as it were, which is actuality, namely, form; something lowest, which is only potential, namely, prime matter; and something in between, namely, the composite of matter and form.

So also should we consider this even in regard to intelligible existing. For the highest intelligible thing (i.e., God) is pure actuality. But other intellectual substances have some actuality and some potentiality in regard to intellectual existing. And the lowest intellectual substance, by which a human being understands, is only potential, as it were, in regard to intellectual existing. Also attesting to this is the fact that a human being understands at first only potentially and is then brought little by little to actual understanding. And so we call the thing by which a human being understands, the potential intellect.

⋘ 81 ⋙

The Potential Intellect Receives Intelligible Forms from Sensibly Perceptible Things

But since the higher an intellectual substance is, the more universal intelligible forms it has, as I have said [I, 78], it follows that the human intellect we call potential has less universal forms than other intellectual substances have. And so the potential intellect receives intelligible forms from sensibly perceptible things.

This can also be made clear in another way to one who considers the matter. For form needs to be proportioned to what receives it. Therefore, as the potential intellect, of all intellectual substances, is closer to corporeal matter, so that intellect's intelligible forms are necessarily the closest to material things.

⋘ 82 ⋙

A Human Being Needs Sense Powers in Order to Understand

And we should consider that the forms in material things are particular and have material existing, whereas the forms in the intellect are universal and immaterial. The way of understanding shows this, since we understand things in a universal and immaterial way. But the way of understanding needs to correspond to the intelligible forms by which we understand. Therefore, since something comes from one terminus to the other only by something in between, the forms from natural things need to come to our intellect by some intermediate things.

Such things are the senses, which receive the forms of material things apart from matter. For example, the form of stone, not the matter, comes to be in the eye. But the forms of things are received in the senses as particular, since the senses know only particular things. Therefore, it was necessary that a human being also have sense powers in order to understand. And an indication of this is that one who lacks a sense power lacks knowledge of the sensibly perceptible things perceived by that sense power. For example, a man born blind cannot have knowledge of colors.

◄ ε 83 ε►

We Need to Posit an Active Intellect

And so it is made clear that the sharing in, or influx of, some intrinsically subsisting actually intelligible forms does not cause the knowledge of things in our intellect, as Platonists and some other philosophers who followed them held. Rather, our intellect acquires knowledge from sensibly perceptible things by means of the senses. But since the forms of things in the senses are particular, as I have said [I, 82], such forms are only potentially, not actually, intelligible, since the intellect understands only universals. And only something active brings what is potential to actuality. Therefore, there needs to be something active that makes the forms existing in the senses actually intelligible. But the potential intellect cannot do this, since it is potential regarding intelligible things rather than productive of them. Therefore, we need to posit another intellect that makes the potentially intelligible forms actually intelligible, as light makes potentially visible colors actually visible. And we call this intellect the active intellect, and we would not need to posit such an intellect if the forms of things were actually intelligible, as the Platonists held.

Therefore, in order to understand, we need, first, the potential intellect, which receives intelligible forms, and, second, the active intellect, which makes things actually intelligible. And when intelligible forms have perfected the potential intellect, we call the intellect habitual, in that it then has the intelligible forms so that it can use them at will, in an intermediate way between pure potentiality and complete actuality. But when the intellect has the aforementioned forms in complete actuality, we call the intellect actual, since the intellect actually understands things when the form of a thing has become the form of the potential intellect. And so we say that the actual intellect is the thing actually understood.

The Human Soul Cannot Pass Away

And a necessary consequence of the foregoing is that the intellect, by which a human being understands, cannot pass away. For each thing acts in the way in which it has existing. But the intellect has an activity in which the body does not share, as I have shown [I, 79], and this makes clear that the intellect is active by itself. Therefore, it is a subsistent substance in its existing. But I have shown before that intellectual substances cannot pass away [I, 74]. Therefore, the intellect, by which a human being understands, cannot pass away.

Second, the proper subject of coming to be and passing away is matter. Therefore, each thing is remote from passing away inasmuch as it is remote from matter. For example, things composed of matter and form are intrinsically capable of passing away; material forms can pass away incidentally, although not intrinsically; and immaterial forms, which exceed proportion to matter, cannot pass away at all. But the intellect is by its nature altogether raised above matter, and its activity shows this, since we understand some things only by separating them from matter. Therefore, the intellect by its nature cannot pass away.

Third, there can be no passing away without contrariety, since only the contrary of something destroys it. And so heavenly bodies, in which there is no contrariety, cannot pass away. But contrariety is remote from the nature of the intellect insofar as things as such contrary are not contrary in the intellect. For there is one and the same intelligible aspect of both contraries, since the intellect by one contrary understands the other. Therefore, the intellect cannot pass away.

There Is Not One and the Same Potential Intellect in All Human Beings

Someone will perhaps say that the intellect cannot pass away, but that there is only one and the same intellect in all human beings, and so that there remains only one after the passing away of all human beings. And the argument that there is only one and the same intellect in all human beings can be affirmed in many ways.

First, the argument can be affirmed regarding the intelligible thing. For, if there is one intellect in me and another in you, there will need to be one intelligible form in me and another in you, and so one understood thing that I understand and another that you understand. Therefore, the number of understanding individuals will multiply the intellectual representation, and so it will be individual, not universal. And it seems to follow from this that it is only potentially, not actually, understood, since individual representations are potentially, not actually, understood things.

Second, I have shown that the intellect is a subsistent substance in its existing [I, 84], and I have also shown before that numerically plural intellectual substances do not belong to the same species [I, 77]. Therefore, if numerically one intellect is in me, and numerically another in you, it follows that the two intellects are also specifically different. And so you and I do not belong to the same species.

Third, since all individuals of a species share in the nature of the species, we need to posit something outside the specific nature by which individuals of the species are distinguished from one another. Therefore, if the specifically same intellect belongs to all human beings, but there are many intellects numerically, we need to posit something that makes one intellect to differ numerically from another. But this cannot be anything that regards the substance of the intellect, since the intellect is not composed of matter and form. And so it follows that every difference that could be understood by what regards the substance of the intellect is one of form and species. Therefore, the only conclusion is that the intellect of one human being can be numerically distinct from the intellect of another human being only because of the diversity of their bodies. Therefore, when the different bodies have been destroyed, it seems that only one intellect, not many, remains.

But this is quite evidently impossible. And to demonstrate this, we need to proceed as one does against those who deny first principles, so that we affirm something that cannot be at all denied. Therefore, let us affirm that a particular human being, say Socrates or Plato, understands. A respondent could not deny the proposition without understanding that it should be denied. Therefore, by denying the proposition, the respondent affirms it, since affirming and denying belong to one who understands. And if this human being understands, that by which the human being formally understands is necessarily the human being's form, since nothing acts except insofar as it is actual. Therefore, that by which the active thing acts is its actuality (e.g., heat, by which something hot warms, is the thing's form). Therefore, the intellect by which a human being understands is the form of this human being. Similarly, the intellect by which another human being understands is the form of that human being. But the numerically same form cannot belong to numerically different things, since the same existing does not belong to numerically different things. And each thing has existing by its form. Therefore, the intellect by which a human being understands cannot be one and the same in all human beings.

But conscious of the difficulty posed by this argument, some tried to find a way to avoid it. For they say that the potential intellect, which I considered before [I, 80 and 81], receives the intelligible forms by which it becomes actual, but these forms are in sense images in some way.[17] Therefore, insofar as an intelligible form is in the potential intellect and in the sense images in us, the potential intellect is connected and united with us, so that we can understand by means of it.

But this is no answer at all. First, it is no answer because the intelligible form, insofar as it is in sense images is only potentially understood, but insofar as the form is in the potential intellect, it is actually understood. Therefore, insofar as it is in the potential intellect, it is abstracted from sense images rather than in them. Therefore, there remains no union of the potential intellect with us. Second, assuming that there is some union, it would not suffice to make us understanding. For, from the fact that the form of something is in the intellect, it does not follow that the thing understands, but that the thing is understood. For example, a stone does not understand even if its form is in the intellect. Therefore, because the forms of the sense images in us are in the potential intellect, it follows that we, or rather the sense images in us, are understood, not that we understand.

And this becomes more clearly evident if one should consider the comparison that Aristotle makes in the *De anima*,[18] saying there that the intellect is related to sense images as sight is to colors. But it is obvious that the fact that forms of the colors in a wall are in our vision does not cause the wall to see but to be seen. Therefore, from the fact that the forms of the sense images in us are in the intellect, it does not follow that we understand, but only that we [i.e., the sense images in us] are understood.

Further, if we formally understand by the intellect, the very understanding of the intellect is necessarily the understanding of a human being, just as the heating action of fire and heat is the same thing. Therefore, if the numerically same intellect is in me and in you, it will necessarily follow that my understanding and yours will be numerically the same with respect to the same intelligible thing, namely, when we simultaneously understand the same thing. But this is impossible, since it cannot belong to different activities to be numerically one and the same activity. Therefore, there cannot be one and the same intellect in all human beings. Therefore, it follows, if the intellect cannot pass away, as I have shown [I, 84], as many intellects as there are human beings abide after their bodies have been destroyed.

And it is easy to answer the contrary arguments. The first argument is defective in many respects. First, it fails because we admit that all human beings understand the same thing, and I call the understood thing the object of the intellect. But a thing's essence, not the intelligible form, is the object of the intellect, since not all intellectual sciences concern intelligible forms. Rather, they concern the natures of things. Just so, the object of the sense of sight is color, not the form of color in the eye. Therefore, although there are plural intellects of different human beings, there is only one understood thing in all human beings, as there is one colored thing that different people see when they look at it. Second, the argument fails because it is not necessary that, if something is individual, it is potentially, not actually, understood. But it is necessary regarding things that matter individuates, since what is actually understood is necessarily immaterial. And so immaterial substances, although they are intrinsically existing individual things, are nonetheless actually understood. And so also intelligible forms, although they are numerically different in me and in you, do not on that account lose being actually intelligible, since they are immaterial. But the intellect, understanding its object by means of the forms, is reflected on itself by understanding its very understanding and the form by which it understands.

Then we should consider that, even if we should posit one and the same intellect of all human beings, there remains the same difficulty, since there still remain many intellects because there are many separately understanding substances. And so, according to their argument, it would follow that the understood things were numerically different and consequently individual and not actually understood. Therefore, it is clear that the foregoing argument, if it were to have any force, would take away the plurality of intellects absolutely and not only in human beings. And so, since this conclusion is false, the argument obviously does not reach a necessary conclusion.

The second argument is also easily answered if one should consider the difference between the intellectual soul and the separate substances. For the intellectual soul by its specific nature has the capacity to be united to a body as the body's form, and so even the body falls within the definition of the soul. And so the intellectual soul's relation to different bodies numerically differentiates it. But this is not so in the case of separate substances.

And this also makes clear how we should answer the third argument, since the intellectual soul by its specific nature has the capacity to be united to a body but does not have the body as part of itself. And so, because the intellectual soul can be united to a body, different bodies numerically differentiate intellectual souls. And this numerical differentiation even remains in the souls when the bodies have been destroyed, since the souls can be united to different bodies, even though they are not actually united to their bodies.

There Is Not One and the Same Active Intellect in All Human Beings

There have been some who, although they conceded that the potential intellect is different in human beings, held that there is one and the same active intellect with respect to human beings.[19] And this opinion, although more tolerable than the foregoing opinion, can be refuted by like arguments. For the activity of the potential intellect is to receive understood things and understand them, whereas the activity of the active intellect is to make the things actually understood by abstracting them. And both of these things belong to a particular human being. For example, this human being, say Socrates or Plato, receives understood things, abstracts intelligible forms, and understands the things abstracted. Therefore, both the potential intellect and the active intellect are necessarily united to this particular human being as a form. And so both intellects are necessarily numerically multiplied according to the number of human beings.

Second, an active thing and the thing acted upon need to be proportioned to each another like matter and form, since an active thing makes matter actual. And so an active power corresponds to a passive power of the same genus, since actuality and potentiality belong to one and the same genus. But the active intellect is related to the potential intellect as active power to passive power, as is clear from what I have said before [I, 83]. Therefore, both intellects necessarily belong to the one and the same genus. But the potential intellect is united to us as a form, not separate from us as an entity, and there are as many potential intellects as there are human beings, as I have shown [I, 85]. Therefore, the active intellect necessarily is something formally united to us, and multiple according to the number of human beings.

The Potential Intellect and the Active Intellect Are Grounded in One and the Same Essence of the Soul

And since both the potential intellect and the active intellect are formally united to us, we need to say that they belong in the same essence of the soul. For what is formally united to something is united to it either by way of a substantial form or by way of an accidental form. Therefore, if the potential intellect and the active intellect should be united to a human being by way of a substantial form, we need to say that the two intellects belong to one and the same essence of the form (i.e., the soul), since there is only one substantial form of one thing. And if the two intellects should be united to a human being by way of an accidental form, clearly neither of them can be an accident of the body, since their activities are apart from a bodily organ, as I have shown before [I, 79]. Thus each is an accident of the soul. But there is only one soul in one human being. Therefore, the active intellect and the potential intellect necessarily belong to one and the same essence of the soul.

Second, every specifically proper activity proceeds from sources resulting from the specific form. But understanding is the activity proper to the human species. Therefore, the active intellect and the potential intellect, which are the sources of understanding, as I have shown [I, 79–83], necessarily result from the human soul, by which human beings have their species. But they do not so result from the soul as things proceeding from it into the body, as it were, since the aforementioned activity is apart from a bodily organ, as I have shown [I, 79], and the potentiality and the activity belong to the soul. Therefore, we conclude that the potential intellect and the active intellect belong to one and the same essence of the soul.

◄⁊ 88 ⱄ►

How the Two Powers Belong to One and the Same Essence of the Soul

And it remains for us to consider how this can be, since a difficulty seems to arise in this regard. For the potential intellect is potential regarding all intelligible things, and the active intellect makes them actually intelligible. And so the active intellect is necessarily related to intelligible things as actuality to potentiality. But it does not seem possible that the same thing in the same regard is potential and actual. Therefore, it seems impossible that the potential intellect and the active intellect belong to the same substance of the soul.

But this difficulty is easily resolved if one should consider how the potential intellect is potential regarding intelligible things, and how the active intellect makes them actually intelligible. For the potential intellect is potential regarding intelligible things insofar as it does not have in its nature a determined form of sensibly perceptible things, as the pupil of an eye is potential regarding colors. Therefore, the sense images abstracted from sensibly perceptible things, insofar as they are likenesses of the determined natures of those things, are related to the potential intellect as actuality to potentiality. But the sense images are still potential regarding something that the intellectual soul has actually, namely, being abstract from the conditions of matter, and, in that respect, the intellectual soul is related to the images as actuality to potentiality.

And it is not repugnant that something is actual and potential regarding the same thing in different respects. Thus, indeed, natural material substances act on one another and are acted upon by one another, since each one is potential with respect to another. Therefore, it is not repugnant that the same intellectual soul is both potential regarding all intelligible things, insofar as we posit the potential intellect in it, and actual regarding those things insofar as we posit the active intellect in it.

And this will be more clearly evident from the way in which the intellect makes things actually intelligible. For the intellect does not make things actually intelligible as if they should flow out of it into the potential intellect, since we would then not need sense images and the senses in order to understand. Rather, the intellect makes things actually intelligible by abstracting them from sense images, just as light in some way makes colors actual, not as if it should have them within itself, but inasmuch as it gives visibility to them in some way. Therefore, we should think that there is one and the same intellectual soul, which lacks the natures of sensibly perceptible things and can receive these natures in an intelligible way, and which makes the sense images actually intelligible, namely, by abstracting intelligible forms from them. And so we call the soul's potentiality by which it receives intelligible forms the potential intellect. And we call the power by which it abstracts intelligible forms from sense images the active intellect, which is an intelligible light, as it were, in which the intellectual soul shares in imitation of higher intellectual substances.

◄₹ 89 ₷►

All the Powers Are Rooted in the Essence of the Soul

Not only the active intellect and the potential intellect but also all the other powers that are sources of the soul's activities belong to one and the same essence of the soul, since all such powers are rooted in some way in the soul. Some powers (e.g., the powers of the vegetative and sensory parts of the soul) are in the soul as their source and in the composite as their subject, since the activities of those powers belong to the composite and not only to the soul. For a power belongs to that to which an activity belongs. But some powers are in the soul as their source and their subject, since the activities of those powers belong to the soul apart from a bodily organ, and such powers are the powers of the intellectual part of the soul. But there cannot be several souls in human beings. Therefore, all powers necessarily belong to the same soul.

◄ẕ 90 ṣ►

There Is Only One Soul in One Body

And that there cannot be several souls in one and the same body is proved as follows. The soul is clearly the substantial form of what possesses the soul, since something alive obtains its genus and species by the soul. And there cannot be several substantial forms of one and the same thing. For a substantial form differs from an accidental form in that the former makes this particular thing to exist without qualification, but the latter comes to what is already this particular thing and makes it to have a quality or quantity, or to be disposed in a certain way. Therefore, if several forms should belong to one and the same thing, the first either does or does not make this particular thing. If the first does not, it is not the substantial form, and if it does, then all subsequent forms come to what is already this particular thing. Therefore, all of the subsequent forms will be accidental, not the substantial form. Therefore, there evidently cannot be several substantial forms of one and the same thing. Therefore, neither can several souls have one and the same existing.

Second, it is clear that we call human beings living things insofar as they have a vegetative soul, animals insofar as they have a sensory soul, and human beings insofar as they have an intellectual soul. Therefore, if there should be three souls in a human being, namely, the vegetative, the sensory, and the rational, then it will follow that we posit the human being in a genus by one soul and assign species by another soul. But this is impossible. For then genus and specific difference would not make anything absolutely one. Rather, genus and specific difference would make something one by accident or aggregation, as it were (e.g., a thing that is a musician and white), which is not to be one thing absolutely. Therefore, there is necessarily only one soul in a human being.

◄ẕ 91 ṣ►

Arguments That Seem to Prove That There Are
Several Souls in Human Beings

But certain things seem to be contrary to this opinion. First, specific difference is related to genus as form is to matter. But animal is the genus of human beings, and rational is their specific difference. Therefore, since an animal is a body enlivened by a sensory soul, it seems that a body enlivened by a sensory soul is still potential with respect to the rational soul, and so the rational soul will be a soul other than the sensory soul.

Second, the intellect does not have a bodily organ, but sense and nutritive powers do. Therefore, it seems impossible that the same soul is both intellectual and sensory, since the same thing cannot be separate and not separate.

Third, the rational soul cannot pass away, as I have shown before [I, 84]. But the vegetative and sensory souls can, since they belong to the activity of bodily organs, which can pass away. Therefore, the same soul is not vegetative, sensory, and rational, since the same thing cannot be capable and incapable of passing away.

Fourth, in generating a human being, the life conferred by the vegetative soul is manifested before sensory activity and movement manifest that the thing conceived is animal, and sensation and movement show that it is animal before it has an intellect. Therefore, let us assume that there is the same soul whereby the thing conceived is first alive with vegetative life, second alive with animal life, and third alive with human life. If so, it will follow either that the vegetative, the sensory, and the rational souls are from an external source, or that the intellectual soul is from the power in semen. But both of these alternatives seem improper. For the activities of the vegetative soul and the sensory soul do not exist apart from the body, and so the sources of those activities cannot. And the activity of the intellectual soul is exercised apart from the body, and so it seems impossible that any power in the body causes the intellectual soul. Therefore, it seems impossible that the same soul is vegetative, sensory, and rational.

◀᎒ 92 ᠄▶

Answers to the Foregoing Arguments

Therefore, in order to eliminate such difficulties, we should first consider that, as in numbers, species are differentiated by one species adding to another, so also, in natural things, one species surpasses another in perfection. For plants have what belongs to the perfection in nonliving material substances, and still more, and animals have what plants have, and something more. And then we finally come to human beings, who are the most perfect of material creatures.

Every imperfect thing is disposed as matter with respect to the more perfect, and this is evident in different kinds of things. For elements are the matter of material substances of like parts, and material substances of like parts in turn are material things with regard to animals. And we should likewise consider this regarding one and the same thing. For what arrives at a higher rank of perfection in natural things has by its form whatever perfection belongs to a lower nature, and by the same form whatever perfection is added to it above other things. For example, a plant by its soul is a substance, a material substance, and a living material substance as well. An animal by its soul has all these things and, in addition, that it is sentient. And above all these kinds of things, human beings by their souls have the power to understand. Therefore, what belongs to the perfection of a lower rank, if we should consider it in a particular thing, will be material with respect to what belongs to the perfection of a higher rank. For example, if we should consider that an animal has vegetative life, this is in a way material with respect to what belongs to the sensory life proper to the animal.

But the genus is not the matter, since we would not then be predicating the genus of the whole thing. Rather, the genus is something taken from the matter. For the designation of a thing from what is material in it is its genus, and we similarly take the specific difference from the thing's form. And so living, or animate, material substance is the genus of animal, and sentient is the specific difference. Similarly, animal is the genus of human being, and rational the specific difference. Therefore, since the form of a higher rank has in itself all the perfections of a lower rank, there is really not one form from which we take the genus and another one from which we take the specific difference. Rather, we take the genus from the same form insofar as that form has the perfection of a lower rank, and we take the specific difference from it insofar as it has the perfection of a higher rank. And so it is clear that, although animal is the genus of human being, and rational is the specific difference, there need not be in a human being one soul that is sensory and another soul that is intellectual, as the first objection argued.

The same things make clear the answer to the second objection. For I have said that the form of a higher species includes in it all the perfections of lower ranks. And we should consider that the more matter has been subjected to form, the higher the natural species is. And so it is necessary that the more excellent a form is, the more it surpasses matter. And so the human soul, which is the most excellent natural form, arrives at the highest rank above matter, namely, that it has an activity without corporeal matter sharing in the activity.

Still, since the same soul includes the perfections of lower ranks, it also has activities in which corporeal matter shares. But activity clearly comes from a thing by the thing's power. Therefore, the human soul necessarily has some forces or powers that are the sources of activities exercised by the body, and these activities are necessarily actions of particular parts of the body. Such powers belong to the vegetative and sensory parts of the soul.

The human soul also needs to have some powers that are the sources of activities exercised apart from the body, and such are the powers of the intellectual part of the soul, which do not belong to the activity of any bodily organs. And so we call both the potential intellect and the active intellect separate, since they do not have bodily organs to which their actions belong, as the powers of sight and hearing do. But they are grounded in the soul that is the form of the body. And so there need not be different sensory and intellectual souls in a human being because, unlike the senses, we call the intellect separate, and it lacks a bodily organ.

And this also makes clear that we are not forced to posit one intellectual soul and another, sensory soul in human beings because the latter soul, but not the former, can pass away, as the third objection argued. For being incapable of passing away belongs to the intellectual part of the soul insofar as it is separate. Therefore, as the separate and conjoined powers are grounded in the same essence of the soul, as I have said [I, 88–89], so nothing prevents some powers of the soul from passing away along with the body, while other powers are indestructible.

The foregoing also makes clear the answer to the fourth objection. For all natural change goes little by little from the imperfect to the perfect, although this happens in one way in alteration and in another way in coming to be. For the same quality takes in more and less, and so the alteration (i.e., the movement) in a quality, being one and continuous, goes from potentiality to actuality, from the imperfect to the perfect. But a substantial form does not take in more and less, since the substantial existing for each thing is one and indivisibly disposed. And so a coming to be does not proceed continuously from the imperfect to the perfect through many intermediate stages. Rather, there needs to be new coming to be and passing away in relation to individual ranks of perfection. Therefore, in generating a human being, the thing conceived is first alive with vegetative life through the vegetative soul. Then, when this form has been taken away by passing away, the thing conceived acquires a sensory soul by another coming to be and is alive with animal life. Then, when this soul has been taken away by passing away, the final and complete form (i.e., the rational soul), which includes in it whatever perfection there was in the preceding forms, is introduced.

<h2 style="text-align:center">◄ɛ 93 ɛ►</h2>

The Rational Soul Is Not Produced by Transmission

And the power in semen does not bring the final and complete form, namely, the rational soul, into existing. Rather, a higher active thing[20] does. For the power in semen is the power of a material substance, but the rational soul surpasses every nature and power of a material substance, since no material substance can reach to the intellectual activity of the rational soul. Therefore, since nothing acts beyond its species, inasmuch as the active thing is more excellent than the thing being acted upon, and the thing producing something more excellent than the thing produced, no power of a material substance can cause the rational soul, and so neither can the power in semen.

Second, insofar as each thing has new existing, so coming to be is proper to it. For coming to be belongs to that thing to which existing also belongs, since something comes to be in order to exist. Therefore, coming to be, as such, is proper to things that as such have existing, namely, subsisting things, and coming to be is not of itself proper to things that as such do not have existing, namely, accidents and material forms. But the rational soul as such has existing, since it as such has activity, as is clear from what I have said before [I, 84]. Therefore, coming to be, as such, is proper to the rational soul. Therefore, since the rational soul is not composed of matter and form, as I have shown before [I, 84], it follows that only creation can bring it into existing. But it belongs only to God to create, as I have shown before [I, 70]. Therefore, God alone brings the rational soul into existing.

This also happens reasonably. For we see in skills ordered to one another that the highest one brings in the final form, while lower skills dispose the matter for the final form. But the rational soul is clearly the final and most perfect form that can be acquired by the matter of things that can come to be and pass away. Therefore, lower natural efficient causes appropriately cause the antecedent dispositions and forms, but the highest active thing, namely, God, causes the final form (i.e., the rational soul).

◄ẕ 94 ṡ►

The Rational Soul Is Not from God's Substance

But we should not believe that the rational soul is from God's substance, as some people erroneously think.[21] For I have shown before that God is simple and indivisible [I, 9]. Therefore, he does not unite the rational soul to the body by separating the soul, as it were, from his substance.

Second, I have shown before that God cannot be the form of any material substance [I, 17]. But the rational soul is united to the body as the body's form. Therefore, the rational soul is not from God's substance.

Third, I have shown before that God is not intrinsically or accidentally changed [I, 4]. But the contrary of this is fully apparent in the case of the rational soul, since it changes from ignorance to knowledge, and from vice to virtue. Therefore, the rational soul is not from God's substance.

3. God's Activity in Creation

◄¿ 95 ｓ►

God Directly Creates Things

And we necessarily conclude from the things I have shown before [I, 69–70] that things that can be brought into existing only by creation come directly from God. And it is clear that only creation can bring the heavenly bodies into existing. For we cannot say that they are made out of any preexisting matter, since they would then be capable of coming to be and passing away and be subject to contrariety. But such things are not proper to them, as their motion makes clear. For they move in orbits, and circular motion has no contrary. Therefore, we conclude that God directly brought the heavenly bodies into existing.

Likewise, whole elements as such do not come from any preexisting matter, since whatever preexisted would have a form. And then, if the matter preexisting the elements were to have a different form than the elements, a material substance other than the elements would necessarily exist prior to them in the order of material causality. Or, if the preexisting matter were to have the form of an element, one of the elements would necessarily exist prior to the others in that order. Therefore, God must have directly produced the elements.

And much more impossible is it that anything other than God creates incorporeal and invisible substances, since all such substances are immaterial. For matter cannot exist without having dimensions, whereby it is thus divisible when many things can be made out of one matter. And so immaterial substances cannot be caused out of preexisting matter. Therefore, we conclude that only creation by God brings them into existing.

And so the Catholic faith professes that God is "the creator of heaven and earth" and "of all things visible and invisible."

◄¿ 96 ｓ►

God Brings Things into Existing by His Will,
Not by a Natural Necessity

And this shows that God by his will, not by a natural necessity, brings things into existing. For only one thing directly results from a natural active thing, while a voluntary active thing can produce different things, and this is so because every active thing acts by its form. And the natural form by which something acts by nature is a single form of one thing, while there are many understood forms by which something acts voluntarily. Therefore, since God directly brings many things into existing, as I have already shown [I, 95], it is clear that God brings things into existing by his will, not by a natural necessity.

Second, something acting by its intellect and will is prior in the order of causes to something acting by a necessity of nature. For something acting by the will has prescribed for itself the end for the sake of which it acts, whereas a natural active thing acts for the sake of an end prescribed for it by another thing. But it is clear from the foregoing that God is the first active thing [I, 3]. Therefore, he is active by his will and not by a necessity of nature.

Third, I have shown before that God has infinite power [I, 19]. Therefore, he is not determined to this or that effect but is indeterminately disposed toward all of them. But what is indeterminately disposed toward different effects is determined to produce one of them by desire (e.g., human beings capable of walking and not walking walk when they will to do so). Therefore, effects necessarily come from God by the determination of his will. Therefore, he acts by his will and not by a necessity of nature.

And so the Catholic faith calls almighty God not only creator but "maker," since making in the proper sense belongs to a craftsman who produces things by his will. And every voluntary active thing acts through a concept of its intellect, which concept we call the intellect's word, as I have said before [I, 37–38], and the Word is the Son of God. Therefore, the Catholic faith also professes of the Son that "all things were made" through him.

◄¿ 97 s►

God in His Activity[22] Is Immutable

Because God brings things into existing by his will, it is clear that he can, without any change in him, bring things newly into existing. For the difference between a natural active thing and a voluntary active thing is that the former acts in the same way as long as it is disposed in the same way, since it makes such things as it is, but the latter does whatever it wishes. And it can happen that one, without any change, wills to act now and not to act before, since nothing prevents one from having the will to act in the future even when one is not acting. Therefore, without change in God, it can happen that he, although eternal, did not bring things into existing from eternity.

◄₹ 98 ₴►

The Argument That Motion Existed from
Eternity, and the Answer to It

And it seems that, although God can produce a new effect by his eternal and immutable will, a motion needs to precede a new effect. For we perceive that the will delays what it wills to do only because of something that either exists now and ceases to exist in the future, or does not exist and is expected to exist in the future. For example, human beings in summer have the will to clothe themselves in warm garments in the future, not then, since there is now heat that will end with the advent of cold weather later.

Therefore, if God willed from eternity to produce an effect but did not produce it from eternity, it seems either that something would be expected to exist in the future that did not yet exist, or that something would have to be taken away that then existed. But neither of these things can happen without motion. Therefore, it seems that an antecedent will could produce an effect in the future only with some motion preceding it. And so, if God's will was eternal regarding the production of things, and the things produced do not exist from eternity, motion and, consequently, movable things, need to precede production of the things. And if God produced the preceding things but not from eternity, it is again necessary that other motions and movable things preexist, and so on in infinite regression.

But one can easily realize the answer to this objection if one should consider the difference between the universal active thing and a particular active thing. For a particular active thing has activity proportioned to the rule and measure that a universal active thing prescribes. And this is evident in civic affairs, since lawmakers lay down laws as the rule and measure, as it were, by which a particular judge should render decisions. Moreover, time is the measure of actions that take place in time, since a particular active thing has activity in relation to time, namely, so that it acts now and not before for a determined reason. But the universal active thing (i.e., God) established the measure that is time and did so by his will. Therefore, even time is among the things produced by God. Therefore, as such quantity and measure belong to each thing as God willed to grant to it, so also the quantity of time is such as he willed to give to it, namely, that time and the things existing in time began when God willed them to exist.

And the foregoing objection argues as if about an active thing that presupposes time and acts in time but did not establish time. For the question whereby one asks why the eternal will produces an effect now and not before presupposes a preexisting time, since now and before are parts of time. Therefore, regarding the universal production of things, among which we also consider time, one should ask why he willed that there is this amount of time, not why the production is now and not before. And why he willed this amount of time depends on the divine will, which is free to assign this or that quantity to time.

And we can also consider this regarding the magnitude of the world. For no one asks why God constitutes the material world in such a place and not above or below or in a different position, since there is no place outside the world. Rather, it comes from the divine will that he gave such magnitude to the material world that nothing belonged to it outside this place in any different position. And although there was no time before the world, or place outside the world, we nonetheless use such a way of speaking. And so we say that there was nothing but God before the world existed, and that there is no material substance outside the world, understanding time by before, and place by outside, only in our imagination.

<h1 style="text-align:center">◄ᵇ 99 ˢ►</h1>

Arguments Showing That Matter from Eternity Necessarily Preceded Creation of the World, and Answers to Them

And it seems that, although the production of perfect things was not from eternity, matter necessarily existed from eternity. For everything that has existing after not existing is changed from nonexisting to existing. Therefore, if created things (e.g., the heavens, the earth, and other such things) did not exist from eternity but began to exist after they had not existed, we need to say that they have been changed from nonexisting to existing. And all change and motion has a subject, since motion is the actuality of what exists potentially. But the subject of the change by which a thing is brought into existing is not the very thing produced, since the latter is the terminus of the motion, and the same thing is not the terminus and the subject of motion. Rather, the subject of the aforementioned motion is that out of which the thing is produced, and we call it the matter. Therefore, it seems that, if things were brought into existing after they had not existed, matter preexisted them, and if, again, the preexisting matter was produced after it had not existed, it necessarily has other, preexisting matter. But an infinite regress is impossible. Therefore, the argument concludes that we need to come to an eternal matter that was not produced after it had not existed.

Second, if the world began to exist after it had not existed, it was either possible or impossible for the world to exist or come to exist before it existed. If it was impossible that the world should exist or come to exist before, then it was with equal force impossible for the world to exist or come to exist now, and necessarily what cannot come to exist does not. Therefore, the world necessarily did not come to exist. But this is obviously false. Therefore, we need to say that, if the world began to exist after it had not existed, it could have existed or come to exist before it did. Therefore, there was something potential regarding the world's coming to exist and existing. But what is potential regarding the coming to exist and existing of something is its matter, as, for example, wood is disposed to become a bench. Therefore, it seems that it is necessary that matter always existed, even if the world did not always exist.

But since I have shown before that even matter is only from God [I, 69], the Catholic faith does not admit that matter is eternal any more than it admits that the world is eternal. For it was necessary to express the divine causality in things themselves in such a way that the things produced by God began to exist after they had not existed, since this evidently and clearly shows that they do not exist from themselves but from their eternal cause.

And the aforementioned objections do not force us to posit the eternity of matter. We cannot call the total production of things change in the strict sense. For in no change is the subject of change produced by change, since the terminus and the subject of change are different, as the objection said. Therefore, since the total production of things by God, which we call creation, extends to all things that are real, such production cannot have the nature of change, strictly speaking, even if created things are brought into existing after they had not existed.

For existing after nonexisting suffices for the true nature of change only if one should suppose a subject at one time deprived of a form and later underlying the form. And so we find one thing after another in some things in which the nature of motion or change in the strict sense is absent, as, for example, when we say that day becomes night. Therefore, although the world began to exist after it had not existed, a change need not have accomplished this. Rather, creation did. And creation is not truly a change but a relation of the created thing dependent on the creator for its existing after previously not existing.

In every change, the same thing needs to be disposed in different ways, as what is now at one terminus and later at another. And this does not really take place in creation but only in our imagination, as we imagine that one and the same thing did not exist before and later does. And so we can call creation change by a similarity.

Likewise, the second objection is not compelling. For, although it is true to say that the world, before it existed, could have existed or come to exist, it is unnecessary that we say this about a potentiality. For we use the word *possible* in propositions to signify a modality of truth, namely, that something is neither necessary nor impossible. And we do not speak of such possibility about a potentiality, as Aristotle teaches in the *Metaphysics*.[23] But if we do use the word *possible* about a potentiality, we need to use it about active, not passive, potentiality. Then we understand the statement that the world could have existed before it did to mean that God could have brought the world into existing before he did. And so we are not compelled to hold that matter preexisted the world.

Therefore, the Catholic faith posits nothing coeternal with God and so professes that he is "the creator" and "maker of all things visible and invisible."

4. *The Purpose of Creation*

◄፨ 100 ፨►

God Does All Things for an End

I have shown before that God brought things into existing by his intellect and will, not by a necessity of nature [I, 96], and everything acting by its intellect and will acts for the sake of an end, since the end of the practical intellect is a source. Therefore, all the things made by God necessarily exist for the sake of an end.

Second, God best produced things, since it belongs to the best to make each thing in the best way. But it is better that something is made for the sake of an end than without intending an end, since the aspect of good in things made comes from the end. Therefore, the things made by God are for the sake of an end. And an indication of this is apparent in things done by nature, each of which is for the sake of an end, and nothing of which is in vain. But it is improper to say that the things done by nature are better ordered than the establishment of nature by the first active thing, since the whole order of nature derives from this. Therefore, God clearly produced things for the sake of an end.

◄≀ 101 ≀►

The Final End of All Things Is the Divine Goodness

And the final end of things is necessarily the divine goodness. For the final end of things made by something acting by the will is what is first and of itself willed by that thing, since the active thing does everything that it does on that account. But the first thing willed by God's will is his goodness, as is clear from what I have said before [I, 32]. Therefore, the final end of all the things made by God is necessarily his goodness.

Second, the end of the coming to be of each thing that has come to be is the thing's form, since the coming to be ceases when the form has been obtained. But each thing that has come to be, whether by a skill or by nature, is by its form in some way like the active thing, since every active thing makes something in some way like itself. For example, the house in matter comes from the house in the mind of the builder, and in natural things, a human being begets a human being. And if something should be begotten or made by nature that is not specifically like the cause of its coming to be, it is still like its cause as the imperfect is like the perfect. For things may not be specifically like the cause of their coming to be because they cannot come to a perfect likeness of the cause. Rather, they imperfectly share in likeness to the cause in some way (e.g., animals and plants generated by the power of the sun). Therefore, the end of generating or making all the things made is the form of the thing that makes or generates them, namely, that the end is achieved according to the form's likeness. But the form of the first active thing, namely, God, is simply his goodness. Therefore, all things have been made in order to be likenesses of the divine goodness.

◄≀ 102 ≀►

Likeness to God Is the Reason for the Diversity of Things

Therefore, we should understand from this end the reason for the diversity and difference in things. For it was impossible that one thing perfectly represent the divine goodness because of the remoteness of each creature from God. Therefore, it was necessary that many things represent him, so that one thing supplied what another thing lacks. For even regarding syllogistic conclusions, the means of proof to demonstrate a conclusion need to be multiplied when one means does not suffice, as happens in rhetorical syllogisms. Nor does even the whole universe of creatures perfectly equivalently represent the divine goodness. Rather, the universe of creatures represents the divine good-ness by the perfection possible in creatures.

Second, what is in a universal cause in a simple and unified way is in the cause's effects in many and different ways, since something is more excellent in the cause than in its effects. But the divine goodness is the one and sim-ple source and the root of the entire goodness found in creatures. Therefore, creatures need to be assimilated to the divine goodness as many and different things are assimilated to something one and simple. Therefore, the multiplicity and diversity does not come about in things by chance or luck but for the sake of the end, just as things are produced for an end, not by chance or luck. For the existing, unity, and multiplicity in things comes from the same source. Nor does matter cause the diversity of things, since the first establishment of things comes about by creation, which does not require matter. In a similar way, things that come about only by a necessity of matter seem to be fortuitous.

Likewise, neither is the multiplicity in things explained by an order of inter-mediate active things. (Some[24] supposed that only one thing could have come directly from a first, simple thing, but that the second thing was so remote from the first in simplicity that many kinds of things could have then come from it. And so they held that the more remote things successively are from the first, simple thing, the greater their number is.) For I have already shown before that there are many things that were able to come into existing only by creation [I, 69 and 72], which belongs only to God, as I have shown before [I, 70]. And so we conclude that God himself directly created many things.

It is also obvious that, according to the position under consideration, the multiplicity and diversity of things would be by chance, as if unintended by the first active thing. But the divine intellect planned and established in things the multiplicity and diversity in order for created things to represent the divine goodness in different ways, and for different things to share in it in different ranks. And this was so that a beauty shone in things from the very gradation of their diversity, and the beauty commended the divine wisdom.

◄⊱ 103 ⊰►

The Divine Goodness Causes Both Things and Every Movement and Action

And not only is divine goodness the end of establishing things, but it is also necessarily the end of every action and movement of any creature. For each thing does such things in the way in which it exists (e.g., something hot heats). But any created thing by its form shares in a likeness of the divine goodness, as

I have shown [I, 102]. Therefore, every action and movement of any creature is ordered to the divine goodness as its end.

Second, every movement and activity of any creature seems to tend toward something perfect. But the perfect has the nature of good, since the perfection of anything is its goodness. Therefore, every movement and action of any creature tends toward something good. But any good is a likeness of the highest good, just as any existing is a likeness of the first being. Therefore, the movement and action of any thing tends toward assimilation of the divine goodness.

Third, if there should be many subordinated active things, the actions and movements of all of them are necessarily ordered to the good of the first active thing as their final end. For, inasmuch as the higher active thing moves the lower ones, and every cause of motion moves toward its own end, the actions and movements of the lower active things necessarily tend toward the end of the first active thing. For example, the actions of all ranks in an army are ordered to victory, which is the objective of the general, as their final end. But I have shown before that the first cause of motion and the first active thing is God [I, 3], and his end is simply his goodness, as I have also shown before [I, 100]. Therefore, all the actions and movements of any creatures are necessarily for the sake of the divine goodness, not to cause or increase it, but in order that it is acquired in the creatures' way, by sharing in a likeness of it.

And created things by their actions obtain the likeness of divine goodness in different ways, just as they by their existing represent it in different ways, since each thing acts insomuch as it exists. Therefore, since it is common to all creatures to represent the divine goodness insomuch as they exist, it is also common to all creatures that they by their actions obtain the divine likeness in preserving their own existing and in communicating it to another. For first, each creature by its activity attempts to preserve itself in perfect existing insofar as it can, and in this it tends in its own way toward likeness of the divine eternity. Second, each creature by its activity attempts to communicate its perfect existing to something else in its own way, and thereby tends toward likeness of the divine permanence.

But a rational creature by its activity tends toward divine likeness in a singular way superior to other creatures, just as it has more excellent existing than other creatures. For matter constricts and limits the existing of other creatures, so that their existing neither actually nor potentially has infinity. But every rational nature either actually or potentially has infinity insofar as its intellect contains intelligible things. Therefore, the intellectual nature in us, considered in its initial existing, is potentially its intelligible objects, and since the latter are infinite, the nature has a potential infinity. And so the intellect is the form of forms, since it has not only a form determined to one thing, as a stone does, but also a form capable of all forms. The intellectual nature in God is actually infinite, as having in itself beforehand the perfection of the whole of being, as I have shown before [I, 21]. And intellectual creatures other than human beings are disposed in a intermediate way between potentiality and actuality.

Therefore, an intellectual creature by its activity tends toward divine likeness not only in that it preserves itself in existing or multiplies existing by somehow communicating it, but also in order to have actually in itself what it has potentially by nature. Therefore, the end of an intellectual creature, which it obtains by its activity, is to make its intellect completely actual by all the intelligible objects that the intellect has potentially, since it will in this respect be most like God.

5. The Purpose of Intellectual Creatures

◄፥ 104 ፥►

The Final End of an Intellectual Creature Is to See God Essentially

And something is potential in two ways. One way is by nature, namely, with regard to those things that can be brought into actuality by an active thing of the same nature. The other way is with regard to those things that can be brought into actuality by a different kind of active thing, not by one of the same nature. This is apparent in material things. For there is a natural potentiality in a boy to become a man, or in semen to become an animal, but there is no natural potentiality in wood to become a bench, or in a blind man to become capable of sight.

And so also it happens regarding our intellect. For our intellect has a natural potentiality with respect to some intelligible things, namely, those that can be brought into actuality by the active intellect, which is the innate source that makes us actually understand. But we cannot obtain our final end by our intellect being brought into actuality in that way. For the power of the active intellect is to make potentially intelligible sense images actually intelligible, as is clear from what I have said before [I, 83], and the senses receive sense images. Therefore, the active intellect brings our intellect into actuality only with respect to those intelligible things that we can come to know through sensibly perceptible things.

But the final end of human beings cannot consist of such knowledge, since natural desire comes to rest when the final end has been obtained. And however much progress one should make in understanding by the aforementioned way of knowing whereby we obtain knowledge from the senses, there still remains a natural desire to know other things. For there are many things that the senses cannot reach, things about which we can receive only a little knowledge through sensibly perceptible things. And so we perhaps know that they exist, but not what they are, since the essences of immaterial substances are of a different kind than the essences of sensibly perceptible things and disproportionately, as it were, transcend them. Also, regarding things that fall under the senses, there are many things whose essence we cannot know with certainty, the essence of some things in no way and the essence of other things weakly. And so there always remains a natural desire with respect to more perfect knowledge.

But a natural desire cannot be in vain. Therefore, we obtain our final end in that a higher active thing than the one connatural to us actualizes our intellect, and this puts to rest our innate natural desire to know. But the desire in us to know is such that we desire to know the cause when we know an effect. And regarding anything, whatever circumstances we know about it, our desire does not rest until we know the thing's essence. Therefore, our natural desire to know cannot be at rest in us until we know the first cause by its essence, not in any way. But the first cause is God, as is clear from what I have said before [I, 68]. Therefore, the final end of an intellectual creature is to see God essentially.

◄⅃ 105 ⅂►

How the Created Intellect Can See the Divine Essence

And we should consider how this is possible. It is clear that our intellect, since it knows a thing only by the thing's form, cannot know the essence of one thing by the essence of another thing. And the more remote the form by which the intellect knows is from the thing known, the more imperfect the knowledge our intellect has about the essence of that thing. For example, the intellect, if it were to know cow by the form of ass, would know the essence of cow imperfectly, namely, only as to the genus. And the intellect, if it were to know cow by stone, would know the essence of cow more imperfectly, since it would know by a more remote genus. And the intellect, if it were to know cow by the form of a thing that did not share in any genus with cow, would in no way know the essence of cow.

But it is clear from what I have said before that no creature shares in a genus with God [I, 12–13]. Therefore, God cannot be known essentially by any created form, whether a sensibly perceptible form or an intelligible form. Therefore, for God to be known essentially, God himself needs to become the form of the intellect knowing him in this way and to be joined to him. I say "joined to him," not so as to constitute one nature, but as the intelligible form is joined to the one understanding, for, just as God is his existing, so he is his truth, and truth is the form of the intellect.

And everything that obtains a form necessarily obtains a disposition toward that form. But our intellect does not by its nature have the final disposition with respect to the form of the thing that is truth, since the intellect would then attain the form from the beginning. Therefore, a newly added disposition needs to elevate the intellect when it obtains the form of the thing that is truth. And we call this the light of glory, by which God, who alone by his nature has this form as his own, fills our intellect. Just so, for example, there can be the disposition of heat for the form of fire only from fire. And Ps. 36:9 says of this light: "We will see light in your light."

⋘ 106 ⋙

How the Natural Desire Comes to Rest by Seeing God Essentially, in Which Blessedness[25] Consists

And when this end has been obtained, the natural desire is necessarily at rest, since the divine essence, which is united to the intellect of the one beholding God in the aforementioned way, is the sufficient source of knowing all things and the fount of all goodness. Consequently, nothing can remain to be desired. And that we know him in the same way in which he knows himself, namely, essentially, is the most perfect way to obtain divine likeness.

But we do not comprehend him as he comprehends himself. It is not that we should not know some part of him, since he has no parts, but that we do not know him as perfectly as he is knowable. This is because the power of our intellect in understanding cannot be equal to the truth of himself as much as he is knowable, since his brilliance or truth is infinite, and our intellect is finite. And his intellect is infinite, just as his truth is, and so he knows himself as much as he is knowable. Just so, one who knows a demonstrable conclusion by demonstration comprehends it, but one who knows it in an imperfect way, namely, by a plausible argument, does not. And because we call our final end blessedness, the happiness or blessedness consists in seeing God essentially. But there is a great remoteness from God in the perfection of blessedness, since he has this blessedness by his nature, while a human being obtains it by sharing in the divine light, as I have said before [I, 105].

◄₹ 107 ₷►

The Movement toward God to Obtain Blessedness
Is like a Natural Movement

And we should consider that, since the process from potentiality to actuality is either a movement or something like it, the process in the course of acquiring this blessedness is like a natural movement or change. For in natural movement we first consider a property by which the movable thing is proportioned or inclined to such-and-such an end (e.g., weight on the earth to being moved downward). For something would by nature be moved to a fixed end only if it were to have a proportion to the end. Second, we consider the movement itself toward the end. Third, we consider the very form or place. And fourth, we consider resting in the form acquired or the place reached.

Therefore, in the intellectual movement to an end, there is, first, the love inclining to the end. Second, there is desire, which is a movement, as it were, toward the end, and there are the actions coming from such desire. Third, there is the form itself that the intellect obtains. And fourth, there is the resulting pleasure, which is simply the state of rest of the will in the end obtained.

Therefore, the end of natural coming to be is a form, and the end of locomotion a place, not rest in the form or the place, although this results from the end. And far less is the movement the end or proportion to the end. Just so, the final end of an intellectual creature is to see God, not to take pleasure in him, although pleasure accompanies the end and perfects it, as it were. And far less can desire or love be the final end, since these are possessed even before the end is reached.

◄₹ 108 ₷►

On the Error of Those Who Put Their
Happiness in Creatures

Therefore, it is clear that some falsely seek happiness in things other than God. Some falsely seek happiness in bodily pleasures, which are common to human beings and irrational animals. Others falsely seek happiness in riches, which are properly ordered to the preservation of those possessing them, and this is the common end of every created being. Others falsely seek happiness in powers, which are ordered to communicating one's own perfection to other things, and we also say that this is common to all things. Others falsely seek happiness in honors and fame, which are owed to someone insofar as that one already has the end or is fittingly disposed toward it. Or others falsely seek happiness in knowledge of any things, even those superior to human beings, although the desire of a human being is at rest only in knowledge of God.

6. Good and Evil

◄₹ 109 ₷►

Only God Is Essentially Good, but Creatures Are Good by Participation

Therefore, the foregoing makes clear that God and creatures are differently related to goodness in the two kinds of goodness that we can consider in creatures. For inasmuch as good has the nature of perfection and end, we note a creature's two kinds of goodness by its two kinds of perfection and end. We note a certain perfection of a creature insofar as the creature persists in its nature, and this is the end of its generation or production. And we note another perfection that a creature obtains by its movement and activity, and this is the end of its movement and activity.

The creature falls short of divine goodness in both of these ways.

For although the form and existing of a thing is its good and perfection insofar as we consider it in its nature, a composite substance is neither its form nor its existing, and a simple created substance, although it is the form itself, is not its existing. But God is his essence and his existing, as I have shown before [I, 10–11]. Likewise, all creatures obtain perfect goodness from an extrinsic end. For the perfection of goodness consists of obtaining the final end, and the final end of any creature is something outside it (i.e., the divine goodness), which is not ordered to a further end.

Therefore, the conclusion is that God is in every way his goodness and essentially good, while simple creatures are not altogether their goodness, both because they are not their existing, and because they are ordered to something extrinsic as their final end. And in composite substances, it is clear that they are in no way their goodness. Therefore, God alone is pure goodness and essentially good, while we call other things good by a sharing in him.

◄₹ 110 ₷►

God Cannot Lose His Goodness

And this makes clear that God can in no way lack goodness. For what is essentially in something cannot be absent from it (e.g., animal cannot be taken away from human being). Therefore, God cannot not be good. And to use a more appropriate example, as a human being cannot not be a human being, so God cannot not be perfectly good.

◄ 111 ►

A Creature Can Fall Short of Its Goodness

And we should consider how there can be lack of goodness in creatures. For it is clear that some goodness is inseparably in a creature in two ways: in one way because the goodness belongs to the creature's essence; in the other way because the creature is determined to one thing. Therefore, in the first way, the very goodness that is the form in simple substances is inseparably related to them, since they are essentially forms. And in the second way, simple substances cannot lose the good that consists of existing. For form is unlike matter, which is disposed to exist and not to exist, but form is equivalent to existing, even though it is not the existing itself. And so it is clear that simple substances cannot lose the good of the nature in which they subsist. Rather, they are inalterably disposed in that good.

But composite substances are neither their forms nor their existing. Therefore, composite substances have the good of their nature in such a way that they can lose it, except in things in which the potentiality of the matter is not disposed to different forms, nor to exist and not to exist, as is evident in heavenly bodies.

◄ 112 ►

How Creatures Lack Goodness in Their Actions

But because we not only consider the goodness of a creature insofar as it subsists in its nature, but rather the perfection of its goodness consists of it being ordered to an end, it is ordered to its end by its action. Therefore, it remains for us to consider how creatures lack goodness regarding their actions, by which they are ordered to their end. Here we should first consider that there is the same judgment about natural actions as there is about the nature that is their source. And so there can be no defect in the natural actions of those things whose nature cannot allow it. But the actions of those things whose nature can allow defects may also be defective.

And so no defective natural action can happen in substances that cannot pass away, whether the substances are material or immaterial. For the natural power in angels always remains capable of performing its proper actions.

Similarly, we find that the movements of the heavenly bodies are never out of their orbits. But in lower material substances, many defective natural actions happen because of weaknesses and defects that happen in their natures. For the sterility of plants, monstrosity in the generation of animals, and other such disorders happen from the defect of a natural source.

◄₹ 113 ₷►

In Created Spiritual Substances, There Can Be Defective Voluntary Action

And there are some actions whose source is the will, not nature, and the object of the will is good, chiefly as the will's end and secondarily as means to its end. Therefore, voluntary action is related to good as natural action is to the form by which a natural thing acts. Defective natural actions can happen only in things that can pass away, things whose forms can be defective, not in things that allow no defect regarding their forms. Just so, therefore, voluntary actions can be defective in things in which the will can fall short of the things' end.

There clearly cannot be defective voluntary action where the will cannot fall short of its end. And the will cannot be defective with respect to a good that by nature belongs to the one willing. For anything seeks its perfect existing (i.e., each thing's good) in its own way. But satisfied with the good connatural to it, the will can be defective with respect to an external good. Therefore, there cannot be defective voluntary action in something if the nature of the willing thing is the final end of its will. And only God is such, since his goodness, which is the final end of things, is his nature. But the nature of other willing things is not the final end of their will. And so there can be defective voluntary action in them because their will remains fixed on its own good, by not tending further to the highest good that is their final end. Therefore, there can be defective voluntary action in all created intellectual substances.

◄₹ 114 ₷►

What the Words *Good* and *Evil* Signify about Things

And we should consider here that, as the word *good* signifies perfect existing, so the word *evil* signifies only the privation of perfect existing. But privation, properly understood, is the lack of what nature constitutes to be possessed, and of when and how nature constitutes it to be possessed. Therefore, it is clear that we for this reason call evil anything that lacks a perfection that it ought to have. And so it is evil for a human being to lack the power of sight, but not for a stone, which nature does not constitute to have the power of sight.

◆ 115 ◆

Evil Cannot Be a Nature

And evil cannot be a nature. For every nature is either an actuality or a potentiality or a composite of both. Actuality is a perfection and has the nature of good, since the potential by nature seeks to be actual, and good is what all things seek. And so also a composite of actuality and potentiality shares in goodness insofar as it shares in actuality. Potentiality also has goodness insofar as it is ordered to actuality, and an indication of this is that the more potentiality is capable of actuality and perfection, the more it is esteemed. Therefore, we conclude that no nature as such is an evil.

Second, becoming actual perfects each thing, since actuality is the perfection of a thing. And mixing one contrary with the other does not perfect either. Rather, both are destroyed or diminished. And so sharing in good does not perfect evil. But having actual existing perfects every nature. And so, since existing is a good that all things desire, sharing in good perfects every nature. Therefore, no nature is an evil.

Third, any nature desires to preserve its existing and avoids destruction as much as it can. Therefore, since good is what all things desire, and, conversely, evil is what all things avoid, we need to say that, for each nature, existing as such is good, and that nonexisting is evil. But being evil is not good. Rather, not being evil is included in the notion of good. Therefore, no nature is an evil.

◆ 116 ◆

How Good and Evil Are Specific Differences of Being, and Contraries and Genera of Contraries

Therefore, it remains that we should consider how we call good and evil contraries and genera of contraries, and differences constituting certain species, namely, moral habits. For each one of two contraries is a nature, and nonbeing cannot be a genus or a specific difference, since we predicate a genus of something regarding what it is, and a specific difference regarding what sort of thing it is. Therefore, we should note that, as natural things get their species from a form, so moral things get their species from the end that is the object of the will, on which all moral things depend.

And as, in natural things, the privation of one form is connected with the reception of another form (e.g., the privation of the form of air or wood with the reception of the form of fire), so, in moral things, the privation of one end is connected with the desire of another end. Therefore, since the privation of a requisite perfection is an evil, it is an evil even in natural things to receive a form with which the privation of a requisite form is connected (e.g., fire is evil for wood) because of the connected privation, not because of the received form. And it is also an evil in moral things to adhere to an end with which the privation of a requisite end is connected, not because of the end adhered to but because of the connected privation. And so two kinds of moral action ordered to contrary ends differ regarding good and evil. And so the actions' contrary habits differ, with good and evil being specific differences, as it were, and contrary to each other, not because of the privation by which we call something evil, but because of the end with which the privation is connected.

Some[26] also understand in this way the dictum of Aristotle[27] that good and evil are the genera of contraries, namely, moral contraries. But if we correctly reflect, the good and evil in the genus of moral things are more like specific differences than species. And so it seems better for us to say that we call good and evil genera according to the position of Pythagoras,[28] who traced all things to good and evil as the first genera. And this position has some truth insofar as one of all two contrary things is perfect, and the other lesser, as is clear in white and black, sweet and bitter, and so forth. But what is perfect always belongs to the nature of good, and what is lesser always belongs to the nature of evil.

◄෫ 117 ෧►

Nothing Can Be Essentially or Supremely Evil, but Evil Destroys Something Good

Therefore, in having considered that evil is the privation of a requisite perfection, it now becomes clear how evil destroys good, namely, insofar as evil is the privation of good. Just so, we say that blindness destroys the power of sight because it is the very destruction of the power of sight. But evil does not destroy the whole good, since, as I have said before [I, 115], both form and potentiality for form are good, and a potentiality is the subject of privation, just as it is the subject of a form. And so the subject of evil is necessarily good, not that it is contrary to evil, but that it is a potentiality regarding evil.

And it is also clear from this that not every good can be the subject of evil, but only a good that is potential with respect to a perfection of which it can be deprived. And so, regarding things that are only actualities, or things in which actuality cannot be separated from potentiality, there cannot be evil in this respect.

This also makes clear that there cannot be anything essentially evil, since evil is necessarily always grounded in a subject. And so nothing can be supremely evil in the way in which something is supremely and essentially good.

The same things also make clear that evil cannot be desired or do anything except by the power of a connected good. For the desirable is a perfection and end, and the source of action is form. But the privation of one perfection or form is connected with the reception of another perfection or form. Therefore, it happens incidentally that a privation, or evil, is desired, and it is the source of an action because of a connected good, not insofar as the privation, or evil, is evil. Just so, a musician builds a house as a builder, not as a musician.

This also makes clear that evil cannot be a first source, since what is a source incidentally is secondary to what is a source intrinsically.

◄ई 118 ऽ►

Evil Is Grounded in Good as Its Subject

And against the aforementioned things, someone may wish to object that good cannot be the subject of evil because one contrary is not the subject of the other, nor do we ever find in other contraries that they exist together. In response, we should consider that other contraries belong to a fixed genus, but good and evil are common to all genera. For every being as such is good, and every privation as such is evil. And so, as the subject of a privation needs to be a being, so also the subject needs to be good. But the subject of a privation does not need to be white or sweet or seeing, since we do not predicate these things of being as such. And so something black is not in something white, or something blind in something seeing, but evil is in good just as blindness is in the subject of the power of sight. And we do not call something seeing the subject of the power of sight because something seeing is not common to every being.

◄ई 119 ऽ►

On the Two Kinds of Evil

Evil is a privation and defect, and there can be defect in a thing both insofar as we consider its nature, and insofar as it is ordered by its action to its end, as is clear from what I have said before [I, 112]. Therefore, it follows that we speak of evil in both senses, namely, regarding defect in the very thing, as blindness is evil for an animal, and regarding defect in action, as limping signifies action with a defect. Therefore, in both natural things and voluntary things, we call the evil of an action directed to an end to which the action is not disposed in the requisite way a defect. For example, doctors fail in their practice when they do not act properly in regard to health. And nature also fails in its action when it does not generate offspring in the proper disposition and form, as when monsters happen in nature.

◄∂ 120 ∂►

On the Three Kinds of Action and the Evil of Sin

But we should note that action is sometimes under the control of an active thing, as all voluntary actions are, and I call an action voluntary whose source is in an active thing that knows the things of which an act consists. But sometimes actions are not voluntary, and these are forced actions, whose source is external, and natural actions or actions done out of ignorance, since the latter do not come from a knowing source. Therefore, if there should happen to be defect in involuntary actions ordered to an end, we speak only of defect. But if there should happen to be defect in voluntary actions, we speak of both defect and sin, since the active thing, being master of its action, deserves blame and punishment. And if the actions are mixed, namely, partially voluntary and partially involuntary, the greater the involuntary element, the less sin there is in them.

And because natural action accompanies a thing's nature, defective natural action clearly cannot happen in things that cannot pass away, whose nature cannot be altered. But the will of any intellectual creature can suffer defect in voluntary action, as I have shown before [I, 113]. And so we conclude that, although it is common to all things that cannot pass away to be free of natural evil, being free by a natural necessity of the evil of sin, of which only a rational nature is capable, belongs to God alone.

◄∂ 121 ∂►

Some Evil Has the Nature of Punishment, Not of Sin

And as defect in voluntary action constitutes the nature of defect and sin, so the deficiency of any good imposed for sin against the will of the one on whom it is imposed has the nature of punishment. For punishment is imposed as medicine for sin and to rectify the order of the will. Punishment is imposed as medicine insofar as human beings withdraw from sin because of punishment. They do so when they, in order not to suffer what is contrary to their will, refrain from doing the disordered action that would be pleasing to their will. Punishment also rectifies the order of the will, since human beings by sinning transgress the bounds of the natural order, indulging their will more than is proper. And so the punishment whereby something is taken away from the will effects a return to the order of justice. And so it is clear that suitable punishment for sin is rendered only if the punishment is more contrary to the will than the sin was pleasing to it.

◄§ 122 §►

Not Every Punishment Is Contrary to the Will in the Same Way

Not every punishment is contrary to the will in the same way. For some punishment is contrary to what a human being actually wishes, and this punishment is most keenly felt. And some punishment is contrary to the habitual, not the actual, will, as when one is deprived of something (e.g., a son or a possession), but does not know about it. And so this does nothing actually contrary to the will of the one deprived, but it would be contrary to the will if such a one were to know about it. And punishment is sometimes contrary to the will by the nature of that faculty. For the will is by nature ordered to good. And so if one should be deprived of virtue, this is sometimes not contrary to one's actual will, since one perhaps contemns virtue. Nor is it contrary to habitual virtue, since one is perhaps habitually disposed to will contrary to virtue. And yet it is contrary to the natural rectitude of the will whereby a human being by nature desires virtue.

And this also makes clear that we can measure grades of punishments in two ways: in the first way by the amount of good that the punishment deprives one of; in the second way insofar as the punishment is more or less contrary to the will. For being deprived of a greater good is sometimes less contrary to the will than being deprived of a lesser good.

7. Divine Providence and Governance

◄§ 123 §►

Divine Providence Governs All Things

And the aforementioned things can make clear that divine providence governs all things. For an active thing directs to its end whatever things are ordered to that end (e.g., all soldiers in an army are ordered to the end of its command-ing general, namely, victory, and he directs them to the end). But I have shown before that all things by their actions tend toward the end of divine goodness [I, 101]. Therefore, God himself, to whom this end belongs, directs all things to that end. And this is to be ruled and governed by a providence. Therefore, divine providence governs all things.

Second, things that are always disposed in the same way are found to order things that can fail and are not always disposed in the same way. For example, the invariable movements of a heavenly body regulate all the movements of lower material substances, which can fail. But all creatures can change and fail. For there can be defective voluntary action in intellectual creatures insofar as their nature allows, and other creatures participate in motion, whether by coming to be and passing away, or only by locomotion. But God is the only one in whom there can be no defect. Therefore, we conclude that he orders all other things.

Third, we trace things that exist by sharing to what exists essentially, as their cause (e.g., all things ignited have fire in some way as the cause of their being ignited). Therefore, since God alone is essentially good, and all other things obtain their complement of goodness by a sharing, God necessarily brings all things to their complement of goodness. And this is to be directed and governed. For particular things are governed and ruled by being established in the order of goodness. Therefore, God governs and rules over all things.

◄ᘒ 124 Sᐅ

God Governs Inferior Creatures by Means
of Superior Creatures

Thus God fittingly governs inferior creatures by means of superior creatures. For we call some creatures, ones more perfect in goodness, superior. But crea-tures obtain their rank in goodness from God inasmuch as he governs them. Therefore, superior creatures share in more of the order of divine governance than inferior creatures do. But what shares more in any perfection is related to what shares less in it as actuality is to potentiality, and an active thing is to a thing being acted upon. Therefore, superior creatures are related to inferior creatures in the order of divine providence as active creatures to passive crea-tures. Therefore, superior creatures govern inferior creatures.

Second, it belongs to the divine goodness to communicate its likeness to creatures. For we say in this way that God made all things on account of his goodness, as is clear from what I have said before [I, 101]. But it belongs to the perfection of God's goodness both that he is good in himself, and that he brings other things to good. Therefore, he communicates to creatures both that they are good in themselves, and that one creature brings another creature to goodness. Therefore, he draws some creatures to good by means of other creatures. But the latter creatures need to be superior. For what shares from an active thing in likeness of its form and action is more perfect than what shares from an active thing in likeness of its form but not of its action. For example, the moon, which is both luminous and illumines, receives light from the sun more perfectly than do opaque material substances, which are only illumined and do not illumine. Therefore, God governs inferior creatures by means of superior creatures.

Third, the good of many things is better than the good of only one thing and so more representative of the goodness that is the good of the whole universe. And if a superior creature, which shares in more abundant goodness from God, were not to cooperate with God to procure the good of inferior creatures, the abundance of goodness would belong only to one thing. But the abundance of goodness becomes common to many things by cooperating with God to procure the good of many things. Therefore, it belongs to the divine goodness that God governs inferior creatures by means of superior creatures.

◀ৈ 125 ৯▶

Superior Intellectual Substances Govern
Inferior Intellectual Substances

Therefore, since intellectual creatures are superior to other creatures, as the foregoing makes clear [I, 75], God clearly governs all nonintellectual creatures by means of intellectual creatures. Likewise, since some intellectual creatures are superior to other intellectual creatures, God governs inferior intellectual creatures by means of superior intellectual creatures. And so it is that superior spirits, who are called angels (i.e., messengers) because they announce divine things to human beings, govern human beings, who by the order of nature hold the lowest place among intellectual substances. And of the angels, superior ones govern inferior ones insofar as different hierarchies among them (i.e., sacred rulers) are distinguished, and different ranks are distinguished in individual hierarchies.

◀ৈ 126 ৯▶

On the Ranks and Orders of Angels

And since every action of an intellectual substance, as such, comes from the intellect, there needs to be different action, preeminence, and rank in intellectual substances according to the different ways in which they understand. And the more excellent and worthy the intellect, the more the intellect can consider the natures of effects in a higher and more universal cause. I have also said before that a superior intellect has more universal intelligible forms [I, 78].

Therefore, the first way of understanding proper to intellectual substances is that they perceive the natures of effects in the first cause itself, namely, God, and so the natures of the their own works when God dispenses inferior effects through them. And this is proper to the first hierarchy, which is divided into three ranks by the three things that we consider in any practical skill. The first of these things is the end from which we derive the natures of the works. The second consists of the natures of the works in the mind of the craftsman. The third consists of the application of the natures to the effects. Therefore, it belongs to the first rank to be fully informed about the effects in the highest good, as it is the final end of things. And so we call the first order of angels Seraphim from the ardor of their love, as if they are glowing and burning, since the object of love is good. And it belongs to the second order to contemplate the effects of God in the intelligible natures themselves as the natures are in God. And so we call the second order of angels Cherubim from the fullness of their knowledge. And it belongs to the third order to consider in God himself how creatures share in the intelligible natures applied to the effects. And so we call angels of the third order Thrones because they have God residing in them.

The second way of understanding is to consider the natures of effects as they are in universal causes, and this is proper to the second hierarchy. And this hierarchy is also divided into three ranks by the three things that belong to universal causes, especially those active by their intellect. The first of these things is to preordain what things are to be done, and so the highest skills in the crafts are prescriptive and called architectonic. And so we call the first order of this hierarchy Dominations, since it belongs to a master to command and preordain. The second thing found in universal causes is something that first moves another to act, having the governing power of execution, as it were. And so Gregory the Great calls the second order of this hierarchy Principalities.[29] (Dionysius calls this order Virtues,[30] in order that we understand them as virtues [powers], since the first action is the most virtuous [powerful].) And the third thing found in universal causes is something that removes hindrances to execution. And so also the third rank of this hierarchy belongs to Powers, whose duty is to restrain everything that could block execution of the divine command. And so also people say that they keep devils away.

The third way of understanding is to consider the natures of effects in the effects themselves, and this is proper to the third hierarchy, which is directly in charge of us, who receive knowledge of the effects from the effects themselves. And this hierarchy also has three orders, and we call the lowest order Angels because they announce to human beings things that belong to the governance of human beings. And so also we call them the guardians of human beings. Above the order of Angels is the order of Archangels, which announces to human beings things that are above reason, such as the mysteries of faith. Gregory calls the highest order of this hierarchy Virtues, since they perform things above nature to prove messages above reason that they announce to us. And so working miracles is said to belong to Virtues.[31] (But Dionysius calls the highest order of this hierarchy Principalities.[32] He does so in order that we understand as princes those in charge of individual peoples, as Angels those in charge of individual human beings, and as Archangels those who announce to human beings things belonging to salvation in general.)

Because a lower power acts in virtue of a higher power, a lower order performs things belonging to a higher order insofar as the lower order acts by the power of that higher order. But higher orders have more excellently things that belong to lower orders. And so all the things in angels are in some way common, but proper names are allotted by reason of things that belong to each order as such. And the lowest order, acting in virtue of all the angels, as it were, retains the common name for itself. And because it belongs to a higher angel to act on a lower angel, and intellectual action consists of instructing or teaching, higher angels, insofar as they instruct lower angels, are said to purify, illumine, and perfect them. Higher angels purify lower angels insofar as they take away ignorance. Higher angels illumine insofar as they by their light strengthen the intellects of lower angels to understand something higher. And higher angels perfect lower angels insofar as the former bring the latter to the perfection of higher knowledge. For these three things belong to acquiring knowledge, as Dionysius says.[33]

Nevertheless, this does not take away from the fact that all angels, even the lowest, behold the divine essence. For, although each of the blessed spirits sees God essentially, one sees him more perfectly than another, as the foregoing can make clear. But the more perfectly one knows a cause, the more of its effects one knows in it. Therefore, higher angels instruct lower angels about the divine effects that the higher angels know in God more clearly than other angels do, not about the divine essence that all angels directly see.

◄◦ 127 ◦►

Higher Material Substances Dispose Lower Material Substances but Not the Human Intellect

Therefore, as one intellectual substance, namely, the higher, by divine providence governs another, namely, the lower, so also higher material substances dispose lower ones. And so the movements of heavenly bodies cause all the movements of lower material substances, and the lower forms and species result from the power of the heavenly bodies. Just so, higher spirits convey the intelligible natures of things to lower spirits. But since an intellectual substance in the order of things is superior to all material substances, it is not proper by the aforementioned order of providence that God govern any intellectual substance by means of a material substance. Therefore, since the human soul is an intellectual substance, the movements of heavenly bodies cannot dispose it insofar as it understands and wills. Therefore, heavenly bodies have no direct influence on the human intellect or will.

Second, material substances act only by movement. Therefore, everything acted upon by a material substance is moved by it. But material motion cannot move the human soul regarding its intellectual part, in which is the will, since the intellect does not belong to the activity of any bodily organ. Therefore, the human soul as to its intellect or will cannot be subject to any influence from heavenly bodies.

Third, things that come about from the influence of heavenly bodies on lower things are natural things. Therefore, if the activities of the intellect and the will were to come from the influence of heavenly bodies, the activities would come from a natural impulse. And so human beings would not differ in their actions from other animals, which are moved by a natural impulse to their actions. And free decision, deliberation, election, and all such things that human beings have beyond other animals would perish.

◀℞ 128 ℠▶

How the Human Intellect Is Indirectly
Subject to Heavenly Bodies

But we should nevertheless consider that the human intellect receives the source of its knowledge from sense powers. And so the intellect's knowledge is disturbed when the soul's powers of fancy, imagination, and memory have been disturbed, and the receptivity of the intellect becomes more suitable when the aforementioned powers are well disposed.

Likewise, change in a sense appetite does something to change the will (i.e., the rational appetite) insofar as the perceived good is the object of the will. For, inasmuch as desire, anger, fear, and other emotions dispose us in various ways, something seems good or evil to us in different ways. But all the powers of the sensory part of the soul, whether cognitive or appetitive, belong to the activity of some bodily parts, and when these bodily parts are altered, the sense powers themselves are also necessarily altered incidentally. Therefore, since change in lower material substances is subject to movement of the heavens, the actions of the sense powers are also subject, albeit incidentally, to the same movement. And so heavenly movement indirectly in some way influences an act of the intellect and human will, namely, insofar as emotions incline the will to something.

But the will is not subject to the emotions such that it necessarily follows their impulse. Rather, the will has it in its power to restrain the emotions by a judgment of reason. Consequently, the human will in human bodies is not subject even to the influences of heavenly bodies but has free judgment to follow or resist emotions when it will seem expedient. And this belongs only to the wise, but it belongs to most people, namely, those who lack wisdom and virtue, to follow bodily emotions and inclinations.

◀ 129

God Alone and No Created Thing Moves
the Will of a Human Being

And we trace every changeable and manifold thing to something unchangeable and one as the cause, and the understanding and will of a human being seem changeable and manifold. Therefore, we need to trace such understanding and will to a higher unchangeable and simple cause. And because we do not trace them to heavenly bodies as the cause, as I have shown [I, 127], we need to trace them to higher causes.

But there are different dispositions regarding understanding and will. For there is an act of the intellect insofar as understood things are in the intellect, but we note an act of the will by the inclination of the will to the things willed. Therefore, nature constitutes the intellect to be perfected by something external related to the intellect as to a potentiality. And so anything external that is more perfect regarding intelligible existing, whether God, an angel, or a more educated human being, can assist human beings in regard to acts of the intellect, albeit in different ways. For one human being assists another human being to understand by one proposing to the other something intelligible that the other was not considering. But this is not such that one human being perfects the light of the intellect of another, since the natural light of both belongs to one and the same species.

But because the natural light of an angel is by nature more excellent than the natural light of a human being, an angel can assist a human being to understand both regarding the object an angel proposes to a human being and regarding the light that the light of an angel strengthens. Nevertheless, the natural light of a human being is not from an angel, since only God established the nature of the rational soul, which receives existing by creation. Therefore, God helps a human being to understand, not only regarding the object that he proposes to a human being, or by adding light, but also because the natural light of human beings whereby they understand is from him. Moreover, God is the first truth from which every other truth has certitude, as the conclusions of deductive syllogisms have from first principles. Therefore, he also helps human beings to understand because only divine power can make something certain for the intellect, as only the power of first principles makes the conclusions in sciences certain.

But an act of the will is an inclination proceeding from the internal to the external and is like natural inclinations. Therefore, as inclinations natural for natural things are from the cause of their nature, an act of the will is from God alone, who is the only cause of the rational nature having a will. And so it is clearly not contrary to free decision if God moves the will of a human being, as it is not contrary to nature that God acts in natural things. Rather, both a natural inclination and a voluntary inclination are from God, each coming about according to the condition of the thing to which the inclination belongs. For God moves things insofar as this is proper to their nature.

Therefore, the aforementioned things make clear that heavenly bodies can influence the human body and its bodily powers, just as they influence other material substances. But heavenly bodies cannot influence the intellect, although an intellectual creature can. And only God can influence the will.

◄≀ 130 ≀►

God Is in All Things, and His Providence
Extends to All Things

But since secondary causes act only by the power of the first cause, as tools act at the direction of a skill, all the other active things by which God implements the order of his governance necessarily act by the power of God himself. Therefore, God causes the action of anyone of them, as a cause's motion causes a moveable thing's motion. But the thing causing motion and the thing being moved need to be simultaneous. Therefore, God is necessarily internally present in any active thing, acting in it, as it were, when he moves it to act.

Second, God causes both the action of secondary active things and their existing, as I have shown before [I, 68]. But we should not understand that God causes the existing of things as a builder causes the existing of a house, which continues to exist when the builder has been removed. For the builder causes the existing of a house only insofar as he moves toward the existing of the house, and this movement consists of building the house. And so he directly causes the coming to be of the house, a process that ceases if the builder has been removed. But God of himself directly causes existing itself, communicating it to all things, as it were, as the sun communicates light to air and other things that the sun illumines. And so, as enduring illumination of the sun is necessary to preserve light in air, so it is necessary that God ceaselessly bestow existing on things to preserve them in it. And so all things are related to God like something made to its maker, not only as the things begin to exist, but also as they are preserved in existing. But the maker and the thing made, like the thing causing motion and the thing moved, need to be simultaneous. Therefore, God needs to be present in all things insofar as they have existing. But existing is what is internally present in all things. Therefore, God needs to be in all things.

Third, one who executes the order of one's providence by some intermediate causes needs to know and order the effects of such causes. Otherwise, the effects would fall outside the order of one's providence. And the more the knowledge and order of the one governing descends to individual things, the more perfect the providence of the one governing. This is because determination of an individual thing escapes the providence of the one governing if particulars of such things are removed from that one's knowledge. But I have shown before that all things are necessarily subject to divine providence [I, 123], and divine providence is clearly most perfect, since whatever we predicate of God belongs to him in the highest degree. Therefore, the order of his providence necessarily extends even to the least effects.

◄❧ 131 ❧►

God Directly Disposes All Things

Therefore, this makes it clear that the disposition and order of divine providence directly extends to all things, although God accomplishes his governance of the world by intermediate secondary causes insofar as this belongs to execution of his providence. For he does not order the first and universal things in such a way as to commit the ultimate and individual things to the disposition of other things. This happens with human beings because of the weakness of their knowledge, which cannot simultaneously have time for many things, and so higher officials dispose about important things and commit the least things for others to arrange. But God can at once know many things, as I have shown before [I, 29]. And so he is not withdrawn from ordering the most important things because he dispenses the least important things.

◄﹩ 132 ﹩►

Arguments That Seem to Show That God Does Not Have Providence about Particular Things

But it could seem to someone that God does not arrange individual things. For one arranges by one's providence only the things that one knows. But God can seem to lack knowledge of individual things because the senses, not the intellect, know individual things. And there can be only intellectual, not sense, knowledge in God, who is altogether immaterial. Therefore, it can then seem to someone that divine providence does not order individual things.

Second, individual things are infinite, and knowledge of infinite things is impossible, since the infinite as such is unknowable. Therefore, it seems that individual things escape divine knowledge and providence.

Third, many contingent things belong to individual things, and there can be no certain knowledge of contingent things. Therefore, since God's knowledge needs to be most certain, it seems that he does not know or dispense individual things.

Fourth, not all individual things exist at the same time, since some things pass away when other things come to be. But there cannot be knowledge of things that do not exist. Therefore, if God should have knowledge of individual things, it will follow that he begins and ceases to know some things, and so that he is mutable. Therefore, it seems that he does not know or dispense individual things.

◄﹩ 133 ﹩►

Answers to These Arguments

But these arguments are easily answered if one should consider the truth of the matter. For, inasmuch as God knows himself perfectly, he necessarily knows everything that is in him in any way. But since every essence and power of a created being is from him, and what is from anything is in it virtually, he, knowing himself, necessarily knows the essence of a created being and whatever is in the being virtually. And so he knows all the individual things that are in him and his other causes virtually.

Nor are the divine intellect and the human intellect similar regarding knowledge, as the first objection argued. For our intellect receives its knowledge of things by abstracted forms, which are likenesses of the forms, not matter or the material dispositions that are the sources of individuation. And so our intellect can know only universal, not individual, things. But God's intellect knows things by his essence, in which, as the first source, both the form and the matter of things are contained virtually. And so he knows both universal and individual things.

Likewise, it is not inappropriate that God knows infinite things, although our intellect cannot. For our intellect cannot at the same time actually consider many things. And so, if it were to know infinite things by considering them, it would need to number them one after the other, and this is contrary to the notion of the infinite. But our intellect can know infinite things virtually and potentially (e.g., all species of numbers or proportions), inasmuch as it has a sufficient source to know all things. On the other hand, God can at once know many things, as I have shown before [I, 29]. And that by which he knows all things, namely, his essence, is the sufficient source of knowing all things, both things that exist and things that can exist. Therefore, as our intellect knows virtually and potentially the infinite things for the knowledge of which it has a source, so God actually considers all infinite things. It is also clear that, although individual destructible and temporal things do not exist simultaneously, God has knowledge of them at once, since he knows them by the way of his existing, which is eternal and without temporal succession. Therefore, as he knows material things in an immaterial way and many things by one thing, so also he in one gaze sees things that do not exist simultaneously. And so nothing needs to be added to, or subtracted from, his knowledge because he knows individual things.

This also makes clear that God has certain knowledge of contingent things. For even before they come to be, he sees them as they are actual in their existing, and not only as they are future things and in their causes virtually, as we can know some future things. Contingent things, as future things existing virtually in their causes, are not determined to one thing, so that we can have certain knowledge of them. But as actual in their existing, they are now determined to one thing, and we can have certain knowledge of them. For example, we can know with the certainty of an eyewitness that Socrates is sitting when he is sitting.

And God likewise knows with certainty all things, anything done throughout the whole course of time, in his eternity, since his eternity in its presence to him extends to, and goes beyond, the whole course of time. And so we may consider that God in his eternity knows the flow of time as one who is perched on the top of a watchtower sees at once the whole transit of travelers passing by.

◀ζ 134 ş▶

Only God Knows Individual Future Contingent Things

And it clearly belongs only to God, to whom eternity properly and truly be-longs, to know future contingent things as actual in their existing (i.e., to have certitude about them). And so the certain foretelling of future things is held to be a sign of divinity, as Is. 41:23 says: "Also foretell the future, and we shall say that you are gods." But to know future things in their causes can also belong to other things, although this knowledge is conjectural, not certain, except regard-ing effects that necessarily result from their causes. A doctor foretells future illnesses, and a sailor forecasts storms, in this way.

◀ζ 135 ş▶

God Is in All Things by His Power, Essence, and Presence, and He Directly Disposes All Things

Therefore, nothing prevents God from having knowledge even of individual ef-fects and ordering them directly by his very self, although he executes the order through intermediate causes. But he is also directly somehow related to all the effects in the execution, inasmuch as all the intermediate causes act in the power of the first cause, so that he himself somehow seems to act in all things. And all the works of secondary causes can be attributed to him as we attribute the work of a tool to a craftsman. For we say more appropriately that a blacksmith rather than his hammer makes a knife. God is also directly related to all the effects inso-far as he is intrinsically the cause of existing and preserves all things in existing. And we say that God is in all things by these three direct ways: essence, power, and presence. He is in all things by his essence, inasmuch as the existing of any-thing is a participation in the divine existing, and so the divine essence is present in any existing thing inasmuch as it has existing, as the cause in its effect. He is in all things by his power, inasmuch as all things act in his power. And he is in all things by his presence, inasmuch as he directly orders and disposes all things.

◀ζ 136 ş▶

It Belongs to God Alone to Work Miracles

The whole order of secondary causes and their power are from God, and he produces his effects by his free will, not by necessity, as I have shown before [I, 96]. Therefore, it is clear that he can act outside the order of secondary causes (e.g., he cures those whom natural activity cannot heal, or causes some such things outside the order of natural causes). But these things are by the order of divine providence, since God has arranged for the sake of an end that he sometimes should do things outside the order of natural causes. And when he does some such things outside the order of secondary causes, we call the deeds miracles, since it is a source of wonder if we see an effect but do not know its cause. Therefore, since God is a cause absolutely hidden from us, if he causes something outside the order of secondary causes known to us, we call such things miracles absolutely. But if another cause hidden from this or that person causes something, the thing is a miracle in relation to the one who does not know the cause, not a miracle absolutely. And so something may seem wondrous to one person that is not to another person, who knows the cause.

And so acting outside the order of secondary causes belongs only to God, who institutes the order and is not bound to it, although all other things are subject to it. And so it belongs only to God to work miracles, as Ps. 72:18 says: "He is the only one who does great marvels." Therefore, when a creature seems to work miracles, they are not true miracles because some powers of natural things cause them, although the powers are hidden from us, as in the case the devils' "miracles" accomplished by magical arts. Or else, if they are true miracles, someone importunes them from God, namely, that God do such things. Therefore, since only God produces all such miracles, they are appropriately understood as proof of faith, which relies on God alone. For the fact that something proposed by a human being is said with divine authority is never more appropriately demonstrated than by works that only God can do.

And such miracles, although done outside the order of secondary causes, are not be called absolutely contrary to nature, since the natural order allows lower things to be subject to the actions of higher things. And so we do not say that things that result in lower material substances from the influence of heavenly bodies are absolutely contrary to nature. But such things are sometimes perhaps contrary to the particular nature of this or that thing, as is evident about the movement of water in the ebb and flow of the sea that the moon's action causes. Therefore, although things that happen in creatures by God's action seem to be contrary to the particular order of secondary causes, the action is in accord with the universal order of nature. Therefore, miracles are not contrary to nature.

◀ 137 ▶

Some Things Are Said to Be by Chance and Fortuitous

And although God dispenses even the least things, as I have shown [I, 130–31], nothing prevents some things from happening by chance and good fortune.

For something, when done outside the aim of a lower cause, may be fortuitous or by chance in relation to that cause but not be fortuitous or by chance in relation to a higher cause, in accord with whose aim the thing is done. For example, this is clear in the case of a master who sends two slaves to the same place in such a way that one slave does not know about the other. Therefore, the meeting of the two is by chance as to each but not as to the master. Therefore, when some things happen outside the aim of secondary causes, they are fortuitous or by chance with the respect had to those causes. And they can be called absolutely by chance, since we denote effects absolutely by the condition of proximate causes. But if we consider the effects' relation to God, they are foreseen, not fortuitous.

◄₹ 138 ₴►

Whether Fate Is a Nature, and What It Is

And this makes clear what is the nature of fate. For, inasmuch as many effects were found to result by chance when considering secondary causes, some wished to trace such effects to no higher cause ordaining them, and they necessarily deny fate completely.[34]

And some wished to trace effects that seem by chance and fortuitous to a higher cause ordaining them, but, not going beyond the order of material things, they attributed the order of the effects to the foremost material substances, namely, the heavenly bodies.[35] And they said that fate is a force from the stars' position, from which they said such effects happen.[36] But I have shown that the intellect and the will, which are the proper sources of human acts, are not subject to the heavenly bodies [I, 127]. Therefore, one cannot say that things that seem to happen by chance or fortuitously in human affairs are traceable to heavenly bodies as the cause ordaining them.

And fate seems to be only about human affairs, in which there is also luck. For some wishing to know the future are accustomed to inquire about human affairs and to find answers about them from fortune-tellers. And so also fate gets its name from foretelling.[37] And so it is alien to faith to posit fate in this way.

But because both natural things and human affairs are subject to divine providence, it is necessary to trace to the order of divine providence things that seem to happen by chance in human affairs. And so it is necessary for those who hold that all things are subject to divine providence to posit fate, since fate so understood is related to divine providence as providence's proper effect. For fate is the unfolding of divine providence applied to things, as Boethius says that fate is "the immovable disposition," that is, order, "inhering in movable things."[38] But insofar as we can, we ought not even to utter words in common with unbelievers, lest those who do not understand can take the occasion to err. Therefore, it is more prudent for the faithful to refrain from using the word *fate*, since fate is more commonly understood by the first understanding. And so also Augustine says in *The City of God* that, if one believes that there is fate in the second sense, such a one "should hold the opinion and correct the language."[39]

◀ᶎ 139 ᶩ▶

Not All Things Are by Necessity

And although the order of divine providence applied to things is certain, by reason of which Boethius says that fate is "an immovable disposition inhering in movable things,"[40] it still does not follow because of this that all things happen by necessity, since we call effects necessary or contingent by the condition of their proximate causes. For it is clear that, if the first cause should be necessary, and a secondary cause contingent, a contingent effect results. For example, the first cause in material things of the coming to be in the lower ones is the movement of a heavenly body. And although that movement happens necessarily, the coming to be and passing away in the lower material things happen contingently, since inferior causes are contingent and can fail. But I have shown that God executes the order of his providence through inferior causes [I, 130]. Therefore, some effects of divine providence will be contingent according to the condition of inferior causes.

◀ᶎ 140 ᶩ▶

Many Things Are Contingent, with Divine Providence Abiding

Nevertheless, the contingency of effects or causes cannot disturb the certainty of divine providence. For three things seem to guarantee the certainty of divine providence, namely, the infallibility of divine foreknowledge, the efficacy of the divine will, and the wisdom of the divine arrangement that devises sufficient ways to obtain an effect. And none of these things is repugnant to the contingency of things.

For God's foreknowledge is infallible even regarding contingent future things, inasmuch as God in his eternity sees future things as actual in their existing, as I have explained before [I, 133].

And God's will, since it is the universal cause of things, regards both that something comes to be, and that it comes to be in this way. Therefore, it belongs to the efficacy of the divine will both that something comes to be that God wills to come to be, and that it comes to be in the way in which he wills that it come to be. But he wills that some things come to be necessarily, and that other things come to be contingently, since each of these things is required for the complete existing of the universe. Therefore, in order that things come to be in both ways, he used necessary causes for some things and contingent causes for other things. And so the divine will is efficaciously fulfilled when some things come to be necessarily, and other things contingently.

It is also clear that the wisdom of the divine arrangement preserves the certainty of providence, with the contingency of things abiding. The practical wisdom of a human being can enable one to assist a cause that can fail to produce an effect, so that the effect sometimes follows without fail, as is evident in a doctor healing a patient or in a vinedresser using a remedy to cure the barrenness of a vine. If so, much more does it happen by the wisdom of the divine arrangement that, although contingent causes can fail to produce an effect insofar as it lies within their power, the effect follows without fail when some supports have been supplied. And this does not take away the effect's contingency.

Therefore, the contingency of things clearly does not exclude the certainty of divine providence.

◄₹ 141 s►

The Certainty of Divine Providence Does
Not Exclude Evils from Things

We can also perceive in the same way that evils can happen in the world because of the defect of secondary causes, with divine providence abiding. For we perceive in ordered causes that evil happens in an effect from the defect of a secondary cause, and yet the first cause in no way causes this deficiency. For example, the crookedness of a leg, not the soul's power of locomotion, causes the evil of limping. And so whatever motion there is in the limping is related to the power of locomotion as the motion's cause, but the crookedness of a leg, not the power of locomotion, causes whatever crookedness there is in the limping. Therefore, we trace to God as the cause whatever evil happens in things as to what has existing or a form or a nature, since there can be evil only in something good, as is clear from what I have said before [I, 118]. But we trace something evil to an inferior defective cause as to the defect that it has. And so, although God is the universal cause of all things, he does not cause evils as such but does cause whatever good is connected to the evils.

◄§ 142 §►

That God Permits Evils Does Not Derogate
from His Goodness

But it is not repugnant to God's goodness that he permits evils to be in things governed by him. First, this is true because it belongs to providence to preserve, not to lose, the nature of things governed. But the perfection of the universe requires that there be some things in which evil cannot happen and other things that can by their nature suffer the defect of evil. Therefore, if divine providence were to exclude evil completely from things, their nature would not govern them, and this would be a greater defect than the individual defects that would be taken away.

Second, this is true because the good of one thing sometimes cannot happen without the evil of another thing. For example, we observe that there is no coming to be of one thing without the passing away of another thing, that the lion is not nourished without the killing of another animal, and that there is no patience of the just without persecution by the unjust. Therefore, if evil were to be completely excluded from things, it would follow that many good things would also be taken away. Therefore, it belongs to divine providence to ordain that evil things result in some good, not to exclude evil completely from things.

Third, this is true because particular evil things render the good things more commendable when the latter are compared to the former. Just so, the darkness of black makes the brilliance of white more manifest. And so the fact that evils are permitted to be in the world manifests more clearly the divine goodness in good things and the divine wisdom in ordering evil things to good things.

◄§ 143 §►

God Specially Provides for Human Beings by Grace

Therefore, because divine providence provides for individual things according to their way, and the rational creature above other creatures is the master of its acts by free decision, provision needs also to be made in an individual way for the rational creature in two regards. First, provision needs to be made regarding aids in the work God gives to the rational creature. Second, provision needs to be made regarding the recompense God gives to the rational creature for its works. For God gives to irrational creatures only the aids to act by which nature moves them to act, but God gives to rational creatures examples and precepts to live by. For it is proper only for those who are masters of their acts to be given precepts, although we say by an analogy that God also gives precepts to irrational creatures, as Ps. 148:6 says: "He established an ordinance, and it will not pass away." And this ordinance is nothing but divine providence's disposition moving natural things to their proper actions.

Likewise, the actions of rational creatures are imputed to them for praise or blame because they have mastery of their acts, actions imputed to human beings by both their human ruler and God, since both a human being and God govern human beings. And whatever a human being does in a praiseworthy or blameworthy way is imputed to the human being by the one to whom the human being is subject. And because reward is due for things done rightly, and punishment for sin, as I have said before [I, 121], rational creatures are both punished for evil things and rewarded for good things according to the justice of divine providence. But in irrational creatures, punishment and reward have no place, nor have blame or praise.

But the final end of a rational creature exceeds the capacity of its nature, and means should be proportioned to that end according to the right order of providence. Therefore, God also confers on rational creatures both aids proportionate to their nature and aids that exceed its capacity. And so God imparts to human beings above the natural capacity of reason the light of grace, which internally perfects them for virtues. The light of grace internally perfects them regarding knowledge when such light elevates their mind to know things that surpass reason. It also internally perfects them regarding action and desire when the light elevates their desire to love God above all created things, to hope in him, and to do the things that such love requires.

And we for two reasons call such aids bestowed on human beings above their nature gratuitous. First, the aids are gratuitous because God gives them gratis. For there cannot be anything in a human being for which such helps are worthily due, since they exceed the capacity of human nature. Second, the aids are gratuitous because such gifts make a human being pleasing to God in a special way. For the love of God causes the goodness in things and is not aroused by preexisting goodness, as our love is. Therefore, we need to consider the special nature of divine love regarding those on whom he bountifully bestows some particular effects of his goodness. And so we say that he especially and absolutely loves those on whom he bountifully bestows such effects of his goodness by which they attain to their final end (i.e., himself, who is the fount of goodness).

8. Sin, Grace, and the Final End of Human Beings

◄≀ 144 ≀►

God Remits Sins by Gifts of Grace

Sins happen because actions lack the right order to the end, and a human being is ordered to the end by both natural aids and the aids of grace. Therefore, the sins of human beings are necessarily contrary to both natural aids and the aids of grace. But contraries drive each other out. And so, as such sins take away the aids of grace from a human being, so the gifts of grace remit sins for a human being. Otherwise, the wickedness of a human being in sinning would be more powerful when it takes away grace than the divine goodness would be to remove sins by the gifts of grace.

Second, God provides for things according to their way. And the way of mutable things is that contraries can be alternated in them (e.g., the coming to be and passing away in corporeal matter, and white and black in colored material substances). But human beings are mutable regarding their will as long as they live in this life. Therefore, God gives gifts of grace to a human being in such a way that the human being can lose the gifts through sin, and God imputes sins in such a way that the gifts of grace can remit them.

Third, we note the possible and the impossible in supernatural acts by divine, not natural, power. For it belongs to divine, not natural, power that a blind man can be restored to sight, or that a dead man can rise. But gifts of grace are supernatural. Therefore, it belongs to divine power that one can obtain them. Therefore, to say that one cannot obtain the gifts of grace after sin is to derogate from divine power. But there cannot be gifts of grace along with sin, since gifts of grace order human beings to the end from which sin turns them away. Therefore, to say that sins cannot be remitted is contrary to divine omnipotence.

◄≀ 145 ≀►

Sins Can Be Remitted

And if one should say that sins cannot be remitted because divine justice requires that one who falls away from grace not be later returned to it, not because of lack of divine power, this is patently false. For the order of justice does not require that what belongs to the end of a journey is given to someone while the person is on the way. But it belongs to the end of life's journey to be immovably disposed in good or evil, since immobility and rest are the termini of movement. And the whole present life is a condition of passage, and the alterability of a human being regarding both the body and the soul demonstrates this. Therefore, divine justice does not require that a human being after sin remain immovably in it.

Second, divine benefits, especially the greatest, do not expose a human being to danger. But it would be dangerous for human beings living a life subject to change to receive grace if they could sin after receiving grace and not return again to grace. This would be especially dangerous because grace remits the sins preceding grace, which are sometimes greater than the sins a human being commits after having received grace. Therefore, we should not say that the sins of a human beings cannot be remitted, whether the sins are committed before or after grace has been received.

◄§ 146 §►

Only God Can Forgive Sins

And only God can forgive sins. For, when an offense has been committed against someone, only the one against whom it is committed can remit it. And both a human being and God impute sins to a human being as an offense, as I have said before [I, 143]. But we are dealing now with sins as imputed to a human being by God. Therefore, only God can forgive sins.

Second, sins, since they turn a human being away from the final end, cannot be forgiven unless the human being is reordered to the end. But gifts of grace, which come only from God, do this, since the gifts exceed the capacity of nature. Therefore, only God can forgive sins.

Third, a sin is imputed to a human being as an offense inasmuch as the sin is voluntary. But only God can change the will. Therefore, only he can forgive sins.

◄§ 147 §►

On Certain Articles of Faith Assumed with the Effects of Divine Governance

Therefore, the second effect of God is his governance of things, and especially his governance of rational creatures, on whom he bestows grace, and whose sins he forgives. The Creed touches on this effect regarding all things being ordered to the end of divine goodness, by our profession that the Holy Spirit is "the Lord," since it belongs to a lord to dispose subjects to his end. The Creed touches on this effect regarding the Holy Spirit moving all things, by saying that he is "the giver of life." For, as the movement from the soul to the body is the life of the body, so the movement by which God moves the universe is the life of the universe, as it were. And because we derive the whole consideration of divine providence from divine goodness, which is appropriated to the Holy Spirit, who proceeds as love, we appropriately posit the effects of divine providence about the person of the Holy Spirit. Regarding the effect of the supernatural knowledge that God causes in human beings by faith, the Creed says, "I believe in the holy Catholic Church," since the church is the assembly of the faithful. Regarding the grace that God communicates to human beings, the Creed says, "I believe in . . . the communion of saints." And regarding the forgiveness of sin, the Creed says, "I believe in . . . the forgiveness of sins."

◄◊ 148 ◊►

God Made All Things for the Sake of Human Beings

All things are ordered to the divine goodness as their end, as I have shown [I, 101], and some of the things ordered to this end are closer to the end than others and share more fully in divine goodness. Therefore, lower created things, which share in less divine goodness, are also ordered in some way to higher beings as their end. For in every ordering of ends, things closer to the final end are also the ends of things more remote. For example, a medicinal potion is for the sake of purgation, purgation for the sake of leanness, and leanness for the sake of health. And so leanness is in a way the end of purgation, just as purgation is the end of a medicinal potion. And this happens reasonably. For, in the order of efficient causes, the power of the first active thing arrives at the final effects through intermediate causes. Just so, in the order of ends, things more remote from an end arrive at the final end by intermediate things closer to the end. For example, a medicinal potion is ordered to health only through purgation. And so also in the universal order, lower things most obtain their final end inasmuch as they are subordinated to higher things.

This is also clearly evident to one who considers the very order of things. For things made by nature are so constituted by nature to be acted upon as they are acted upon, and we perceive that less perfect things submit to being used by more excellent things. For example, the earth nourishes plants, plants nourish animals, and animals submit to being used by human beings. Therefore, non-living things exist for the sake of living things, plants for the sake of animals, and animals for the sake of human beings. And since I have shown that an intellectual nature is superior to a material nature [I, 75], the whole of material nature is ordered to an intellectual nature. But of intellectual natures, the one closest to a material substance is the rational soul, which is the form of a human being. Therefore, the whole of material nature seems to be in some way for the sake of human beings, inasmuch as they are rational animals. Therefore, we see that the perfection of the whole material creation depends in some way on the perfection of human beings.

◄ξ 149 ξ►

The Final End of Human Beings

And the perfection of human beings lies in attaining their final end of perfect blessedness or happiness, which consists of seeing God, as I have shown before [I, 106]. And inalterability of both the intellect and the will results from the vision of God. Inalterability of the intellect results because intellectual inquiry ceases when one has arrived at the first cause in which one can know all things. And alterability of the will ceases because nothing remains to be desired when the final end, in which there is the fullness of all goodness, has been obtained. (The will is alterable because it desires something that it does not yet have.) Therefore, it is clear that the final perfection of human beings consists of perfect rest, or inalterability, regarding both the intellect and the will.

◄ξ 150 ξ►

How Human Beings Come to Eternity

And I have shown in the foregoing matter that the consideration of eternity results from immobility [I, 5]. For, as motion causes time, in which there is before and after, so before and after necessarily cease when motion has been taken away. And then the consideration of eternity, which is entirely simultaneous, remains. Therefore, human beings in their final perfection obtain eternal life, not only regarding the fact that they, as to the soul, live immortally, which the rational animal has by its nature, as I have said before [I, 84], but also regarding the fact that they are brought to perfect immobility.

9. The Death and Resurrection of the Body

◄፨ 151 ፨►

The Rational Soul Needs to Be Reunited to the Body for Perfect Blessedness

And we should consider that the will can be completely immovable only if its natural desire is completely fulfilled. But any things constituted by their nature to be united desire naturally to be united, since each thing desires what is proper to it by its nature. Therefore, since the human soul is by nature united to a body, as I have shown before [I, 85], there is in the rational soul a natural desire for union with the body. Therefore, there will be able to be perfect rest of the will only if the soul should be reunited to the body, and this is that human beings rise from death.

Second, the final perfection requires the first perfection. But the first perfection of each thing is to be perfect in its nature, and the final perfection consists of obtaining its final end. Therefore, the human soul needs to be perfect in its nature in order to be made completely perfect in its end, and this can be only if it should be united to the body. For the nature of the soul is to be part of a human being as the form. But a part is perfect in its nature only if it should be in the whole of which it is a part. Therefore, it is necessary for the final blessedness of a human being that the soul be reunited to the body.

Third, what is accidental and contrary to nature cannot be everlasting. But it is necessarily accidental and contrary to nature for the soul to be separate from the body if it is intrinsically and naturally innate to the soul to be united to the body. Therefore, the soul will not be perpetually separated from the body. Therefore, since the soul's substance cannot pass away, as I have shown before [I, 84], we conclude that the soul will be reunited to the body.

◄፨ 152 ፨►

How the Separation of the Soul from the Body Is According to Nature, and How Contrary

And it seems that the soul is separated from the body according to nature, not by accident. For the body of a human being is composed of contraries. But every such thing can by nature pass away. Therefore, the human body by nature can pass away. But the separated soul, if it is immortal, necessarily remains after the body has passed away, as I have shown before [I, 84]. Therefore, it seems that the separation of the soul from the body is according to nature. Therefore, we should consider how this is according to nature, and how contrary.

For I have shown before that the rational soul, contrary to the way of other forms, surpasses the capacity of the whole of corporeal matter [I, 93]. And the rational soul's intellectual activity, which it has apart from the body, demonstrates this. Therefore, in order that corporeal matter should be suitable for the rational soul, it was necessary that a disposition by which the matter became suitable for such a form needed to be added to the human body. And as this form comes into existing only from God by creation, so only God allotted to the human body the disposition surpassing material nature, namely, the disposition that preserved the body itself from destruction. And so the body would befit the perpetuity of the soul.

And this disposition in the body of Adam remained as long as his soul adhered to God. But when sin turned his soul away from God, his body also appropriately lost the supernatural disposition by which it was immovably subject to the soul. And so humankind incurred the necessity of dying.

Therefore, death is natural if one should regard the nature of the body. But if one should regard the nature of the soul and the disposition supernaturally implanted from the beginning in the human body for the sake of the soul, death is accidental and contrary to nature, since it is natural for the soul to be united to the body.

◄ 153 ►

The Soul Regains the Completely Same Body

And since the soul is united to the body as its form, and proper matter corresponds to each form, the body to which the soul will be reunited needs to belong to the same nature and kind as the body that death put an end to. Therefore, the soul in the resurrection regains a human body composed of flesh and bones, with the same organs of which it now consists, not a celestial or brazen body, or the body of another animal, as some have fantasized.[41]

Second, as there ought to be the specifically same matter for the specifically same form, so there ought to be the numerically same matter for the numerically same form. For, as an ox's soul cannot be the soul of a horse's body, so the soul of this ox could not be the soul of another ox's body. Therefore, since the numerically same rational soul abides, it is necessarily reunited to the numerically same body in the resurrection.

◂ఢ 154 ⲋ▸

The Soul Regains the Numerically Same Body
Only by the Power of God

But nature's action repeats things that substantially pass away only as specifically the same, not as numerically the same. For example, the cloud from which rain is generated and the one that is regenerated by the rainfall and its subsequent evaporation are not numerically the same. Therefore, since death substantially destroys the human body, nature's activity cannot restore the numerically same body. But the nature of the resurrection requires such a restoration, as I have shown [I, 153]. Therefore, no action of nature causes the resurrection of human beings, as some held that the numerically same human beings return again when the heavenly bodies return to the same location after many annual cycles.[42] Rather, only divine power causes the restoration of those who rise.

Second, nature's activity clearly cannot restore sense powers that are lacking or any of the things received only through generation, since the numerically same thing cannot be generated again. But if any such thing should be restored to anyone (e.g., a plucked eye or an amputated hand), this will be by divine power, which acts above the order of nature, as I have shown before [I, 136]. Therefore, since all the sense powers and all the bodily members perish through death, only divine action can restore a dead human being to life.

And because we posit future resurrection by divine power, we can easily see how the numerically same body is restored. For I have shown before that all things, even the least, are included in divine providence [I, 130–33]. Therefore, it is clear that the matter of this human body, whatever form it should take after the death of a human being, does not escape from divine power or knowledge. And the numerically same matter remains, inasmuch as we understand it as quantified, by reason of which we can call it, and it is, the source of individuation. Therefore, if the same matter remains, if divine power has restored the human body out of it, and if the rational soul, which remains the same because it cannot pass away, has been united to the same body, then the numerically same human being is restored.

Nor can numerical identity be prevented because there is no numerically same humanity, as some argue.[43] For, according to them, humanity, which is called the form of the whole human being, is only the form of the part that is the soul. But they call humanity the form of the body insofar as it gives life to the body, and the form of the whole human being insofar as it gives the whole human being its species. And if this is true, it is clear that the numerically same humanity also abides, since the numerically same rational soul abides.

But humanity is what the definition of human being signifies, just as the essence of anything is what the thing's definition signifies. And the definition of human being signifies both the form and the matter, since we necessarily posit matter in the definition of natural things. Therefore, others say more properly that both the soul and the body are included in the notion of humanity but otherwise than in the definition of human being.[44] For only the essential sources of human being are included in the notion of humanity, with the elimination of other things. For we say that humanity is that by which a human being is a human being. Therefore, it is clear that all the things about which it is false to say that a human being is such by reason of them are eliminated from humanity. But we call one who has humanity a human being, although the fact that one has humanity does not exclude one from also having other things (e.g., whiteness or any such thing). Therefore, the word *human being* signifies the essential sources of being human but without eliminating other things, although other things are included in its notion only potentially, not actually.

And so we signify human being by way of the whole human being, but we signify humanity by way of part of a human being and do not predicate it of a human being. But particular matter and a particular form are included in Socrates or Plato. And so, as the notion of human being is derived from the fact that a human being is composed of body and soul, so, if Socrates were to be defined, the notion of him would be that he is composed of particular flesh and bones and a particular soul. Therefore, since humanity is not another form in addition to the soul and the body but something composed of both, it is clear that there will be the numerically same humanity if the same body has been restored, and if the same soul abides.

Nor is the aforementioned numerical identity prevented because the numerically same corporeity does not return, since the corporeity is destroyed when the body has been destroyed. For, if we understand by corporeity the substantial form by which something is classified in the genus of material substance, such corporeity is only the soul, since only one substantial form belongs to each thing. For a particular animal by reason of a particular soul is animal, living body, material body, and a particular thing existing in the genus of substance. Otherwise, the soul would come to an actually existing body and so be an accidental form. For the subject of a substantial form is a particular thing only potentially, not actually. And so, when the subject receives a substantial form, we do not say that only this or that comes to be, as we say in the case of accidental forms, but we say that this or that comes to be absolutely, receiving existing absolutely, so to speak. And so the corporeity received remains numerically the same, since the rational soul is indestructible.

But if one should understand the word *corporeity* to mean a form by which we designate a material substance that we classify in the genus of quantity, then corporeity is an accidental form, since it only signifies three-dimensional. And so, although the numerically same accidental form does not return, the subject's identity, for which the unity of the subject's essential sources suffices, is not prevented. And the argument is the same regarding all other accidents, whose difference does not take away numerical identity. And so, since such a union of an accidental form is a relation and thereby an accident, its numerical difference does not take away the identity of the subject. Likewise, neither does the numerical difference of sensory and vegetative powers, even if we should hold that they pass away, since they are conjoined natural powers existing in the genus of accident. Nor do we derive the sensibly perceptible from the senses insofar as the senses constitute the specific difference of animal. Rather, we derive the sensibly perceptible from the very substance of the sensory soul, which in human beings is substantially the same as the rational soul.

◄₹ 155 ₷►

Human Beings Rise to a Condition of Indestructible Life

And although the numerically same human beings rise, they will have a different way of living, since they now have a perishable life, but then an imperishable life. For if nature in generating a human being strives for perpetual existing, far more does God in restoring a human being. Nature has its striving for perpetual existing because God so moves nature. But in restoring the human being who rises, God does not intend the perpetual existing of the species, since he could have achieved this by continuous generation. Therefore, we conclude that he intends the perpetual existing of the individual. Therefore, the human being who rises lives forever.

Second, if the human beings who rise should die, the souls separated from bodies will not remain forever without a body, since this is contrary to the nature of the soul, as I have said before [I, 152]. Therefore, it will be necessary that they rise again. And the same thing will happen if they should die again after the second resurrection. Therefore, death and life will be repeated in cycles regarding the same human being, which seems pointless. Therefore, it is more appropriate to rest in the first position, namely, that human beings rise immortal in the first resurrection.

Nor does taking away mortality introduce specific or numerical difference. For mortal by its nature cannot be the specific difference of human being, since it denotes a condition of being acted upon. But we posit it as a substitute for the specific difference of human being. And so what we call mortal designates the matter of a human being, namely, that a human being is composed of contraries, as what we call rational designates a human being's form in the proper sense. For natural things cannot be defined without matter. And taking away a human being's proper matter will not take away mortality, since the soul recovers a human body composed of contraries, not a celestial or brazen body, as I have maintained before [I, 153]. But indestructibility will come by divine power, by which the soul will be master over the body to the point that the body cannot pass away, since a thing is preserved in existing as long as its form is the master over its matter.

◄ 156 ►

Consumption of Food and Carnal Generation Will Cease after the Resurrection

And because it is fitting that means to an end are removed when the end has been taken away, things ordered to the condition of mortal life are also necessarily taken away when mortality has been taken away from those who rise. But food and drink, which are necessary to sustain mortal life, when food restores what natural heat dissipates, are such. Therefore, there will be no consumption of food or drink after the resurrection. Likewise, there will also be no use of clothes, since a human being needs clothes lest external things destroy the body by heat or cold. Likewise, it is necessary that sexual intercourse cease, since it is ordered to the generation of animals. But generation is of service to mortal life in order to preserve at least in the species what cannot be preserved in the individual. Therefore, since the numerically same human beings will be preserved forever, generation will have no place in their regard. And so there will also be no sexual intercourse.

Second, since semen is surplus food, sexual intercourse necessarily ceases when the consumption of food ceases. And we cannot properly say that the consumption of food and drink, and sexual intercourse, remain only for pleasure. For there will be nothing inordinate in the final condition, since all things will then receive perfect consummation in their own way, and disorder is contrary to perfection. Besides, since the restoration of a human being is directly from God through the resurrection, there cannot then be any disorder in that condition. For "things from God are ordered," as Rom. 13:1 says. But it is inordinate that one should seek the consumption of food or drink, or sexual intercourse, only for the sake of pleasure, and so even now human beings consider it vicious. Therefore, in those who rise, there cannot be the consumption of food or drink, or sexual intercourse, only for the sake of pleasure.

◄᛭ 157 ᛭►
But All the Bodily Members Will Rise

And those who rise, although they lack the use of such things, do not lack the bodily members ordered to such uses, since, without the members, the whole body of one who rises would not be integral. But it is appropriate that, in the restoration of the risen human being, which will be directly by God, whose works are perfect, the nature is wholly restored. Therefore, there will be such bodily members in those who rise, for the sake of preserving the integrity of nature, not for the sake of the acts for which the members are now assigned.

Second, if human beings in that condition will obtain punishment or reward for the acts they now do, as I shall make clear later [I, 172–84], it is appropriate that human beings have the same bodily members by which they were slaves to sin or observed justice in this life. This is so that they are punished or rewarded in the members in which they sinned or merited.

◄᛭ 158 ᛭►
Bodies Will Rise without Any Defect

And it is likewise appropriate that all natural defects be taken away from the bodies of those who rise, since all such defects derogate from the integrity of nature. Therefore, if it is appropriate that God wholly restore human nature in the resurrection, then such defects should also be taken away.

Second, such defects come from the defect of the natural power that was the source of human generation. But there will be in the resurrection only divine active power, which admits of no defect. Therefore, there will be in human beings restored by the resurrection no such defects as were in human beings as begotten.

◄᛭ 159 ᛭►
Only Things Proper to True Nature Will Rise

And we need to relate what I said about the integrity of those who rise to what belongs to true human nature, since what does not belong to true human nature will not be restored in those who rise. Otherwise, if whatever has been converted from food into flesh and blood will be restored in those who rise, their size would necessarily be immense. But we note each thing's true nature by its species and form. Therefore, all the parts of a human being specifically will be wholly in those who rise, both the organic parts and the exactly similar parts (e.g., flesh, nerves, and the like) of which the organic members are composed. And as much as will be sufficient to reintegrate the arrangement of these parts, not the whole of whatever was materially in the parts, will be restored.

But if the whole of whatever was materially in a human being will not rise, the human being will not on that account not be numerically the same or integral. For it is clear that a human being remains numerically the same in the condition of this life from birth to death, but what is materially in the human being beneath the outer form of the parts does not remain the same. Rather, what lies underneath gradually flows in and out, as if the same fire were to be kept burning by logs being consumed and replaced. And a human being is whole when the outer form and the proper size of the outer form are preserved.

◄؟ 160 ؟►

God Will Supply All Things If Anything Was Materially Lacking

And as God, at the restoration of the body of one who rises, will not restore the whole of what was materially in the body of a human being, so also God will supply whatever was materially lacking. For the service of nature can bring it about that external matter taken in as food and drink adds to a boy, who lacks the requisite size of a man, only enough for him to have perfect size, nor does he cease to be the numerically same one he was. If so, then far more can divine power bring it about that those having less external matter are supplied with what they lacked in this life regarding the integrity of natural bodily members or requisite size. Therefore, although some persons in this life lacked some bodily members or had not yet attained perfect size to whatever degree at the time of their death, they will in the resurrection obtain the requisite perfection of bodily members and size by divine power.

◄؟ 161 ؟►

Answers to Possible Objections

And this enables us to answer objections that some pose against the resurrection.[45] For they say that a man can eat human flesh and further, so fed, can beget a son who consumes similar food. Therefore, if the food is converted into the substance of the flesh, it seems impossible that each wholly rises, since the flesh of one has been converted into the flesh of another. And what seems more difficult, if semen comes from surplus food, as philosophers teach,[46] then the semen from which a son is conceived is taken from the flesh of another. And so it seems impossible that a son begotten of such semen rises if the human beings whose flesh both the father and the son had consumed rise entirely.

But this is not repugnant to the general resurrection. For I have said before that only as much matter as suffices to preserve the measure of requisite size, not whatever was materially in a human being, needs to be restored in one who rises [I, 159]. And I have also said that divine power will supply even anything anyone lacks of the matter for perfect size [I, 160].

Moreover, we should consider that we find that something existing materially in the body of a human being belongs to true human nature in different grades. For, first and chiefly, the formative power perfects what human beings take from their parents in the human species as the simplest thing. Second, what food adds is necessary for the requisite size of bodily members. And so, since the admixture of something external always weakens a thing's power, it is also finally necessary that growth cease, and that the body grow old and disintegrate. Just so, the addition of water eventually makes wine watery.

Further, food also produces superfluities in the body of a human being, some of which are necessary for a use (e.g., semen for generation, and hair for covering and adornment). But other superfluities are completely useless (e.g., the superfluities expelled by sweat and various discharges), or are retained internally in natural weight.

Therefore, divine providence in the general resurrection will see to it that the numerically same thing, if it existed materially in different human beings, will rise in the one in whom it obtained the more important grade. And if it existed in two human beings by one and the same grade, it will rise in the one in whom it first existed, but divine power will supply it in the other. And so it is clear that human flesh consumed by someone will rise in the one to whom it first belonged, not in the one consuming it. But the human flesh consumed will rise in the one begotten of such semen regarding what was from the nutritive fluid in the flesh, and the rest of the flesh will rise in the one in which it first existed, with God supplying to each what each lacks.

◄ 162 ►

The Resurrection of the Dead Is Expressed
in the Articles of Faith

Therefore, in order to profess this belief in the resurrection, the Apostles' Creed posited: "The resurrection of the flesh." Nor was "of the flesh" added without reason, since there were some, even in the time of the Apostles, who denied the resurrection, professing only the spiritual resurrection by which a human being rises from the death of sin. And so Paul in 2 Tim. 2:18 says of certain persons that they said that "the resurrection has already happened, and they subverted the faith of many." And in order to remove their error, so that the future resurrection is believed, the Creed of the Fathers says: "I await the resurrection of the dead."

◄? 163 ?►

What Kind of Activity Will Belong
to Those Who Rise

And we need to consider further what is the kind of activity of those who rise, since there needs to belong to any living thing an activity for which the thing chiefly strives, and we say that its life consists of this. For example, we say that those who chiefly devote their time to pleasures live a voluptuous life, that those who devote their time to contemplation live a contemplative life, and that those who govern political communities live a political life. And I have shown that, for those who rise, there will be no consumption of food and no sexual intercourse [I, 156], to which all bodily practices seem to be related. But when these bodily practices have been taken away, there remain spiritual activities, of which we say that the final end of human beings consists. Obtaining this end belongs to those who rise freed from the condition of dissolution and mutability, as I have shown [I, 155]. And the final end of a human being consists of beholding God essentially, not in any kind of spiritual acts, as I have shown before [I, 104 and 105]. But God is eternal. And so the intellect united to God is necessarily united to eternity. Therefore, as we say that those who devote their time to pleasure live a voluptuous life, so those who possess the vision of God obtain eternal life, as Jo. 17:3 says: "This is eternal life, that they may know the true God."

◄? 164 ?►

Those Who Rise Will See God Essentially,
Not by a Likeness

And the created intellect sees God essentially, not by a likeness of himself. The thing understood in the present intellect by a likeness can be remote (e.g., a stone is present to the eyes by a likeness, not by its substance). But, as

I have shown before [I, 105], the very essence of God is united to the created intellect in such a way that the created intellect can see God essentially. Therefore, as one will see in the final end what one hitherto believed about God, so one will possess as present what one hoped for as remote. And we call this comprehension, as Paul says in Phil. 3:12: "But I press on as if I may somehow comprehend." And we should understand this insofar as comprehension signifies the presence and a possession of what we say is comprehended, not insofar as comprehension signifies confinement.

◄ 165 ◄

Seeing God Is the Highest Perfection and Pleasure

Again, we should consider that the perception of something suitable causes pleasure (e.g., the power of sight takes pleasure in beautiful colors, and the power of smell in sweet smells). But such sensibly perceptible pleasure in one of the senses can be prevented because of the indisposition of a bodily organ. For "light, which is lovable to pure eyes, is hateful to diseased eyes."[47] But because the intellect does not understand by a bodily organ, as I have shown before [I, 79], no distress is contrary to the pleasure in considering truth. Still, distress can incidentally result from the intellect's contemplation inasmuch as one apprehends the understood thing as harmful. Then there is pleasure in the intellect about knowing truth, but sadness results in the will about the known thing inasmuch as the thing's action causes harm, not inasmuch as it is known. But God is truth itself. Therefore, the intellect seeing God cannot fail to take pleasure in seeing him.

Second, God is goodness itself, which is the cause of love. And so all who apprehend his goodness necessarily love it. For, although something good can be unloved or even hated, this will be inasmuch as it is understood as harmful, not inasmuch as it is apprehended as good. Therefore, in the vision of God, who is goodness itself and truth, as comprehension is necessarily present, so is pleasure or pleasurable enjoyment, as Is. 66:14 says: "You will see, and your heart will rejoice."

◄ 166 ◄

The Soul Seeing God Has a Will Confirmed in Him

And this makes clear that the soul seeing God, or any other spiritual creature doing so, has a will confirmed in him, so that it is not deflected to the contrary in other things. For, inasmuch as the object of the will is the good, the will can be inclined to something only under an aspect of good. But something can be lacking in any particular good, and this leaves the knower free to seek the good in something else. And so the will of one perceiving any particular good does not necessarily rest content only in that good so as not to turn outside its order. But God, who is the universal good and goodness itself, lacks nothing good that can be sought elsewhere, as I have shown before [I, 106]. Therefore, those who see his essence cannot turn their will away from him without tending to all things according to his plan.

We also see this by the like in intelligible things. For our intellect can turn this way and that by doubting until it comes to the first principle in which the intellect is necessarily confirmed. Therefore, since the end in desirable things is like the first principle in intelligible things, the will can be deflected to contrary things until it comes to enjoyment of the final end, in which the will is necessarily confirmed. It would also be contrary to the nature of perfect happiness if human beings could be turned to the contrary, since the fear of losing the end would not be completely excluded, and so desire would not be completely at rest. And so Rev. 3:12 says of one who is blessed: "He will depart from it no more."

◄ぇ 167 s►

Bodies Will Be Completely Obedient to the Soul

And because the body is for the sake of the soul, as matter is for the sake of form, and a tool for the sake of a craftsman, God in the resurrection will unite to the soul that will obtain the aforementioned life the kind of body that befits the soul's blessedness. For means for the sake of an end should be disposed according to what the end requires. And it does not belong to a soul reaching the height of intellectual activity to have a body that impedes or retards the soul to any degree. But the human body by reason of its destructibility impedes and retards the soul, so that the soul can neither remain continually in contemplation nor arrive at the height of contemplation.

And so abstraction from bodily senses renders human beings more fit to grasp some divine things. For prophetic revelations are manifested to those sleeping or in a trance, as Num. 12:6 says: "If anyone among you should be a prophet of the Lord, I shall speak to him in a dream or a vision." Therefore, the bodies of the blessed who rise will be indestructible and completely obedient to the soul, so that their bodies do not resist the soul in anything, and will not be destructible and retarding the soul as is the case now.

◄≈ 168 ≈►

On the Qualities of Glorified Bodies

And we can perceive from this how the bodies of the blessed are disposed, since the soul is the form of the body and the cause of its movement. And inasmuch as the soul is the form, it is the source of the body regarding both its substantial existing and its proper accidents, which the union of the form to the matter causes in the subject. And the stronger the form, the less any external active thing can hinder the imprint of the form on the matter. This is evident in the case of fire, whose form, which is the most excellent of elementary forms, enables fire not to be easily altered from its natural disposition by any active thing acting on it.

The blessed soul, as united to the first cause of things, will be at the height of excellence and power. Therefore, first of all, it will confer substantial existing in the most excellent way on the body united to it by God, by keeping the body completely subject to it. And so the body will be subtle, or spiritual. It will give itself the most excellent quality, namely, glorious brilliance. And because of the power of the soul, no active thing will be able to alter it from its disposition (i.e., it cannot suffer). And because it will completely obey the soul, as a tool obeys the one who moves it, it will be rendered agile. Therefore, there will be four conditions of the blessed bodies: subtleness, brilliance, incapacity to suffer, and agility. And so Paul in 1 Cor. 15:42–44 says that the body that by death "is sown in corruption will rise in incorruption," regarding the body's incapacity to suffer; that the body that "is sown in weakness will rise in power," regarding the body's agility; that the body that "is sown in baseness will rise in glory," regarding the body's brilliance; and that the body that "is sown as animal will rise as spiritual," regarding the body's subtleness.

◄≈ 169 ≈►

The Material Creature Will Receive a Different Condition

And means to an end are clearly disposed according to what the end requires. And so, if the perfect and the imperfect differentiate the end of different things, the means ordered to it need to be disposed in different ways, so that they are of service to it according to each condition. For example, food and clothes are provided for a child in one way and for an adult in another way. But I have shown before that the material creature is ordered to rational nature as its end [I, 148]. Therefore, the material creature necessarily receives a different condition when the human being receives final perfection through the resurrection. And we accordingly say that the world is renewed when the human being rises, as Rev. 21:1 says: "I saw a new heaven and a new earth"; and Is. 65:17 says: "Behold, I create new heavens and a new earth."

◄¿ 170 ¿►

Which Creatures Will Be Renewed, and Which Will Remain

But we should consider that different kinds of material creatures are ordered to human beings in different respects. For plants and animals serve human beings to assist the latter's weakness, when human beings have from plants and animals the food, clothing, means of travel, and other such things that support human weakness.

But the resurrection will take away all such weakness from human beings in their final condition. For they will no longer need food for eating, since they are indestructible, as I have shown before [I, 155]. Nor will they, as then clothed in brilliant glory, any longer need clothing for covering. Nor will they, who will have agility, need animals for travel. Nor will they, as then incapable of suffering, need any remedies to preserve health. Therefore, it is appropriate in the condition of final perfection that there remain no such material creatures, namely, plants, animals, and other such mixed material substances.

But the four elements, namely, fire, air, water, and earth, are ordered to human beings, not only regarding their use in this perishable life but also regarding the constitution of human beings' bodies, since the human body is constituted of the elements. Therefore, the elements have an essential order to the human body. And so, when human beings have been perfected in body and soul, it is appropriate that the elements also remain, although altered to a better arrangement.

And human beings do not appropriate heavenly bodies regarding the bodies' substance for use in this perishable life, nor do the heavenly bodies enter the substance of the human body. But they serve human beings inasmuch as their form and size demonstrate the excellence of their creator. And so the Scriptures frequently admonished human beings to consider heavenly bodies so that those bodies may bring human beings to reverence God. Is. 40:26 makes this clear, saying: "Raise your eyes to the heavens and see who created them."

It is true that sensibly perceptible creatures do not bring human beings in the condition of final perfection to knowledge of God, since human beings then see God in himself. But even for one who knows the cause, it is pleasurable and joyful to contemplate how his likeness shines forth in his effects. And so also it will give the saints joy to contemplate the refulgence of the divine goodness in material things, especially heavenly bodies, which seem to surpass the others. Heavenly bodies also have an essential order to the human body in one respect, by reason of being the body's active cause, as the elements do by reason of being the body's material cause. For "a human being and the sun beget a human being."[48] And so also it is appropriate even for this reason that the heavenly bodies remain.

Not only the relation of heavenly bodies to human beings but also the natures of the aforementioned other material creatures make this clear. For what is in no intrinsic regard imperishable ought not to abide in the condition of freedom from destruction. Heavenly bodies are imperishable in whole and in part. Elements are imperishable in whole but not in part. Human beings are imperishable in part, namely, the rational soul, but not in whole, since death dissolves the composite. But other animals, and plants and all mixed material substances, are perishable both in whole and in part. Therefore, human beings, elements, and heavenly bodies appropriately remain in the final condition of freedom from destruction, but other animals, and plants and mixed substances, do not.

The same thing is also rationally evident from the nature of the universe. For, inasmuch as a human being is part of the material universe, it is necessary that it remain when human beings reach their final perfection, since a part does not seem to be perfect if it should be separate from the whole of which it is a part. And the material universe cannot remain unless its essential parts should remain. Its essential parts are the heavenly bodies and the elements, as the whole cosmic system consists of these things. But the other things do not seem to belong to the integrity of the material universe. Rather, they seem to belong to the ornament and beauty of the material universe appropriate for its condition of mutability, insofar as animals, plants, and minerals are produced by a heavenly body as the active thing, and the elements as the material things. But a different ornament, one becoming to the condition of freedom from destruction, will be given to the elements in the condition of final perfection. Therefore, in that condition, human beings, elements, and heavenly bodies, but not animals, plants, or minerals, will remain.

◄ξ 171 ς►

The Heavenly Bodies Will Be Stationary

But since we see that the heavenly bodies are continuously in motion, it can seem to someone that they are also in motion in the condition of perfection if their substance should remain. And the assertion would be reasonable if heavenly bodies were to have movement for the same reason that the elements do. For heavy or light elements have movement in order to obtain their perfection, since they tend by their natural movement to their proper place, where it is better for them to be. And so each element and any part of it will be in its proper place in the final condition of perfection.

But we cannot say this about the movement of heavenly bodies, since a heavenly body does not come to rest in any place that it has occupied. Rather, as it naturally moves toward whatever place, so also it naturally moves away from it. Therefore, if movement is taken away from heavenly bodies, they do not lose anything by which they have a movement to perfect them.

But it is silly to say that, as the nature of a light material substance is moved upwards by its nature, so a heavenly body is moved in an orbit by its nature as the active cause. For it is manifest that nature always tends toward unity. And so what is by its nature contrary to unity cannot be the final end of nature. But movement is contrary to unity, inasmuch as what is moved is disposed in one or another way when it is moved. Therefore, nature does not produce movement for its own sake but causes movement striving for the terminus of the movement (e.g., the nature of a light thing in its ascent strives for a higher place, and so forth). Therefore, since the circular movement of a heavenly body is not for a fixed place, we cannot say that nature is the cause of the orbit of a heavenly body as nature is the active cause of the movement of heavy and light things.

And so nothing prevents heavenly bodies, if their nature remains the same, from coming to rest, although fire, if its nature remains the same, cannot come to rest when it is outside its proper place. Nonetheless, we call the movement of a heavenly body natural because it is a movable thing that has the capacity to be so moved, not because it is the active cause of its movement. We conclude that the movement of a heavenly body comes from an intellect.

But since the intellect causes movement only by intending an end, we need to consider what is the end of the movement of heavenly bodies. We cannot say the very movement is the end, since the movement, inasmuch as it is the way to perfection, has the nature of a means to an end, not the nature of an end. Likewise, we cannot say that the repetition of positions is the end of the movement of a heavenly body, namely, that the heavenly body is moved in order actually to gain every place for which it has a potentiality. For such a process is endless, and an endless process is contrary to the nature of end.

Therefore, we need further to consider the end of the heavens' movement. For every material substance moved by an intellect is clearly the intellect's instrument. And the end of the instrument's movement is the form conceived by the chief active thing, and the instrument's movement brings this form into actuality. And the divine intellect's form that the heavens' movement fulfills is the perfection of things by way of their coming to be and passing away. But the final end of coming to be and passing away is the most excellent form (i.e., the human soul, whose final end is eternal life, as I have shown before [I, 104–106]). Therefore, the final end of the heavens' movement is multiplication of the human beings to be brought to eternal life.

But this multitude cannot be infinite, since the intention of any intellect rests in something definite. Therefore, when the number of human beings to be brought to eternal life has been fulfilled, and when they have been constituted in eternal life, the heavens' movement will cease, as any instrument's movement ceases after it has completed its work. But when the heavens' movement ceases, all movement in lower material substances will consequently cease, except the movement that will be in human beings from the soul. And so the whole material universe will have a different disposition and form, as Paul says in 1 Cor. 7:31: "The shape of this world is passing away."

10. The Reward and Punishment of Human Beings

◄≀ 172 ≀►

On the Reward or Wretchedness of Human Beings According to Their Deeds

And we should consider that, if there is a fixed way of arriving at an end, those who proceed by the contrary way or defect from the right way cannot reach the end. For example, sick people are not cured if they use contrary things that their doctor prohibits, except, perhaps, by chance. And the fixed way of arriving at happiness is by virtue. For something obtains its end only by doing rightly what is proper to it. For a plant would produce no fruit if nature's way of action were not observed in it. Nor would a runner attain the prize, or a soldier the palm of victory, unless each was to act rightly regarding the proper function of each. But for human beings to perform their proper activity rightly is for them to perform it virtuously, since the virtue of each thing is what makes the possessor of virtue good, and the possessor's work good. Therefore, since the final end of a human being is eternal life, about which I have spoken [I, 104–106 and 149], only those who act virtuously, not all human beings, arrive at it.

Second, I have shown before that both natural things and human things, both collectively and severally, are included in divine providence [I. 123 and 130]. But it belongs to the one who has charge of individual human beings to give rewards for virtue and punishments for sin, since punishment is remedial and corrective of sin, as I have maintained before [I, 121]. But happiness is the reward of virtue, and divine goodness gives this reward to a human being. Therefore, it belongs to God not to give happiness to those who act contrary to virtue, but to give them the contrary, namely, the worst wretchedness, as punishment.

<hr />

◄§ 173 §►

The Reward and Wretchedness of Human Beings Are after This Life

And we need to consider that contrary effects belong to contrary things. But wicked activity is contrary to virtuous activity. Therefore, wretchedness, at which human beings arrive by wicked activity, is contrary to the happiness that virtuous activity merits. But contraries belong to one and the same genus, and final happiness, at which human beings arrive by virtuous activity, is a good after this life, not one of this life, as is clear from what I have said before [I, 104–106 and 149]. Therefore, final wretchedness, to which wickedness leads, is also an evil after this life.

Second, we find that all the good or evil things of this life are ordered to something else. For both external goods and bodily goods are instrumentally in the service of virtue, which is the direct way of arriving at blessedness with those who use the aforementioned things rightly. Just so, with those who use them wrongly, the things are instruments of wickedness, through which one arrives at wretchedness. And likewise, the evils contrary to these goods (e.g., sickness, poverty, and the like) are for some the means for perfect virtue, and for others the means for increased wickedness, as human beings use the evils in different ways. But what is ordered to something else is not the final reward or punishment. Therefore, neither final happiness nor final wretchedness consists of the goods or evils of this life.

<hr />

◄§ 174 §►

Of What the Wretchedness of a Human Being Regarding the Pain of Loss Consists

Therefore, since the wretchedness to which wickedness leads is contrary to the happiness to which virtue leads, we need to understand the things belonging to wretchedness by contrasting them to the things we say about happiness. But I have said before that the final happiness of a human being regarding the intellect consists of the full vision of God, and regarding desire consists of the will being confirmed immovably in the first goodness [I, 105–106 and 165–166]. Therefore, there will be the worst wretchedness of a human being in the intellect being completely deprived of the divine light and in desire being resolutely turned away from God's goodness. And this is the chief wretchedness of the damned, which we call the pain of loss.

Still, we should consider, as I have said before [I, 118], that evil cannot totally exclude good, since everything evil is grounded in something good. Therefore, wretchedness, although contrary to the happiness that will be free of every evil, needs to be grounded in the good of nature. And the good of an intellectual nature consists of the intellect contemplating the true and of the will tending toward the good. But everything true and everything good is derived from the first true and good thing (i.e., God). And so the intellect of a human being constituted in the worst wretchedness necessarily has some knowledge and some love of God, namely, insofar as God is the source of natural perfections, and this is natural love. But the intellect of such a human being does not have knowledge or love of God as he is in himself, or as he is the cause of virtues and graces, or of any goods by which he perfects the intellectual nature, and this is love of virtue and glory.

But human beings constituted in such wretchedness do not lack free decision, although they have a will immovably confirmed in evil, just as the blessed do not lack free decision, although they have a will confirmed in good. For freedom of decision in the strict sense extends to election, and election is of those things that are means to an end. But each thing by nature seeks its final end, and so all human beings, because they are intellectual, by nature desire happiness as their final end, and so immovably that no one can will to become wretched. Nor is this contrary to freedom of decision, which extends only to means to an end.

And that these human beings posit their final end in this particular thing, and those in another particular thing, does not belong to these or those human beings inasmuch as they are human beings, since human beings differ in such evaluation and desire. Rather, it belongs to each of them insofar as they are a certain kind of human being.

And I say "a certain kind of human being" by reason of an emotion or habitual disposition. And so, if an emotion or habitual disposition should be altered, something else will seem best to a human being. And this is especially clear in the case of those who out of emotion desire something as best and, when the emotion (e.g., of anger or desire) ceases, do not judge that good the same as before. But habits are more permanent. And so human beings persevere more strongly in things that they habitually pursue. Still, both the estimation and the desire of human beings about the final end are mutable as long as the habit can be altered.

This happens only to human beings in this life, in which they are in a mutable condition. For the soul after this life cannot be affected by alteration, since such change belongs to the soul only incidentally as a consequence of an alteration in the body. But when the body has been restored, the soul will not be affected by bodily changes. Rather, the converse will be true. For the soul is now infused into a begotten body, and so the soul is fittingly affected by bodily changes. But the body will then be united to the preexisting soul, and so the body will be completely affected by the soul's conditions. Therefore, the soul will remain forever in whatever final end it is found to have prescribed for itself at death, desiring that thing as best, whether it should be good or evil. Just so, Eccl. 11:3 says that wood when cut "will be wherever it fell." Therefore, after this life, those who are found good at their death will have a will forever confirmed in good, and those who will then be found evil will be forever confirmed in evil.

◄¿ 175 ട►

Mortal Sins Are Not Forgiven after This Life,
but Venial Sins Are Duly Forgiven

And this enables us to consider that mortal sins are not forgiven after this life, but that venial sins can be. For sins are mortal by reason of turning away from the final end, regarding which human beings are immovably confirmed after death, as I have said [I, 174], but venial sins regard the way to the final end, not the final end. But if the will of the wicked after death is resolutely confirmed in evil, they will always desire as best what they had desired before. Therefore, they will not grieve that they have sinned, since no one grieves that one has pursued what he thinks to be best.

But we should note that the damned, regarding their final wretchedness, will not be able after death to possess the things they had desired as best. For the opportunity for lust will not then be available to the lustful, nor the opportunity to offend others to the irate, nor the opportunity to obstruct others to the envious, and it is the same about particular vices. But they will know that those who lived virtuously obtain what they desired as best. Therefore, they grieve that they committed sins. They do not grieve because their sins displease them, since they even then will prefer to commit the sins, if the opportunity to do so were available, than to possess God. Rather, they grieve because they cannot have what they chose, and would have been able to have what they rejected. Therefore, both their will remains forever confirmed in evil, and they will nonetheless most heavily grieve about the sin committed and the glory lost. And we call this pain remorse of conscience, which Scripture metaphorically calls the worm, as Is. 66:24 says: "Their worm will not die."

⮜ 176 ⮞

The Bodies of the Damned Will Be Capable
of Suffering and Yet Be Integral, without
the Qualities of Glory

And as the blessedness of the soul in the saints is channeled in some way into their bodies, as I have said before [I, 168], so also even the wretchedness of the soul is channeled into the bodies of the damned. But we note that, as wretchedness does not exclude the good of nature from the soul, so also wretchedness does not exclude the good of nature from the body. Therefore, the bodies of the damned will be whole in their nature but will not have the conditions that belong to the glory of the blessed. For example, their bodies will not be subtle or incapable of suffering. Rather, the bodies will remain in their bulkiness and be capable of suffering, or these things will be increased in them. They will be scarcely moveable by the soul, not agile. They will be dark, not brilliant, so that the darkness of the soul is shown in the bodies, as Is. 13:8 says: "You shall set their countenances aflame."

⮜ 177 ⮞

The Bodies of the Damned, Although Capable
of Suffering, Will Be Indestructible

But we should note that, although the bodies of the damned will be capable of suffering, they will be indestructible. This is so despite the fact that this seems to be contrary to the nature of the things we now experience, since greater suffering takes away from the body's substance. But there will be two reasons why suffering continuously forever will not destroy the bodies capable of continuous suffering.

The first is because all natural change necessarily ceases when the heavens' movement ceases, as I have said before [I, 171]. Therefore, something will be able to be affected only by a change in the soul, not by a natural change. I say "natural change" to mean, for example, when something hot becomes cold, or any variation regarding the natural existing of qualities. But I say "change in the soul" to mean, for example, when something receives a quality according to its immaterial existing, not according to its natural existing (e.g., the pupil of an eye receives the form of color in order to perceive the color, not to be colored). Therefore, so also will the bodies of the damned suffer, whether by fire or any other material thing, so as to perceive characteristics of the qualities of fire, not so as to be changed into the outward form or quality of fire. And this will inflict pain, inasmuch as such characteristics are contrary to the harmony of which sense perception consists, and in which it takes pleasure. But this will not destroy the body, since the immaterial reception of forms does not change the nature of the body, except, perhaps, incidentally.

The second reason will regard the soul, to whose perpetuity divine power will hand over the body. And so the soul of the damned, insofar as it is the form and nature of such a body, will give the body perpetual existing. But the soul, because of its imperfection, will not give to the body inability to suffer. Therefore, these bodies will always suffer but not be destroyed.

◄₂ 178 ₅►

Before the Resurrection, the Souls of Some Obtain Happiness, and the Souls of Others Will Live in Wretchedness

Therefore, the foregoing makes clear that both happiness and wretchedness consist of the soul chiefly but of the body secondarily and by a derivation. Therefore, the happiness or wretchedness of the body depends on the happiness or wretchedness of the soul, not the converse. But souls abide after death before the restoration of their bodies, some with the reward of blessedness, others with the punishment of wretchedness. Therefore, it is clear that the souls of some, even before the resurrection, obtain the aforementioned happiness. Just so, Paul says in 2 Cor. 5:1: "We know that, if our earthly home of this life should be dissolved, we have from God a home not made by human hands, a home preserved in the heavens." And he adds in v. 8: "We make bold and have the righteous will to be away from the body and present with God." But the souls of some live in wretchedness, as Lk. 16: 22 says: "The rich man died and was buried in hell."

◄₂ 179 ₅►

The Punishment of the Damned Consists of Both Spiritual and Material Evils

Still, we should consider that the happiness of the holy souls will consist only of spiritual goods, and the punishment of the damned souls before the resurrection will consist not only of spiritual evils, as some have thought,[49] but the damned souls will also sustain corporal punishments.

The reason for this difference is that the saints' souls, while they were united to bodies in this world, observed their right order by not subjecting themselves to material things but to God alone. And their entire happiness consists of enjoying him, not in any material goods. But the souls of the wicked, which did not observe the order of nature, subjected themselves to material things by their desire, contemning divine and spiritual things. And so they are punished both by being deprived of spiritual goods and by being subjected to material things. And so, if there should be any things in sacred Scripture that promise the reward of material goods to holy souls, such things should be explained mystically, insofar as Scripture is accustomed to designate spiritual things by analogies to material things. But we should understand literally things in Scripture that predict corporal punishments for the souls of the damned, such as being tormented by the fire of hell.

◄₹ 180 ₷►

Can Material Fire Inflict Pain on the Soul?

And lest it seem absurd to someone that a soul separated from the body suffers from material fire, we need to consider that being fettered to a body is not contrary to the nature of a spiritual substance. For nature also does this, as, for example, is evident in the union of the soul with the body, and magical arts, which fetter a spirit to pictures, rings, or some such things, do this. Therefore, divine power can bring it about that particular spiritual substances are fettered to particular material substances such as hellfire, although the spiritual substances are by their nature superior to all material things. Divine power can do this so that the spiritual substances are fettered to a material substance in some way, not so that the spiritual substances enliven a material substance. And the very fact, namely, that a spiritual substance is in some way subject to so inferior a thing, when considered by the spiritual substance, torments it.

Therefore, inasmuch as such consideration torments a spiritual substance, the statement that "the soul, by the very fact that it sees itself being consumed by fire, is so consumed"[50] is verified. It is also verified that the fire is spiritual, since the immediate thing that torments is the fire apprehended as fettering. And inasmuch the fire to which the soul is fettered is material, then what Gregory said,[51] that both seeing the fire and experiencing it inflict pain on the soul, is verified. And because the fire has from divine power, not from its nature, the power to fetter a spiritual substance, some say appropriately that the fire acts on the soul as an instrument of retributive divine justice.[52] The fire acts on the spiritual substance by fettering it, as I have just said, not as it acts on material substances by heating, drying, and consuming them. But the proximate thing tormenting the spiritual substance is the apprehension of the fire fettering the spiritual substance as punishment. Therefore, we can evidently consider that the torment does not cease even if the fire should by dispensation happen not to fetter the spiritual substance for a moment. For example, one condemned to chains forever would feel continual torment from this even if such a one were to be freed from the chains for a moment.

◄≀ 181 ≀►

There Are Temporal Punishments in Purgatory after This Life

And although some souls gain eternal blessedness at the moment that they are freed from their bodies, as I have said [I, 178], some are for a time impeded from attaining this. For sometimes some may not have performed penance in this life for the sins they have committed but at last repented. And because the order of divine justice requires that punishments be inflicted for sins, we need to say that souls after this life discharge the punishment that they did not discharge in this world. But they do not discharge the punishment so as to come to the final wretchedness of the damned, since repentance has brought them back to the state of charity, by which they adhere to God as their final end. And they have merited eternal life by this. And so we conclude that there are after this life some purgatorial punishments, the penances for which are not completely satisfied.

◄≀ 182 ≀►

There Are Also Punishments of Venial Sins in Purgatory after This Life

At the same time, it also happens that some depart from this life without mortal sin but still with venial sin, which does not turn them away from their final end, although they sinned by adhering unduly regarding means to the end. And fervent charity purges such sins in certain perfect individuals. But some punishment needs to purge such sins in other individuals, since only one who has been freed of every sin and defect is brought to obtain eternal life. Therefore, we need to posit some purgatorial punishments after this life. But such punishments have the capacity to be purgatorial from the condition of those who undergo them. They have charity, by which they conform their will to the divine will, and the punishments they undergo benefit them as purification by the power of this charity. And so, in those without charity (i.e., the damned), punishments do not cleanse. Rather, the stain of sin always remains, and so punishment endures forever.

◄ੲ 183 ട►

Is the Eternal Punishment Inflicted for Temporal Sin Contrary to Divine Justice?

And it is not contrary to the nature of divine justice if one should suffer perpetual punishment, since not even human laws require that punishment be commensurate with the offense in duration. For the sin of adultery or homicide, which is committed in a moment, human law sometimes imposes perpetual exile or even death, both of which perpetually exclude a person from the association of a political community. Exile may by happenstance not last forever, since the life of a human being does not last forever, but the aim of the judge seems to be to punish the wrongdoer forever insofar as the judge can. And so also it is not unjust if God inflicts eternal punishment for a momentary and temporal sin.

We should also consider at the same time that eternal punishment is inflicted on the sinner who does not repent of his sin, and so he persists in it up to death. And because the sinner remains eternally in sin, God reasonably punishes the sinner eternally. And any sin committed against God also has a certain infinity in relation to God, against whom it is committed. For it is clear that the greater the one against whom a sin is committed, the more serious the sin is. For example, one who boxes the ear of a soldier is judged more severely than if one were to box the ear of a peasant, and one is judged still more severely if one were to box the ear of a ruler or king. And so, inasmuch as God is infinitely great, an offense committed against him is in some way infinite, and so also infinite punishment is in some way due for the offense. But the punishment cannot be infinite in intensity, since nothing created can be infinite in this way. And so we conclude that punishment infinite in duration is due for mortal sin.

Likewise, on those who can be corrected, temporal punishment is inflicted for their correction or purification. Therefore, if one cannot be corrected from sin, and one's will is resolutely confirmed in sin, as I have said before about the damned [I, 174], the punishment of such a one should not be terminated.

◄꜠ 184 ꜱ►

The Aforementioned Things Are Also Appropriate
for Other Spiritual Substances

Human beings in their intellectual nature are like the angels, in whom there can be sin just as in human beings, as I have said before [I, 113]. Therefore, we should also understand any things said of the glory and punishment of souls about the glory of the good angels and the punishment of the wicked angels. But human beings and angels differ in only one respect. Human souls have conformity of the will in good or resolution of the will in evil when they are separated from the body, as I have said before [I, 174], whereas angels have such a will when they first deliberately prescribe the end for themselves, either God or something created. And angels became blessed or wretched from that moment on. For there can be mutability in human souls by reason of both the will's freedom and the body's mutability, but there can be mutability in angels only by reason of freedom of decision. And so angels acquire immutability by their first choice, but human souls only when they have been taken from their bodies.

Therefore, to show the reward of the good, the Apostles' Creed says: "Life everlasting." And we should understand life as eternal both because of its duration and because of the enjoyment of eternity. But there are in this regard many other things to be believed, things said about the punishments of the damned and the final state of the world. Therefore, the Creed of the Fathers, in order to include all of these things, posits: "The life of the world to come." For the world to come includes all such things.

SECOND TREATISE: THE HUMANITY OF CHRIST

◄꜠ 185 ꜱ►

On Faith in the Humanity of Christ

Christian faith, as I said at the beginning [I, 2], is chiefly concerned about two things, namely, the divinity of the Trinity and the humanity of Christ. Therefore, with the things belonging to divinity and its effects set forth, it remains for us to consider about things belonging to the humanity of Christ. But "Christ Jesus came into this world to save sinners," as Paul says in 1 Tim. 1:15. Therefore, it seems that we should first explain how humankind fell into sin, so that we know more clearly how the humanity of Christ freed human beings from sins.

1. Original Justice and Original Sin

◄୫ 186 ୫►

On the Perfection of Human Beings in Their First Constitution

And as I have said before [I, 152], God instituted human beings in their condition in such a way that the body was completely subject to the soul. And also, of parts of the soul, he instituted human beings such that the lower powers were, without resistance, subject to reason, and that the reason of human beings was subject to God. And because the body was completely subject to the soul, no emotion could happen in the body that would be contrary to the mastery of the soul over the body. And so neither death nor sickness had any place in human beings. And there was complete peace of mind in human beings due to the subjection of the lower powers to reason, since human reason was not disturbed by any inordinate emotions. And because the will of human beings was subject to God, they related all things to God as their final end, of which their righteousness and innocence consisted.

And of these three things, the last caused the others. For it was not by the nature of the body, if we should consider its components, that dissolution or any life-threatening suffering would not take place in it, since it was composed of contrary elements. Likewise, it was not by the nature of the soul that its sense powers were, without resistance, subject to reason, since nature moves sense powers to things that are sensibly pleasurable, and such things are often contrary to right reason. Therefore, this was by the power of something higher, namely, God. He united to the body the rational soul that transcends every proportion of the body and bodily powers such as the senses. Just so, he gave to the rational soul the power to be able to control the body itself above its condition, and to control sense powers, insofar as such control befitted the rational soul. Therefore, in order for reason to keep lower things firmly under its control, it was necessary that reason itself was firmly under the control of God, from whom it had the aforementioned power above the natural condition.

Therefore, human beings were so constituted that, unless their reason were to be drawn away from God, their body could not be drawn away from the life of the soul, nor sense powers from the rectitude of reason. And so human beings were in a way immortal and incapable of suffering, namely, in that they could neither die nor suffer had they not sinned. But with their will not yet confirmed by obtaining their final end, they could sin, and they could both die and suffer if they did.

And the incapacity to suffer and die that the first man had differs in this respect from the incapacity to suffer and die that the saints will have after the resurrection. The saints, with their will altogether confirmed in God, as I have said before [I, 166], will never be capable of suffering or dying. And there was another difference. For human beings after the resurrection will neither consume food nor have sexual intercourse, but the first man was so constituted that he necessarily had to sustain life by food, and it was incumbent on him to engage in the task of generation in order to multiply the human race from one man. And so he in this condition received two precepts. Regarding the first belongs what God said to him in Gen. 2:16: "Eat from the fruit of every tree in the garden of paradise." Regarding the second belongs what God said to him in Gen. 1:28: "Increase and multiply and fill the earth."

◄ᵌ 187 ᵌ►

We Call That Perfect State Original Justice

We call this so well ordered state of the human being original justice, by which both the human being himself was subject to his superior, and all inferior things were subject to him. Just so, Gen. 1:26 says: "Let him rule over the fish of the sea and the birds of the heavens." And even of the parts of the human being, the lower was also without resistance subject to the higher. And this state was granted to the first man, not as an individual person but as the first source of human nature, so that he transmitted the state along with human nature to his descendants. And since each thing should have a place suitable for that thing's condition, the human being so orderly constituted was placed in a most temperate and pleasant place, so that every vexation from internal or external annoyances was removed from him.

◄ᵌ 188 ᵌ►

Of the Tree of Knowledge of Good and Evil and the
First Precept for Human Beings

But the aforementioned state of human beings depended on the human will being subject to God. Therefore, in order that human beings became accustomed from the beginning to following the will of God, he laid down certain precepts for them. The precepts were that they were to eat of all the other trees

of paradise but were not, under threat of death, to eat of the tree of the knowledge of good and evil.

    And God did not thus forbid eating of the latter tree because the eating as
such was evil, but so that human beings, at least in this slight matter, observed
something for the sole reason that God commanded it. And so eating from
the aforementioned tree became evil because it was prohibited. And Gen. 2:17
called the tree one "of the knowledge of good and evil" because of the subsequent event, namely, that human beings by eating of it learned by experience
the difference between the good of obedience and the evil of disobedience, not
because the tree possessed the power to cause the knowledge.

◄ 189 ►

On the Devil's Seduction of Eve

Therefore, the devil, who had already sinned, seeing the man so constituted
that he could arrive at the perfect happiness from which the devil had fallen
away, and that he could nonetheless sin, tried to lead him away from the rectitude of righteousness. The devil approached him on his weaker side, tempting
the woman, in whom the benefit of wisdom was less vigorous. And in order to
incline her more easily to disobey the precept, he mendaciously shut out the
fear of death. And he promised her things that human beings by nature desire
(Gen. 3:5), namely, avoidance of ignorance, saying: "Your eyes will be opened";
the excellence of honor, saying: "You will be gods"; and perfect knowledge, saying: "You will know good and evil." For regarding the intellect, human beings
by nature avoid ignorance and desire knowledge, and regarding the will, which
is by nature free, they desire preeminence, so as to be subject to no one, or as
few as possible.

◄ 190 ►

What Induced the Woman to Disobey

Therefore, the woman desired the promised preeminence and perfect knowledge. The beauty and sweetness of the fruit also added to this, attracting her
to eat it, and so she, contemning the fear of death, disobeyed the command of
God by eating of the forbidden tree. And so her sin was manifold. First, there
was a sin of pride, in which she inordinately desired excellence. Second, there
was a sin of curiosity, in which she desired knowledge beyond the limits determined for her. Third, there was a sin of gluttony, in which the sweetness of the

food induced her to eat it. Fourth, there was a false esteem of God, when she believed the words of the devil speaking against God. Fifth, there was disobedience by transgressing the precept of God.

◄₹ 191 §►

How Sin Came to the Man

And sin came also to the man by the influence of the woman, but, as Paul says in 1 Tim. 2:14, he "was not tempted" as she was, namely, in believing the words that the devil spoke against God. For he could not think that God had mendaciously threatened something or uselessly prohibited something useful. But he, by inordinately desiring eminence and knowledge, was enticed by the promise of the devil. And because his will had departed from the rectitude of righteousness, he, wishing to bring his will to hers, followed her in disobeying God's precept by eating the fruit of the forbidden tree.

◄₹ 192 §►

On the Rebellion of the Lower Parts against Reason

The subjection of the human will to God caused the whole, so well-ordered integrity of the aforementioned state, as I have said [I, 186]. Therefore, the perfect subjection of the lower powers to reason and of the body to the soul was lost when the human will was withdrawn from subjection to God. And so the human being experienced, in a lower sense appetite, inordinate movements of desire, anger, and other emotions. Such movements are contrary to, rather than in accord with, the order of reason, very often obscuring reason and enticing it, as it were. And this is the battle of the flesh against the spirit of which Scripture speaks (Gal. 5:17). For, inasmuch as a sense appetite and other sense powers act through a bodily organ, while reason acts without a bodily organ, Scripture properly imputes to the flesh what belongs to a sense appetite. And Scripture properly imputes to the spirit what belongs to reason, as people customarily call substances that are separate from matter spiritual substances.

◄₹ 193 §►

On the Capacity to Suffer and the Necessity of Dying

The human being also consequently experienced in the body the defects of corruption and thereby incurred the necessity of dying, with the soul no longer able to keep the body forever, so to speak, by bestowing life on it. And so the human being became able to suffer and die, having a necessity, so to speak, to suffer and die and not merely the capacity to do so, as before.

◄≥ 194 ≤►

On Other Resulting Defects

Consequently, many other defects also resulted in the human being. For, along with the abundant inordinate emotional movements in the lower appetite, the light of wisdom, by which God illumined the human being when the will was subject to God, was lacking in reason. Consequently, human beings subjected their desire to sensibly perceptible things, and, deviating from God, sinned in many ways regarding these things. And further, they subjected themselves to unclean spirits, which they believed offered them help in acquiring such things, and so idolatry and different kinds of sins transpired in the human race. And the more human beings were corrupted in these things, the more fully they withdrew from knowing and desiring spiritual and divine goods.

◄≥ 195 ≤►

How Those Defects Were Transmitted to Descendants

And God gave the aforementioned good of original justice to the human race in our first parent, but in such a way that it was to be transmitted through him to his descendants. But an effect is taken away when its cause is taken away. The consequence was that, when the first man's own sin deprived him of the aforementioned good, all his descendants were deprived of it. And so, of the others, namely, after the sin of our first parent, all his descendants were born without original justice and with the defects resulting from his sin.

Nor is this contrary to the order of justice, as if God is punishing in the offspring the crime that our first parent committed, since this punishment only takes away things that God supernaturally granted the first man to be transmitted by him to others. And so these things were owed to others only insofar as they were to be transmitted to them by our first parent. Just so, if a king should give an estate to a soldier to be transmitted by him to his heirs, it cannot subsequently devolve to his descendants if the soldier commits a crime against the king so as to merit forfeiture of the estate. And so the crime of the parent justly deprives his descendants of the estate.

Does the Lack of Original Justice in Descendants
of Adam Have the Nature of Sin?

But a more pressing question remains: Can the lack of original justice in those who descended from our first parent have the nature of sin? For it seems to belong to the nature of sin that the evil called culpable is in the power of the one who is reckoned guilty, as I have said before [I, 120]. For no one is guilty of what one does not have the power to do or not to do. But it is not in the power of one who is born to be with or without original justice. And so it seems that such lack cannot have the nature of sin.

But this question is easily answered if we should distinguish between the person and the nature. For, as there are many bodily members in one person, so there are many persons in one human nature. And so we understand many human beings as if one human being by reason of their participation in the human species, as Porphyry says.[53] And we should note in regard to the sin of one human being that different bodily members of that human being perform different sinful acts. Moreover, the nature of sin does not require individual sins to be voluntary by the will of the bodily members that perform the sinful acts. Rather, the nature of sin requires that sins be voluntary by the will of what is the chief thing in a human being, namely, the intellectual part. For the hand cannot fail to strike, or the foot to walk, when the will so commands.

Therefore, the lack of original justice is a sin of nature in this way, inasmuch as the lack in human nature originates from the inordinate will of the first source in human nature, namely, our first parent. And so the sin is voluntary in relation to human nature, namely, by the will of the first source of the nature. And so the sin is transmitted to all who receive human nature from their first parent, as if to some of his bodily members. And so we call this sin original sin, since it is transmitted to descendants by their origin from the first parent. And so, although other sins, namely, actual sins, directly regard the person sinning, this sin directly regards human nature. For our first parent by his sin corrupted human nature, and the corrupted human nature corrupts the persons of the offspring who receive it from him.

Not All Sins Are Transmitted to Descendants

But it is not necessary that all other sins, whether of our first parent or other parents, be transmitted to descendants, since the first sin of our first parent took away the whole gift that was supernaturally conferred on the human nature of his person. And so we say that he corrupted or tainted nature. And so subsequent sins do not find any such thing that they can subtract from the whole nature. Rather, subsequent sins take away a personal good from a human being, or lessen it, and the sins corrupt nature only inasmuch as the nature belongs to this or that person. And a human being begets descendants as in the human being's nature, not in the human being's person. And so a parent transmits to descendants the first sin that corrupted the nature, not a sin that corrupts the person.

◆℥ 198 ℥►

The Merit of Adam Did Not Benefit His Descendants
to Restore Human Nature

And although the sin of our first parent corrupted the whole human nature, his repentance or any merit of his was unable to restore the whole nature. For it is clear that the repentance of Adam or any other merit of his was the act of an individual person, and the act of an individual has no power regarding the whole nature of the species. For causes that have power regarding the whole species are equivocal, not univocal, causes. For the sun causes generation in the whole human species, but a particular human being causes the generation of a particular human being, not the whole human species. Therefore, the individual merit of Adam or any mere human being was unable to suffice to restore the whole nature. And it resulted incidentally that the individual act of the first man corrupted the whole nature, inasmuch as he, when deprived of the state of innocence, was unable to transmit that state to others. And although he returned to grace by repentance, he could not return to his former innocence, for which God had granted the aforementioned gift of original justice.

It is at the same time also clear that the aforementioned state of original justice was a special gift of grace. And grace is not acquired by one's merits. Rather, God freely bestows it. Therefore, as the first man had original justice from the beginning by God's gift, not by his own merit, so also, and far less, was he able to merit it after his sin by repenting or performing any other work.

2. Christ's Incarnation

◆℥ 199 ℥►

On the Restoration of Human Nature by Christ

And it was necessary that divine providence restore the human nature corrupted in the aforementioned way. For human nature was unable to arrive at perfect happiness except with such corruption being removed. This is because happiness, since it is the perfect good, is incompatible with any defect, and especially the defect of sin. Sin is in some way contrary to virtue, and virtue is the way to happiness, as I have said [I, 172]. And so, inasmuch as human beings have been made for the sake of happiness, since happiness is their final end, God's work in so excellent a creature would then have been in vain. And the Psalmist in Ps. 89:47 reckons this inappropriate, saying: "For have you constituted the sons of men for no purpose?" Therefore, it was necessary to restore human nature.

Second, divine goodness surpasses the potentiality of a creature for good. But what I have previously said makes clear that the condition of human beings is such that they, as long as they live in this mortal life, are not immovably confirmed in evil, just as they are not immovably confirmed in good [I, 174]. Therefore, it belongs to the condition of human nature that it can be purged of the corruption of sin. Therefore, it was not appropriate for divine goodness to have left this potentiality completely empty, which would have been the case if God were not to have procured a remedy to restore it.

200

The Nature Needed to Be Restored by God and by Him Incarnate

And I have shown that neither Adam nor any other mere human being was able to restore human nature, both because no individual human being was preeminent over the whole of nature, and because no mere human being can cause grace [I, 198]. By the same argument, neither was an angel able to restore human nature, since no angel can cause grace, nor was an angel preeminent over human beings regarding the final perfect happiness to which they needed to be recalled, since angels and human beings are equal regarding it. Therefore, we conclude that only God was able to effect the restoration.

But if God were to have restored human beings only by his will and power, the order of divine justice, which requires satisfaction for sins, would not be observed. God does not make satisfaction, nor does he merit, since this belongs to one who is subject to another. Therefore, neither was it proper for God to make satisfaction for the sin of the whole human nature, nor was a mere human being able to do so, as I have shown [I, 198]. Therefore, it was appropriate that God became a human being, so that the one who was able to repair human nature and the one who was able to make satisfaction for sin would be one and the same. And Paul in 1 Tim. 1:15 assigns this reason of the divine incarnation: "Christ Jesus came into this world to save sinners."

◄ 201 ►

On Other Reasons for the Incarnation of the Son of God

But there are also other reasons for the divine incarnation. For human beings had withdrawn from spiritual things and given the whole of themselves to material things, from which they were unable to return to God by their own efforts. Therefore, divine wisdom, which had made human beings, by the material nature assumed visited human beings immersed in material things, so that he, by the mystery of his body, recalled them to spiritual things.

It was also necessary for the human race that God became a human being in order to demonstrate the excellence of human nature, so that human beings did not subject themselves to devils or material things.

At the same time, God, by having willed to become a human being, also clearly showed the immensity of his love for human beings, so that they as a result would now be subject to God by the desire of love, not the fear of death, which the first man contemned.

This also gives human beings an example of the blessed union by which the created intellect will be united to the uncreated spirit by understanding. For it does not remain unbelievable that a created intellect can be united to God by seeing his essence, since God has been united to a human being by assuming the nature of a human being.

The universe of God's whole work of creation is in a way perfected when human beings, who were created last, return cyclically to their source, united by the work of the incarnation to the very source of things.

◄ 202 ►

On the Error of Photinus Regarding the Incarnation of the Son of God[54]

And Photinus, inasmuch as he could, emptied the mystery of the divine incarnation. For he, following Ebion, Cerinthus, and Paul of Samosata, asserted that the Lord Christ Jesus was a mere man and did not exist before the Virgin Mary. But he claimed that Jesus by the merit of his blessed life and the suffering of his death merited the glory of divinity, so that he was called God by the grace of adoption, not by his nature. Therefore, grace would have made the human being divine, but there would have been no union of God and the human being. This is common to all the saints, not singular to Christ, although some would be considered more excellent in the grace than others.

But this error contradicts the authorities of divine Scripture. For example, Jo. 1:1 says: "In the beginning was the Word"; and adds in v. 14: "The Word became flesh." Therefore, the Word that "was in the beginning with God" (v. 2) took on flesh and was not a previously existing human being made divine by the grace of adoption.

Likewise, the Lord says in Jo. 6:38: "I came down from heaven to do the will of him who sent me, not my will." But according to the error of Photinus, it would have belonged to Christ only to have gone up, not to have come down, although Paul says the contrary in Eph. 4:9: "What is it for him to go up except that he first came down to the lower parts of the earth?" And this clearly gives us to understand that ascension would have had no place in Christ unless his descent were to have preceded.

◄₹ 203 ₷►

The Error of Nestorius Regarding the Incarnation, and Its Refutation

Therefore, Nestorius, wishing to avoid this, partially departed from the error of Photinus, since Nestorius held that we call Christ Son of God not only by the grace of adoption but by the divine nature in which Christ existed coeternal with the Father. But Nestorius partially agrees with Photinus, saying that the Son of God has been united to the human being only by an indwelling, not in such a way that God and the human being constituted one person. And so, as Photinus calls the human being God only by grace, so also Nestorius calls the human being the Son of God because of the indwelling of the Son of God in him that is by grace, not because he is truly God.

This error, too, is contrary to the authority of sacred Scripture. For Paul calls this union of God and the human being an emptying, saying about the Son of God in Phil. 2:6: "He who was in the form of God did not think it robbery to be equal to God but, taking the form of a slave, emptied himself." But there is no emptying of God because he dwells in the rational creature by grace. Otherwise, both the Father and the Spirit would have been emptied, since they also dwell in a rational creature by grace. The Lord says of himself and the Father in Jo. 14:23: "We shall come to him [one who loves me and keeps my word] and make our home with him"; and Paul says of the Holy Spirit in 1 Cor. 3:16: "The Spirit of God dwells in you."

Second, it would not have belonged to the human being to utter the words of divinity if he were not personally God. Therefore, he would have said most presumptuously: "I and the Father are one" (Jo. 10:30), or "Before Abraham was, I am" (Jo. 8:58). For the word *I* shows the person of the one speaking, and it was the human being who was speaking. Therefore, the person of God and the person of the human being are the same.

Therefore, in order to exclude these errors, both the Apostles' Creed and the Creed of the Fathers, after mentioning the person of the Son, add: "Who was conceived, born, suffered, died, and rose." For the Creeds would not have predicated of the Son of God things belonging to the human being unless the person of the Son of God and the person of the human being were the same. This is because the things belonging to one person are by that very fact not predicated of another person. For example, the things belonging to Paul are by that very fact not predicated of Peter.

◀፨ 204 ፨▶

On the Error of Arius Regarding the Incarnation, and Its Refutation

Therefore, in order to profess the unity of God and the human being, some heretics went to the other extreme, saying that there is both one person and one nature of God and the human being. And the first source of this error was Arius, who held that the only soul in Christ is the Word of God, which he said took the place of the soul for the body of Christ. He held this so that what the Scriptures say about Christ showing him less than the Father could be related only to the very Son of God regarding his assuming nature. And so, when Christ says, "The Father is greater than I" (Jo. 14:28), or when we read that Christ prayed or was distressed, these statements should be related to the very nature of the Son of God. And so, with this posited, it follows that there was effected a union of the Son of God with the human being in both the person and the nature, for soul and body clearly constitute the unity of human nature.

And when I showed that the Son is equal to the Father [I, 41–43], I made clear the falsity of this position regarding the assertion that the Son is less than the Father. But regarding the assertion that the Word of God took the place of the soul for Christ, the foregoing can show the falsity of this error. For I have shown before that the soul is united to a material substance as its form [I, 90], and that God cannot be the form of the body [I, 17]. And lest Arius were perchance to say that this should be understood about the supreme God the Father, we can also show the same about the angels. That is, we can show that angels by their nature cannot be united to a body by way of a form, since they are by their nature separate from bodies. Therefore, far less can the Son of God, who made the angels, as even Arius professes, be the form of a body.

Second, the Son of God, even if he should be a creature, as Arius falsely says, still surpasses all created spirits in happiness, according to Arius. The angels have so much happiness that they cannot have distress, since there would not be true and full happiness if they were to lack anything they desired. For it belongs to the nature of happiness to be the final and perfect good completely satisfying desire. Therefore, far less can the Son of God by his nature be distressed or have fear. But we read that he was sad: "Jesus began be fearful and weary and distressed."[55] And he himself professes his distress in Mk. 14:34, saying: "My soul is distressful even unto death." But this is clearly the distress of an intellectual substance, not a body. Therefore, besides the Word and the body in Christ, there needs to have been another substance that was able to suffer distress, and we call this substance the soul.

Third, let us grant that Christ took on things that are ours in order to cleanse us from our sins, and that it was more necessary for us to be cleansed regarding the soul, from which sin had come, and which is the subject in which sin inheres. Therefore, if so, he chiefly took on the soul, and the body with the soul, not the body without the soul.

◄◊ 205 ◊►

On the Error of Apollinaris Regarding the Incarnation, and Its Refutation

And this also excludes the error of Apollinaris, who at first followed Arius and did not posit in Christ any soul other than the very Word of God. But Apollinaris did not follow Arius in calling the Son of God a creature, and Scripture says many things about Christ that can neither be attributed to his body nor belong to the creator (e.g., distress, fear, and the like). Therefore, Apollonaris was at last compelled to posit a soul in Christ that made his body capable of sensation and could be the subject of such emotions but lacked reason and intellect. And the Word itself took the place of the intellect and reason in Christ the human being.

But many reasons show this to be false. First, it is contrary to the notion of nature that an irrational soul can be the form of a human body, since [...],[56] and we should not think that there was anything monstrous or unnatural about the incarnation of Christ. Second, it would have been contrary to the end of the incarnation, which is to restore human nature, and the restoration of human nature chiefly begins regarding its intellectual part, which can share in sin. And so it was especially appropriate that Christ assumed the intellectual part of human beings. We also read in Mt. 8:10 and Lk. 7:9 that Christ marveled, and to marvel belongs only to the rational soul and cannot belong at all to God. Therefore, as distress compels us to posit a sensory part of the soul in Christ, so marveling compels us to posit an intellectual part of the soul in him.

◄₹ 206 ₴►

On the Error of Eutyches, Who Posited
Only One Nature in Christ

And Eutyches followed them in one respect, since he held that there was one nature of God and human being after the incarnation, but he did not hold that Christ lacked either the soul or the intellect or any things that regard the integrity of human nature.

But the falsity of this opinion is also patently obvious, since the divine nature in itself is perfect and cannot be shared. And a nature perfect in itself cannot be united into one nature with a second unless the first should be converted into the second (e.g., food into something fed); or the second thing should be converted into the first thing (e.g., logs into fire); or both things are changed into a third thing (e.g., elements into a mixed material substance). But divine immutability removes all of these alternatives. For neither a thing converted into another thing nor a thing into which another thing can be converted is immutable. Therefore, since the divine nature in itself is perfect, it can in no way be united with another nature into one nature.

Second, if one should consider the order of things, the addition of a greater perfection changes the specific nature. For what exists and lives belongs to a different species than what only exists. And what exists, lives, and sensibly perceives, such as an animal, belongs to a different species than what only exists and lives, such as a plant. And likewise, what exists, lives, sensibly perceives, and understands, such as a human being, belongs to a different species than what only exists, lives, and sensibly perceives, such as an irrational animal. Therefore, if the one nature that Eutyches holds to belong to Christ had above all these things what is divine, then that nature would have belonged to a different species than human nature. Just so, human nature belongs to a different species than the nature of an irrational animal. Therefore, Christ was not a human being of the same species as other human beings. But this is demonstrably false, since he was begotten from human beings according to the flesh, as Mt. 1:1 shows, saying: "The book of the generation of Jesus Christ, son of David, son of Abraham."

Against the Error of Mani, Who Said That Christ Had an Imaginary, Not a Real, Body

And as Photinus emptied the mystery of the incarnation by taking the divine nature away from Christ, so Mani emptied the mystery by taking the human nature away from him. For Mani, since he held that the devil created the whole material creation, and it was inappropriate that the Son of the good God take on the creature of the devil, held that Christ had only imaginary, not real, flesh. And he asserted that all the things belonging to human nature related in the Gospel about Christ were done in appearance, not in fact. But this position clearly contradicts sacred Scripture, which says that Christ was born of the Virgin, circumcised, hungry, ate, and bore other things belonging to the nature of human flesh. Therefore, the passages of the Gospels relating these things about Christ would be false.

Second, Christ says about himself in Jo. 18:37: "I was born for this, and I came into the world for this, that I bear witness to the truth." But he would have been a false, not a true, witness if he were to have shown in himself what he was not. This is especially so because he predicted that he was about to suffer things that he could not have suffered without real flesh, namely, that he would be betrayed into the hands of human beings, spat upon, scourged, and crucified. Therefore, to say that Christ did not have real flesh, and that he suffered such things only in appearance, not in reality, is to impute falsity to Christ.

Third, it belongs to a human deceiver to remove true opinion from the hearts of human beings, and Christ removed from the hearts of his disciples the opinion that he did not have real flesh. For, after his resurrection, he appeared to his disciples, who thought he was a spirit or apparition. Therefore, to take away such a suspicion from their hearts, he said in Lk. 24:39: "Touch and see, since a spirit does not have flesh and bones as you see me to have." And in another place (Jo. 6:20), when he walked on the sea, and his disciples thought that he was an apparition and were beset with fear because of it, the Lord said: "It is I. Do not fear." Therefore, if the opinion that Christ did not have real flesh is true, we need to say that he was a deceiver. But Christ is the truth, as he says about himself (Jo. 14:6). Therefore, the opinion is false.

◄۶ 208 ۶►

Christ Had a Real Body, Not One from Heaven, against Valentine

Valentine, although he professed that Christ had a real body, said that Christ did not take on flesh from the Virgin. Rather, he said that Christ brought an already formed body from heaven that passed through the Virgin, receiving nothing from her, like water through a canal.

This, too, contradicts the truth of Scripture. For Paul says about Christ in Rom. 1:3: He "issued from the seed of David according to the flesh." And Paul says in Gal. 4:4: "God sent his Son born of a woman." Also, Mt. 1:6 says that "Jacob begot Joseph, the husband of Mary, from whom was born Jesus, who is called the Christ," and v.18 calls her his mother, adding: "When his mother Mary was betrothed to Joseph." But these things would not be true if Christ were not to have taken on flesh from the Virgin. Therefore, it is false that he brought a heavenly body. But we should understand what Paul says in 1 Cor. 47, "The second, heavenly man come down from heaven," to refer to what came down from heaven regarding Christ's divinity, not his bodily substance.

Second, there would be no reason why the Son of God bringing a body from heaven would have entered the womb of the Virgin if he were to take nothing from her. Rather, it would seem to be a deceit, since coming out of the womb of his mother would indicate that he received flesh from her that he had not. Therefore, since all falsehood by Christ is alien to him, we should absolutely profess that Christ came out of the womb of the Virgin in such a way that he received flesh from her.

◄۶ 209 ۶►

The Judgment of Faith Regarding the Incarnation

Therefore, we can gather from the foregoing that, according to the true Catholic faith, there was in Christ a real body of our nature, a real rational soul, and, along with these, perfect divinity as well. And these three substantial elements are united into one person, not one nature.

But some have proceeded to explain this truth in certain erroneous ways. For example, some considered that everything that comes to something after its complete existing is accidentally united to it, like clothing to a human being.[57] They held that the humanity was united to the divinity in the person of the Son by an accidental union, namely, such that the nature assumed was related to the person of the Son of God as clothing to a human being. And to confirm this, they introduced what Paul says about Christ in Phil. 2:7, that "he was found in appearance like a human being."

Moreover, they considered that the union of a soul and a body produces an individual of a rational nature, which one calls a person. Therefore, if the soul in Christ were to have been united to a body, they were unable to see it not to follow that such a union would constitute a person. Therefore, it would follow that there are two persons in Christ, namely, the person assuming and the person assumed. For there are not two persons in a clothed human being, since clothing does not have the nature of a person. But if the clothing were to be a person, then there would be two persons in the clothed human being. Therefore, to exclude this, they held that the soul of Christ was never united to his body, but that the person of the Son of God took on the soul and the body separately.

But while this opinion attempts to avoid one inappropriate thing, it falls into something more inappropriate, since it necessarily follows from the opinion that Christ was not a true human being. For true human nature requires union of the soul and the body, since a human being is composed of both. It would also follow that the flesh of Christ was not true flesh, nor were any of his bodily members true members, since, without a soul, there is no eye, hand, flesh, or bone except equivocally, as in a painting or a statue. It would also follow that Christ did not really die. For death is the privation of life, but death obviously could not take away divine life, and the body was unable to be alive unless a soul was united to it. Further, it would also follow that the body of Christ was incapable of sensibly perceiving, since the body does so only by the soul united to it.

Second, this opinion slips back into the error of Nestorius, although it strives to avoid it. For Nestorius erred in that he held that the Word of God was united to Christ the human being by the indwelling of grace, so that the Word of God was in the human being as in a temple. But it does not at all matter regarding the proposed opinion whether one says that the Word of God is in a human being as in a temple, or that human nature comes to the Word like clothes to the one wearing them. (There may be a difference insofar as the latter opinion is worse, since it cannot profess Christ as a real human being.) Therefore, this opinion is deservedly condemned.[58]

Third, we cannot say that a clothed human being is a person of clothes or a garment, nor can we in any way say that such a human being belongs to the species of clothes. Therefore, if the Son of God took on human nature as clothing, we will in no way be able to call him a person of human nature. Nor will we be able to say that the Son of God belongs to the same species as other human beings, although Paul says of him in Phil. 2:7 that he was "made in the likeness of human beings." And so it is clear that this opinion should be completely avoided.

◄◊ 210 ◊►

There Are Not Two Existing Subjects in Christ

And others, wishing to avoid the aforementioned inappropriate things, held that the soul in Christ was united to the body, and that such a union constituted a human being that they say the Son of God assumed into the unity of the person.[59] And by reason of this assumption, they say that the human being is the Son of God, and that the Son of God is the human being. And because they say that the aforementioned assumption had the unity of the person as its terminus, they profess one person of God and the human being in Christ. But because this human being, whom they say the soul and the body constituted, is an existing subject or hypostasis of human nature, they posit two existing subjects and two hypostases in Christ: one, created and temporal, of the human nature; the other, uncreated and eternal, of the divine nature.

But this position, although it seems nominally to retreat from the error of Nestorius, slips into the same error with him if one should scrutinize it more deeply. For a person is clearly nothing but an individual substance of rational nature, and human nature is a rational nature. And so, because this position posits in Christ a hypostasis or temporal and created existing subject of a rational nature, it also posits a temporal and created person in Christ. For this is what the terms *existing subject* or *hypostasis* mean, namely, individual substance. Therefore, when they posit in Christ two existing subjects or hypostases, if they understand what they say, they necessarily have to posit two persons.

Second, any things that differ as existing subjects are so disposed that things proper to one cannot belong to the other. Therefore, if the Son of God and the human son are not the same existing subject, then it will follow that things belonging to the human son cannot be attributed to the Son of God, and vice versa. Therefore, we will be unable to say that God was crucified or born of the Virgin, and this belongs to the Nestorian impiety.

And regarding these things, one may wish to say that we attribute things belonging to the human being to the Son of God, and the converse, because of the unity of the person, although the human being and the Son of God are different existing subjects. But this is altogether impossible. For it is clear that the eternal existing subject of the Son of God is nothing but his very person. Therefore, any things predicated of the Son of God by reason of his person will be predicated of him by reason of his existing subject. But things belonging to the human being are not predicated of the Son of God by reason of the existing subject, since the Son of God is supposed to differ from the human son by reason of the existing subject. Therefore, things proper to the human son (e.g., being born of the Virgin, dying, and the like) will not be able to be predicated of the Son of God by reason of the person.

Third, if we should predicate the name *God* of a temporal existing subject, this will be fresh and new. But everything that we freshly and newly call God is only God because it has become God, and what has become God is God by adoption, not by nature. Therefore, it will follow that the human being was God only by adoption, not truly and by nature, and this also belongs to the error of Nestorius.

◄§ 211 §►

There Is Only One Existing Subject and Only One Person in Christ

Therefore, we need to say both that there is in Christ one person of God and the human being, and that there is one existing subject and one hypostasis. But there are two natures, not one.

And in order to show this, we need to consider that the terms *person, hypostasis,* and *existing subject* designate something integral. For we can call the whole that is a particular human being, but not a hand, flesh, or any other part, a person or hypostasis or existing subject. But we can apply terms such as *individual* and *particular,* which are common to the individual things of substances and accidents, to both a whole and its parts. For parts have something in common with accidents, namely, that parts exist in other things, not by themselves, although parts do so in a different way than accidents do. Therefore, we can say that the hand of Socrates or Plato is an individual and singular thing, although it is not a hypostasis, existing subject, or person.

Further, we should also consider that the conjunction of some things, considered in itself, sometimes produces something integral, but the conjunction does not constitute anything integral in another thing because something else needs to be added. For example, the mixture of the four elements in a stone produces something integral. And so we can call what the elements in the stone constitute an existing subject or hypostasis, which is the particular stone, but we cannot call it a person, since the stone is not the hypostasis of a rational nature. But the composition of the elements in an animal does not constitute anything integral. Rather, the composition of the elements constitutes part of the animal, namely, its body, since something else, namely, the soul, needs to be added to complete the animal. And so the composition of the elements in an animal does not constitute an existing subject or hypostasis. Rather, the whole particular animal is the hypostasis or existing subject. Still, the composition of the elements in an animal is far more, not less, efficacious in an animal than in a stone, since the composition is ordered to something more excellent.

Therefore, the union of the soul and the body in other human beings constitutes a hypostasis and existing subject, since nothing else besides these two components is added. But in the Lord Jesus Christ, a third essential, divinity, is added to the soul and the body. And so what is composed of body and soul is not a distinct existing subject, hypostasis, or person. Rather, the existing subject, hypostasis, or person is something that exists from three essentials, namely, the body, the soul, and the deity. And so, as there is only one person in Christ, so there is only one hypostasis and one existing subject in him.

And the soul comes to the body in one regard, and divinity to both in another regard. For the soul comes to the body as the body's existing form, and so these two things constitute one nature, which we call human nature. But divinity does not come to the soul and the body by way of a form or a part, since this is contrary to the nature of divine perfection. And so divinity, the soul, and the body do not constitute one nature. Rather, the divine nature, being in itself whole and simple, united the human nature constituted of soul and body to itself in an incomprehensible and ineffable way. And this came from the infinite power of the divine nature. For we see that the greater power that an active thing has, the more it attaches to itself an instrument to carry out a work. Therefore, as divine power is infinite and incomprehensible because of its infinity, so the way by which it united the human nature of Christ to itself as an instrument, as it were, to effect human salvation is ineffable to us and surpasses every other union of God to a creature.

And person, hypostasis, and existing subject signify a whole, as I said above. Therefore, if the divine nature in Christ is like a part, as the soul is in the composition of a human being, and not like a whole, the person of Christ would be something constituted of three things, not held together only by the divine nature. (Just so, the person, hypostasis, and existing subject in a human being is something constituted of the soul and the body.) But because the divine nature is a whole that took human nature to itself by an ineffable union, the person of Christ is held together by the divine nature, and so are the hypostasis and the existing subject. And the soul and the body are drawn into the personhood of the divine person, so that the person of the Son of God is also the person, hypostasis, and existing subject of the human son.

And we can find such an equivalent example in creatures. For a subject and its accidents are not united in such a way that they constitute a third thing.

And so the subject in such a union is not disposed as a part but is a whole that is a person, hypostasis, and existing subject. And the accidents are drawn into the personhood of an existing subject, so that the person, as well as the hypostasis and the existing subject, of a human being and of the human being's whiteness are the same. Therefore, the person, hypostasis, and existing subject of the Son of God are analogously the person, hypostasis, and existing subject of the human nature in Christ. And so some, not distinguishing reality from analogy, presumed to say because of such an analogy that the human nature in Christ degenerates into an accident and was accidentally united to the Son of God.[60]

Therefore, the foregoing makes clear that there is no other person in Christ than the eternal person, which is the person of the Son of God, nor is there another hypostasis or existing subject. And so, when we say "this human being" about Christ, we introduce the eternal existing subject. Still, we do not on this account equivocally predicate the term *human being* about Christ and other human beings. For we note equivocation by the different meanings of a term, not by the different suppositions. And the term *human being* attributed to Peter and to Christ means the same thing, namely, human nature, but does not suppose the same thing, since the latter attribution supposes the eternal existing subject of the Son of God, and the former attribution a created existing subject.

But we can predicate of each existing subject of a nature things proper to the nature to which the existing subject belongs, and there is in Christ the same existing subject of the human and divine natures. Therefore, we clearly can without difference predicate both things belonging to the divine nature and things belonging to the human nature of this existing subject of both natures. This is true whether the existing subject is presupposed by a word signifying the human nature or one signifying the divine nature or person. This is as if, for example, we should say that the Son of God is eternal, and that the Son of God was born of the Virgin. And we can likewise say that this human being is God and created the stars, and that he was born, died, and was buried.

And what we predicate of an existing subject we predicate by a form or nature (e.g., Socrates is white by whiteness, and rational by the soul). But I have said above that there are in Christ two natures and one existing subject. Therefore, if the reference should be to the existing subject, we should predicate human and divine things of Christ without difference. But we should distinguish in what respect we predicate each, since we predicate divine things of him by his divine nature, and human things of him by his human nature.

◄⅋ 212 ⅋►

On the Things We Call One or Many in Christ

Therefore, because there is one person and two natures in Christ, we should
next consider what we should call one in Christ, and what many. For we need
to profess that any things multiple by reason of the different natures are many
in Christ. One of the first things that we should consider is that, since one receives a nature by begetting or birth, it is necessary that, as there are two natures
in Christ, so also there are two generations or births. One generation or birth
is eternal, by which he received the divine nature from the Father; the other is
temporal, by which he received the human nature from his mother. Likewise,
we need to call many in Christ any things belonging to nature commonly attributed to both God and human beings. But we attribute to God intellect, will, and
their perfections (e.g., knowledge or wisdom, and charity and justice), which
we also attribute to human beings as things belonging to human nature. For
the will and the intellect are parts of the soul, and their perfections are wisdom,
justice, and the like. Therefore, we need to posit in Christ two intellects, the
human and the divine, two wills, and two kinds of knowledge, and justice or
charity, namely, the created and the uncreated.

But we need to profess that things belonging to the existing subject or hypostasis are only one thing in Christ. And so, if we should understand existing
insofar as one existing belongs to one existing subject, it seems that we should
say that there is only one existing in Christ. For separate individual parts clearly
have their own existing, but the individual parts, insofar as they are considered
in a whole, do not have their own individual existing. Rather, all of them exist
by the existing of the whole. Therefore, if we should consider Christ himself as
a whole existing subject of two natures, only one existing will belong to him,
just as there is one existing subject.

And because activities belong to existing subjects, it seemed to some
that, as there is only one existing subject in Christ, so there is only one activity.[61] But they did not correctly consider the matter. For several kinds of
activities are found in each individual thing if there are several sources of
the activities. For example, a human being has one activity of understanding
and another activity of sense perception because of the difference between
a sense and an intellect. Even fire has one activity of heating and another of
rising because of the difference between heat and lightness. And nature is
related to activity as the source of activity. Therefore, Christ has two kinds of
activity because of his two natures, not one kind of activity because of his one

existing subject, just as, conversely, there is in the holy Trinity one activity of the three persons because of their one nature.

But the activity of the humanity in Christ shares in part of the power of divine activity. For, of all the things that belong to one existing subject, other things serve as instruments of the most important thing (e.g., other parts of a human being are instruments of the intellect). Therefore, we regard the humanity in the Lord Jesus Christ as an instrument of his divinity, as it were. But an instrument clearly acts in the power of the chief active thing. And so we find both the power of the instrument and the power of the chief active thing in the activity of the instrument (e.g., an axe's action makes a box inasmuch as a carpenter directs the action). Therefore, so also did the activity of the human nature in Christ have a power from his divinity beyond human power. For example, touching a leper was an action of his humanity, but it came from the power of his divinity that the touch cured the leper of leprosy. And all his human actions and sufferings were in this way salutary by the power of his divinity. And so Dionysius calls Christ's human activity *theandric* (i.e., divine-human), namely, that it proceeded from his humanity but in such a way that the power of his divinity was active in it.[62]

Some also raise a question about the sonship, whether there is only one sonship in Christ because of the unity of the existing subject, or two sonships because of the duality of his birth.[63] But it seems that there are two sonships, since multiple causes produce multiple effects, and birth causes sonship. Therefore, since there are two births of Christ, it seems that there are also two sonships.

Nor is it an obstacle that his sonship is a personal relation (i.e., a relation constituting a person). For this is true about his divine sonship, but his human sonship happens to a constituted person and does not constitute a person. Likewise, it is no obstacle that a human being is related to his father and mother by one and the same sonship, since a human being is born from both by the same birth. And where the cause of a relation is the same, the relation also is really one and the same, although the respects are multiple. For nothing prevents something from having a relation to something else without the relation being really in it, as, for example, a knowable object is related to knowledge of it by a relation that is not in it. Just so, nothing prevents only one real relation from having several respects. For, as a relation has from its cause to be a certain kind of thing, it also has from its cause to be one or many things. And so, since Christ is not born by the same birth from the Father and his mother, there seem to be two real sonships in him because of the two births.

But there is another obstacle, because of which there cannot be plural real sonships in Christ, since we can call only the complete existing subject, not everything that is born from someone, a son. For we call the whole individual thing that is Peter or John a son, not the hand of a human being a daughter, or the foot of a human being a son. Therefore, the subject of sonship in the proper sense is the complete existing subject itself. But I have shown before that there is in Christ only the uncreated existing subject [I, 211], to which no real temporal relation can be added. Rather, every relation of God to a creature is only conceptual, as I have said before [I, 54]. Therefore, the sonship by which the eternal existing subject of the Son is related to his Virgin mother is necessarily only a conceptual, not a real, relation.

Nor is Christ because of this prevented from being truly and really the son of his Virgin mother, as one really born of her. Just so, God is truly and really the Lord of a creature, as one having real power to compel creatures, although we attribute the relation of lordship to God only conceptually.

But if there were to be several existing subjects in Christ, as some have held,[64] nothing would prevent positing two sonships in Christ, since the created existing subject would be subject to temporal sonship.

◄§ 213 §►

Christ Was Necessarily Perfect in Grace and True Wisdom

And the humanity of Christ is related to his divinity as an instrument, as it were, of the latter, as I have already said [I, 212], and we chiefly judge the disposition and quality of instruments both by their end and by the fitness of the one using the instrument. Therefore, it is appropriate that we consider in these ways the quality of the human nature assumed by the Word of God. But the end of the Word of God's assumption of human nature is the salvation and restoration of human nature. Therefore, Christ, regarding his human nature, needed to be such that he could appropriately cause human salvation. But human salvation consists of enjoying God, which makes a human being blessed. And so Christ, regarding his human nature, needed to have been perfectly enjoying God, since the source in any genus needs to be perfect.

And there is enjoyment of God in two ways, namely, by the will and by the intellect: by the will perfectly adhering to God by love, and by the intellect perfectly knowing him. And perfect adherence of the will to God by love is through grace, which makes human beings righteous, as Rom. 3:24 says: "His freely bestowed grace makes them righteous." For human beings are righteous because they adhere to God by love. And perfect knowledge of God is through the light of wisdom, which is knowledge of divine truth. Therefore, the incarnate Word of God needed to be perfect in grace and true wisdom. And so also

Jo. 1:14 says: "The Word became flesh and dwelt among us, and we saw his glory, glory as the only-begotten of the Father, full of grace and truth."

◄≀ 214 ≀►

On the Fullness of Christ's Grace

First, we should inquire about the fullness of his grace. And about this, we should consider that we can understand the word *grace* in two ways.[65] We can understand the word in one way because it means to be pleasing, since we say that one enjoys the favor of another because one is pleasing to the other. We can understand the word in a second way because it means to be given something gratis, since we say that one who confers a benefit on another gratis does a favor to the other. Nor are these two understandings of grace completely distinct, since one gives something gratis to another because the recipient is pleasing to the donor, either absolutely or in some respect.

The recipient is absolutely such when the recipient is pleasing to the donor to the extent that the donor unites the recipient to the donor in some way. For we as much as possible draw to ourselves persons we consider pleasing, by the degree and way in which they are such. And the recipient is pleasing to the donor in some respect when the recipient is pleasing to the extent that the recipient receives something from the donor but not pleasing to the extent that the donor accepts the recipient as an associate. And so it is clear that everyone who enjoys someone's favor has something given gratis, but not everyone having something given gratis is pleasing to the donor. And so we are accustomed to distinguish two kinds of grace, namely, one given absolutely gratis and the other a grace that also makes someone pleasing.

And we say that something in no way owed is given gratis. And things are owed in two ways: in one way, owed regarding nature; in the other way, owed regarding activity. Regarding nature, what the natural order of a thing demands is owed to the thing (e.g., it is owed to human beings that they have reason, or hands and feet). And things are owed regarding activity (e.g., pay is owed to a worker). Therefore, there are gifts God gives gratis to human beings that both surpass the order of nature and are not acquired by one's merits. But even things that God at times gives for one's merits do not lose the character of grace. This is both because the source of meriting such things was from grace, and because God gives them more abundantly than human merits require, as Rom. 6:23 says: "The grace of God is eternal life."

And some of such gifts both surpass the capacity of human nature and are not rendered for merits. But a human being is not rendered pleasing to God because the human being has such gifts (e.g., the gifts of prophecy, working miracles, knowledge and learning, or if God confers any like gifts). For these and like gifts do not unite a human being to God, except, perhaps, analogously, as a human being shares in some of God's goodness, and all things are like God in this way. But other gifts render a human being pleasing to God and unite the human being to him, and we call such gifts graces both because they are given gratis, and because they make human beings pleasing to God.

The union of a human being with God is a double union. The first is by desire, and this is by charity, which in a way makes a human being one with God by desire, as 1 Cor. 6:17 says: "One who adheres to God is one spirit with him." God also dwells in a human being by this union, as Jo. 14:23 says: "If any-one loves me, he will keep my word, and my Father will love him, and we shall come to him and make our home with him." For the union causes a human being to be in God, as 1 Jo. 4:16 says: "Anyone who abides in charity abides in God, and God in him." Therefore, a human being is made pleasing to God by the gratuitous gift received and is brought so far as to become one spirit with God by the love of charity, the human being in God, and God in the human being. And so Paul says in 1 Cor. 13:1–3 that, without charity, other gifts do not profit a human being, since the other gifts can make a human being pleasing to God only if charity is present.

But this grace is common to all the saints. And so Christ the human being, when petitioning in prayer that this grace be given to his disciples, says in Jo. 17:21: "That they be one" in us, namely, by the union of love, "as we also are one."

And there is a second union of a human being with God, not only by desire or indwelling, but by the hypostatic or personal union, namely, that one and the same hypostasis or person is God and the human being. And this union with God is particular to Jesus Christ, and I have already said many things about this union [I, 202–212]. Therefore, this is the singular grace of Christ the human being, that he is united to God in the unity of his person. For this gift has also been given gratis, since it surpasses the ability of nature, and no merits precede it. And the gift also makes him most pleasing to God, so that Mt. 3:17 and 17:5 say uniquely of him: "This is my beloved Son with whom I am well pleased."

But the difference between the two graces seems to be that the grace that unites the human being to God by desire exists in the soul as something ha-bitual. For, inasmuch as an act of love effects this union, and perfect acts come from a habit, it follows that a habitual grace is poured into the soul for this most perfect act that joins the soul to God by love. But the very natures to which hypostases or persons belong, not a habit, constitute personal or hypostatic existing. Therefore, the very union of the two natures in the one person, not a habitual grace, causes the union of human nature with God in the unity of the person.

And the nearer a creature comes to God, the more of his goodness it shares, and the more abundant the gifts with which it is filled by his power, just as things closer to fire share in more of its heat. But no way can exist or be conceived by which a creature adheres more closely to God than what is united to him in the unity of the person. Therefore, from the very union of human nature to God in the unity of the person, it follows that the soul of Christ was also filled with habitual gifts of graces beyond other souls. As a result, the habitual grace in Christ is an effect of the union rather than a disposition for the union. And the very way of speaking that John uses in the aforementioned text (Jo. 1:14) makes this very clear: "We saw him as the only-begotten of the Father, full of grace and truth." But the only-begotten Son of the Father is Christ the human being, inasmuch as the Word became flesh. Therefore, from having become flesh, it follows that he Word was filled with grace and truth.

But in things full of any perfection or goodness, the one from which there is also an overflow into other things is fuller (e.g., what can illumine other things shines more fully). But Christ the human being, as the only-begotten Son of the Father, obtained the greatest fullness of grace. Therefore, grace also overflowed from him into others, so that the Son of God, having become a human being, made human beings gods and sons of God, as Paul says in Gal. 4:4: "God sent his Son, born of a woman, so that we received adoption as sons."

And because grace and truth come from Christ to others, it is belongs to him to be head of the church. For sensation and movement come in some way from the head to the other bodily members, which are conformed to it in nature. Just so, grace and truth come from Christ to other human beings. And so Eph. 1:22 says: "And he has made him head over the whole church, which is his body." We can also call him the head of angels as well as human beings regarding excellence and influence, although not regarding conformity to the specifically same nature. And so Paul says before the just cited text (vv. 20–21) that God "established him," namely, Christ, "at his right hand in the heavens over every principality, authority, power, and domination."

Therefore, according to the foregoing, we customarily assign three graces in Christ. First, there is the grace of union, insofar as human nature, without any antecedent merits, received the gift to be united to the Son of God in his person. Second, there is the individual grace, by which the soul of Christ was filled with grace and truth beyond other souls. Third, there is the grace of the head, insofar as grace overflows from him into others. And John treats of these three things in a fitting order. For Jo. 1:14 says regarding the grace of union: "The Word became flesh"; and in the same verse regarding the individual grace: "We saw him as the only-begotten of the Father, full of grace and truth"; and in v. 16 regarding the grace of the head: "And we have all received of his fullness."

◄ 215 ►

On the Infinity of Christ's Grace

And it is particular to Christ that his grace is infinite, since God does not give his spirit to Christ the human being to a degree, according to the testimony of John the Baptist, as Jo. 3:34 says. But God gives his spirit to others to a degree, as Eph. 4:7 says: "Grace is given to each according to the measure of Christ's gift." And if this should be related to the grace of union, the statement admits no doubt. For it was given to other holy persons to be gods or children of God by participation through the influx of a gift, which, because created, needs to be finite, just like other creatures. But it was given to Christ regarding his human nature to be the divine Son of God by nature, not by participation, and natural divinity is infinite. Therefore, he receives an infinite gift by the very union. And so the grace of union is beyond any doubt infinite.

But there can be doubt whether his habitual grace was infinite. For, inasmuch as such grace is also a created gift, one needs to profess that it has a finite essence. Still, we can call it infinite for three reasons. The first reason regards the recipient. For the capacity of any created nature is clearly finite, since, although a created nature can receive infinite good by knowing, loving, and enjoying the good, such a nature does not receive it infinitely. Therefore, each creature's species and nature is the measure of the creature's capacity. But this does not preclude divine power from having been able to make a creature of greater capacity, although the creature would not then be of same specific nature. Just so, if we should add one to the number three, there will then be another specific number.

Therefore, when less divine goodness is given to something than its species has a natural capacity for, it seems given to it in a measure. But when a thing's whole natural capacity is filled, divine goodness does not seem to be given to it in a measure. This is because there is no measure regarding the donor, who was ready to give the whole, although there is a measure regarding the recipient. This is as if someone bringing a jug to a stream finds unlimited water ready at hand, although that person receives in a measure because of the fixed size of the jug. Therefore, the habitual grace of Christ is essentially finite, but we say that it was given without limit and not in a measure, since as much is given as a created nature can receive.

And the second reason regards the very gift received. For we should consider that nothing prevents something from being essentially finite but infinite by reason of a special form. For the essentially infinite has the whole fullness of existing, and this belongs to God alone, who is existence itself. And if one should suppose that there is a special form not existing in a subject (e.g., whiteness or heat), it would not have an infinite essence, since its essence would be limited to a genus or species, but it would still possess the fullness of its species. And so it, having whatever can belong to its species, would be without limit or measure regarding its specific nature. But if whiteness or heat should be received in a subject, it does not always have all of whatever belongs necessarily and always to the nature of this form. Rather, it does so only when it is possessed as perfectly as it can be, namely, so that the way of possessing it equals the power of the thing possessed.

Therefore, the habitual grace of Christ was essentially finite, but we say that it was without limit or measure, since Christ received all of whatever was able to belong to the nature of grace. But other human beings do not receive all of it, but one in this way, another in that way, as 1 Cor. 12:4 says: "For there are diverse graces."

And the third reason regards the cause, since an effect is contained in some way in its cause. Therefore, anything in which a cause with infinite power to cause is present has what is caused, beyond measure and in a way infinitely. For example, if one were to have a fountain that was able to pour out water endlessly, we would say that such a one has water beyond measure or limit. Therefore, the soul of Christ has infinite grace and beyond measure because he has united to him the Word, which is the unfailing and infinite source of the entire emanation of creatures.

And because the individual grace of Christ's soul is infinite in the aforementioned ways, we evidently conclude that his grace is also infinite insofar as he is the head of the church. For grace pours out from what he has. And so he has the power to pour out the gifts of the spirit beyond measure because he has the gifts beyond measure, and having the power belongs to the grace of the head. That is to say, his grace is enough not only for the salvation of some human beings but for the salvation of human beings of the whole world. Just so, 1 Jo. 2:2 says: "He himself is the propitiation for our sins, and not only for ours, but also for those of the whole world." And we can add, "of many worlds," if there were to be any.

◄≈ 216 ≈►

On the Fullness of Christ's Wisdom

And we need to speak next about the fullness of Christ's wisdom. The thing to be considered first in this matter is that, inasmuch as there are two natures in Christ, namely, the divine and the human, anything belonging to both natures needs to be two-fold in Christ, as I have said before [I, 212]. And wisdom belongs to both the divine and human natures. For Job 9:4 says of God: "He is wise in mind and strong in strength." But Scripture also sometimes calls human beings wise, whether in worldly wisdom, as Jer. 9:23 says: "Let the wise man not glory in his wisdom"; or in divine wisdom, as Mt. 23:34 says: "Behold, I send you wise men and scribes."

Therefore, we need to profess that there are two wisdoms in Christ by reason of his two natures, namely, the uncreated wisdom that is proper to him insofar as he is God, and the created wisdom that is proper to him insofar as he is a human being. And insofar as he is God and the Word of God, he is the begotten wisdom of the Father, as 1 Cor. 1:24 says: "Christ, the power and wisdom of God." For the internal word of anyone who understands is nothing but the conception of that one's wisdom. And I have said before that the Word of God is perfect and unique [I, 41–44]. Therefore, the Word of God is necessarily the perfect conception of God the Father's wisdom, namely, that anything contained in the wisdom of God the Father in the way of the one not begotten is contained whole in the Word in the way of the one begotten or conceived. And so Col. 2:3 says: "All the treasures of the wisdom and knowledge of God have been hidden in him," namely, Christ.

And there are two kinds of knowledge of Christ the human being. One is godlike, insofar as he sees God essentially and other things in God, just as God in understanding himself understands all things. This vision makes both God himself and every rational creature perfectly enjoying him blessed. Therefore, since Christ causes human salvation, as I have said [I, 200, 205, 213, and 215], we need to say that such knowledge, as befitting such a cause, belongs to Christ's soul.

But the source of human salvation needs to be both unmovable and outstanding in power. Therefore, it was appropriate that the vision of God, of which the blessedness of human beings and their eternal salvation consist, belongs to Christ more excellently than to the others and as the unmovable source of their blessedness and salvation. But movable and unmovable things differ in that movable things acquire their proper perfection in the course of time and do not, as movable, possess it from the beginning, whereas unmovable things as such always obtain their perfections from when they begin to exist. Therefore, it was appropriate that Christ, the cause of human salvation, had possessed the full vision of God from the very beginning of his incarnation and had not arrived at it in the course of time, as other holy persons do.

It was also appropriate that, above other creatures, the vision of God beatified the soul that was united more closely to God. And we note grades in this vision, insofar as some see God, who is the cause of all things, more clearly than others do. And the more fully one knows a cause, the more of its effects one can perceive in it, since one knows a cause more only if one knows its power more fully, and there cannot be knowledge of the power without knowledge of the power's effects. For we usually measure the amount of power by the power's effects. And so some of those who see the essence of God see more effects or natures of divine works in God himself than do others, who see less clearly. And accordingly, higher angels instruct lower angels, as I have said before [I, 126].

Therefore, Christ's soul, which, of all creatures, obtains the highest perfection of the vision of God, fully intuits in God himself all his works and their natures, whatever things exist, will exist, or have existed. Hence Christ enlightens both human beings and the highest angels. And so Paul says in Col. 2:3: "All the treasures of the wisdom and knowledge of God have been hidden in him"; and in Heb. 4:13 says: "All things are laid bare and open to his eyes."

Nonetheless, Christ's soul cannot extend to comprehending divinity. For something is comprehended in knowledge when one knows it as much as it is knowable, as I have said before [I, 106]. But each thing is knowable inasmuch as it is a being and true, and God's existing as well as his truth are infinite. Therefore, God is infinitely knowable. But no creature can know infinitely, even if what the creature knows is infinite. Therefore, no creature by seeing God can comprehend him. And Christ's soul is a creature, and anything in Christ belonging only to his human nature was created. Otherwise, the nature of humanity in Christ would not differ from the nature of his divinity, which is the only uncreated nature.

And the hypostasis or person of the Word of God, which is one in two natures, was uncreated. And by reason of this, we do not call Christ a creature, absolutely speaking, since his name signifies the hypostasis. But we say that Christ's soul or body is a creature. Therefore, Christ's soul does not comprehend God, but Christ comprehends God by his uncreated wisdom, as the Lord says in Mt. 11:27 about his comprehensive knowledge: "No one knows the Son except the Father, nor does anyone know the Father except the Son."

And we should note that it belongs to the same consideration to comprehend the essence of something and to comprehend its power. For each thing can act inasmuch as it is actual. Therefore, if Christ's soul cannot comprehend the essence of divinity, as I have shown above, his soul cannot comprehend divine power. But his soul would comprehend God's power if it were to know whatever God can do, and by what natures he could produce effects. Therefore, Christ's soul does not know whatever God can make, or by what natures he could act. But because God the Father has set Christ, even as a human being, over every creature, it is appropriate that he have full knowledge in the vision of the divine essence itself of all things that God has created in whatever way. And accordingly, we call Christ's soul omniscient, since it has full knowledge of all the things that exist, will exist, or have existed. But of other creatures seeing God, some perceive knowledge of the aforementioned effects in the vision of God itself more fully, and others less fully.

And besides this knowledge of things whereby the created intellect knows things in the vision of the divine essence itself, there are other ways of knowing whereby creatures have knowledge of things. For angels, besides the initial knowledge whereby they know things in the Word, have later knowledge, whereby they know things in the things' own natures. But such knowledge belongs to human beings according to their nature in one way, and to angels in another way. For human beings by the order of their nature acquire intelligible truth about things from the senses, as Dionysius says,[66] namely, such that the intelligible forms in their intellects are abstracted from sense images by the action of the active intellect. But angels acquire knowledge of things by an influx of the divine light, namely, that, as God brings things into existing, so also he imprints the natures or likenesses of things in the angelic intellect. And in both human beings and angels, there is, above the knowledge of things that belong to them by nature, a supernatural knowledge of the divine mysteries, about which both angels enlighten other angels, and prophetic revelation instructs human beings.

And because no perfection bestowed on creatures should be denied to Christ's soul, which is the most excellent of creatures, three other kinds of knowledge should appropriately be attributed to him besides the knowledge whereby he sees the essence of God and all things in it. One kind is experiential, just as for other human beings, insofar as he knew some things by the senses, as befits human nature.

And God infused a second kind of knowledge in order for him to know all the things that the natural knowledge of a human being can reach. For it was appropriate that the human nature assumed by the Word of God, as the one by which human nature was to be restored, lacked no perfection. But everything potential is imperfect before it is brought into actuality, and the human intellect is potential in relation to the intelligible things that a human being can know by nature. Therefore, Christ's soul received from God knowledge of these things by infused forms, which brought the whole potentiality of his human intellect into actuality.

But Christ by his human nature was both the restorer of the nature and the distributor of grace. Therefore, a third kind of knowledge was present in him whereby he knew most fully whatever can belong to the mysteries of grace, which surpass the natural knowledge of human beings, but which human beings know by the gift of wisdom or by the spirit of prophecy. For the human intellect also has potentiality to know such things, although a higher active thing brings it into actuality. The light of the active intellect brings the human intellect into actuality to know natural things, and the human intellect acquires knowledge of the mysteries of grace by the divine light.

Therefore, the aforementioned things make clear that Christ's soul obtained the highest grade of knowledge among creatures regarding the vision of God, whereby one sees the essence of God and other things in it. And he likewise obtained the highest grade of knowledge regarding the mysteries of grace and knowable natural things. And so Christ could not grow in knowledge in any of these three things. But he evidently increased in knowledge of sensibly perceptible things by experiencing them with his bodily senses over the course of time. And so he was able to grow only in his experiential knowledge, as Lk. 2:52 says: "The boy increased in wisdom and age." (But one can also understand this in another way, to affirm Christ's progress in wisdom because wisdom increased in others, namely, those whom his wisdom was progressively instructing, not because he himself is wiser.) And this was done designedly, to show that he was like other human beings, lest the mystery of the incarnation would seem a fiction were he to have shown perfect wisdom in boyhood.

◄ह 217 ş►

On the Matter of Christ's Body

Therefore, the foregoing makes quite clear how the body of Christ needed to be formed. God was able to form Christ's body out of the dirt of the earth or whatever matter, as he formed the body of Adam, but this would not have been appropriate for the human restoration for the sake of which the Son of God took on flesh, as we have said [I, 200]. For the nature of the human race derived from Adam was the nature to be healed. And that nature would not have been adequately restored to its former honor if the victor over the devil and the conqueror of death, under both of which [the devil and death] the human race was held captive because of the sin of Adam, were to assume a body from another source. But the works of God are perfect, and he brings to a perfect state what he intends to restore, so that he adds still more than had been subtracted, as Paul says in Rom. 5:20: "The grace of God has abounded more than the sin of Adam." Therefore, it was more appropriate that the Son of God assumed a body from the nature propagated by Adam.

Second, faith renders the mystery of the incarnation beneficial to human beings. For, unless human beings were to believe that he whom they saw as a human being was the Son of God, they would not follow him as the cause of their salvation. And this happened to the Jews, who, because of their incredulity, gained damnation rather than salvation from the mystery of the incarnation. Therefore, in order that this ineffable mystery might be more easily believed, the Son of God arranged all things to show that he was a real human being, which would not seem so if he were to receive the matter of his body from a source other than human nature. Therefore, it was appropriate that he assumed a body propagated by Adam.

Third, the Son of God, having become a human being, brought salvation to the human race both by conferring the remedy of grace and by offering an example that cannot be rejected. For the teaching and life of another human being can come into question because of the imperfection of human knowledge and virtue. But, as one believes without question that what the Son of God teaches is true, so one believes without question that what he does is good. And it was necessary that we understand in him an example both of the glory that we hope for and of the virtue whereby we merit it. And the example of each would be less efficacious if he were to have taken his bodily matter from another source than the one from which other human beings take theirs. For, if it were to be urged on someone to bear sufferings as Christ bore his, and to hope to rise as Christ rose, such a one could allege an excuse from the different condition of the body. Therefore, in order to render the example of Christ more efficacious, it was appropriate that he took the matter of his body from no other source than the nature propagated by Adam.

<< 218 >>

On the Formation of Christ's Body Not Being from Semen

Nonetheless, it was not appropriate for Christ's body to be formed from human nature in the same way that the bodies of other human beings are. For, inasmuch as the Son of God took on human nature in order to cleanse it of sin, it was necessary that he assumed it in such a way that he incurred no infection of sin. But human beings incur original sin because they are begotten by the active power in a man's semen (i.e., to have preexisted, as to the seminal aspect, in Adam sinning). For, as Adam would have transmitted original justice to his descendents in the course of transmitting human nature, so also he transmits original sin by transmitting the nature, which is through the active power of a man's semen. Therefore, it was necessary that Christ's body be formed without a man's semen.

Second, the active power of a man's semen acts in a natural way, and so a human being begotten of a man's semen is brought to a perfect state in fixed stages, not all at once, since all natural things progress through intermediate stages to fixed ends. But it was necessary that Christ's body at its assumption should be perfect and informed by a rational soul, since the Word of God can assume a body inasmuch as it is united to a rational soul, although it was not perfect as to its requisite size. Therefore, Christ's body ought not to be formed by the power of a man's semen.

◄﹖ 219 ﹖►

On the Cause of the Formation of Christ's Body

And since nature forms the human body from a man's semen, the formation of Christ's body, howsoever it was formed, was above nature. But only God, who establishes nature, acts supernaturally in things of nature, as I have said before [I, 136]. And so we conclude that only God miraculously formed Christ's body from the matter of human nature. But although every action of God in creatures is common to the three persons, we by an appropriation attribute the formation of Christ's body to the Holy Spirit. For the Holy Spirit is the love of the Father and the Son, whereby they love one another and us. But God established that his Son became incarnate "because of the abundant love with which he loved us," as Paul says in Eph. 2:4. Therefore, we appropriately attribute the formation of his flesh to the Holy Spirit.

Second, the Holy Spirit causes all graces, since he is the first gift, in whom all gifts are freely bestowed. But it belonged to superabundant grace that human nature was assumed into the unity of the divine person, as aforementioned things make clear [I, 214]. Therefore, we attribute the formation of Christ's body to the Holy Spirit in order to show such grace.

This is also appropriate by analogy to a human word and breath. For a human word existing in the mind bears a likeness to the eternal Word insofar as the Word exists in the Father. And as a human word assumes expression in order that it become sensibly known to human beings, so also the Word of God assumed flesh in order to appear visibly to human beings. And the breath of a human being forms human sound. And so also the Spirit of the Word of God ought to have formed the flesh of the Word of God.

◀ꝫ 220 ꜱ▶

Explanation of the Article in the Creed about the Conception and Birth of Christ

Therefore, in order to exclude the error of Ebion and Cerinthus, who said that Christ's body was formed from a man's semen, the Apostles' Creed says: "Who was conceived by the Holy Spirit"; and the Creed of the Fathers substitutes: "And he became flesh by the Holy Spirit." The Creeds say this so that we believe that he assumed true flesh, not the imaginary body of the Manicheans. And the Creed of the Fathers adds, "for us human beings," to exclude the error of Origen, who held even devils to be freed by the power of Christ's passion;[67] and also in the same place, "for our salvation," to show that the mystery of the incarnation is sufficient for human salvation. The latter is against the heresy of the Nazarenes, who did not think that faith in Christ suffices for human salvation without works of the Law.[68] The Creed of the Fathers also adds, "he came down from heaven," to exclude the error of Photinus, who claimed that Christ is a mere human being, saying that he took his beginning from Mary. And so Photinus held that Christ, having a beginning on earth, ascended to heaven by the merit of a good life rather than that he, having a heavenly origin, by assuming flesh descended to earth. The Creed of the Fathers also adds, "and he became man," to exclude the error of Nestorius, according to whose position the Son of God, about whom the Creed speaks, would be said to dwell in a human being rather than to be one.

3. Christ's Birth

◀ꝫ 221 ꜱ▶

It Was Proper That Christ Was Born of the Virgin

And since I have shown that it was proper that the Son of God assume flesh from the matter of human nature [I, 217], and a woman provides the matter in human generation, it was proper that Christ assumed flesh from a woman. Just so, Paul says in Gal. 4:4: "God sent his Son, born of a woman." And a woman needs sexual union with a man for the matter she provides to be formed into a human body. But the power of a man's semen ought not to have accomplished the formation of Christ's body, as I have already said before [I, 218]. And so the woman from whom the Son of God assumed flesh conceived without the mingling of a man's semen.

And the more one is separated from fleshly things, the more one is filled with spiritual gifts. For spiritual things draw human beings upward, but fleshly things draw them downward. And since the formation of Christ's body ought to have been accomplished by the Holy Spirit, it was necessary that the woman from whom Christ assumed flesh should be filled with spiritual gifts to the greatest extent. As a result, the Holy Spirit enriched both her soul with virtues and her womb with the divine offspring. And so it was necessary both that her soul be free from sin, and that her body be remote from every corruption of carnal desire. And so she not only did not experience sexual union with a man in conceiving Christ, but also did not either before or after.

This was also appropriate for him who was born of her. For the Son of God came into the world with the flesh assumed in order to promote us to the condition of the resurrection, in which "they will neither marry nor be given in marriage but will be human beings like the angels in heaven" (Mt. 22:30). And so he introduced the teaching of continence and purity, so that the image of future glory may to a degree shine forth in the life of the faithful. Therefore, it was also proper that he in his birth commended purity by being born of the Virgin. And so the Apostles' Creed says that Christ was "born of the Virgin Mary," and the Creed of the Fathers says that he "became flesh of the Virgin Mary." And this excludes the error of Valentine and others, who said that Christ's body was either imaginary or of another nature, and was not taken and formed from the body of the Virgin.

◄₹ 222 ₷►

The Blessed Virgin Is the Mother of Christ

This also excludes the error of Nestorius, who was unwilling to profess the blessed Mary as the mother of God. Both Creeds say that the Son of God was born or became flesh of the Virgin, and the woman from whom he is born is called his mother because she provides the matter for the human conception. And so we should call the blessed Virgin Mary, who provided the matter for the conception of the Son of God, the true mother of the Son of God. For it does not matter in regard to the nature of mother by what power the matter provided by her is formed. Therefore, the mother that provided the matter to be formed by the Holy Spirit is no less a mother than one who provides the matter to be formed by the power of a man's semen.

But if one should wish to say that one ought not to call the blessed Virgin the mother of God, since only the flesh, not the divinity, is taken from her, as

Nestorius said, one clearly does not know what one is talking about. For we do not call a woman the mother of someone because the whole of what is in her offspring is taken from her. For a human being consists of soul and body, and human beings are what they are by reason of their souls rather than by reason of their bodies. But the soul of no human being is taken from the mother. Rather, either God immediately creates it, as truth holds, or, if it were to be transmitted, as some held,[69] it would be taken from the father rather than the mother. This is because, according to the teaching of philosophers,[70] the male bestows the soul in begetting other animals, and the female the body.

Therefore, as we call a woman the mother of any human being because the offspring's body is taken from her, so we ought to call the blessed Virgin Mary the mother of God if the body assumed from her is the body of God. But we need to say that the body assumed from Mary, if assumed into the unity of the person of the Son of God, who is true God, is the body of God. Therefore, those who profess that the Son of God assumed human nature into the unity of his person need to say that the blessed Virgin Mary is the mother of God. But because Nestorius denied that one person belongs to God and Jesus Christ the human being, so also he consequently denied that the Virgin Mary is the mother of God.

◄? 223 s►

The Holy Spirit Is Not the Father of Christ

And although we call the Son of God incarnate by the Holy Sprit and from the Virgin Mary, and conceived by the Holy Spirit, we should not say that the Holy Spirit is the father of Christ the human being even though we call the blessed Virgin Mary Christ's mother.

First, we should not because we find in the blessed Virgin Mary all of what belongs to the nature of mother, since she provided for the conception of Christ the matter to be formed by the Holy Spirit, as the nature of mother requires. But regarding the Holy Spirit, we do not find all of what is required as regards the nature of father. For it belongs to the nature of father that a father by his nature produces an offspring of the same nature. And so, if there should be an active thing that does not produce something out of its substance or make the thing into the likeness of its nature, we will not be able to call the active thing the thing's father. For example, we do not say that a human being is the father of things that he makes by a skill, except, perhaps, metaphorically.

The Holy Spirit is of the same nature as Christ regarding the divine nature, regarding which the Spirit is not the father of Christ but rather proceeds from him. But the Spirit is not of the same nature as Christ regarding human nature, since the divine and human natures in Christ are different, as I have said before [I, 211]. Nor is anything of the divine nature turned into human nature, as I have said before [I, 206]. Therefore, we conclude that we cannot call the Holy Spirit the father of Christ the human being.

Second, the chief thing in any offspring is from the father, and what is secondary is from the mother. For the soul in other animals is from the father, and the body from the mother. And although the rational soul in a human being is not from the father but created by God, the power of the father's semen acts dispositively toward the form. But the chief thing in Christ is the person of the Word, and the person of the Word is in no way from the Holy Spirit. Therefore, we conclude that we cannot call the Holy Spirit the father of Christ.

◄ 224 ►

On the Sanctification of the Mother of Christ

Therefore, since, as the aforementioned things make clear [I, 219 and 222], the blessed Virgin Mary, conceiving by the Holy Spirit, became the mother of the Son of God, it was fitting that she was cleansed with the most excellent purity, which made her fit for so great a mystery. And so we should believe that she was free from every stain of actual sin, both mortal and venial, and such freedom cannot belong to any holy person after Christ, since the Apostle John says in 1 Jo. 1:8: "If we should have said that we do not have sin, we deceive ourselves, and the truth is not in us." But we can understand about the blessed Virgin mother of God what the Song of Songs 4:7 says: "You are all beautiful, my loved one, and there is no stain in you."

She was both free of actual sin and cleansed of original sin by special privilege. It was necessary that she, as one conceived by sexual intercourse, should have been conceived with original sin. For the privilege that she conceived the Son of God as a virgin was reserved for her alone, and sexual intercourse, which cannot exist after the sin of Adam without lust, transmits original sin to offspring. Also, were she not to have been conceived with original sin, she would not need to be redeemed by Christ, and so Christ would not have been the universal redeemer of all human beings. And this derogates from the dignity of Christ.

Therefore, we should hold that she was conceived with original sin but purified of it in a special way, as I have just said. For some are purified of original sin after birth from the womb, as, for example, those sanctified in baptism. And we read that some are sanctified in their mothers' wombs by a privilege of grace, as Jer. 1:5 says of Jeremiah: "Before I formed you in the womb, I knew you"; and the angel in Lk. 1:15 says of John the Baptist: "He will be filled with the Holy Spirit even from his mother's womb." And we ought not to believe that what was bestowed on the forerunner and foreteller of Christ has been denied to the mother of Christ. And so we believe that she was sanctified from the womb, namely, before she was born from the womb.

But such sanctification did not precede the infusion of the soul, since she would then never have been subject to original sin and would not have needed redemption. For only a rational nature can be the subject of sin. Likewise, the grace of sanctification is first rooted in the soul and can come to the body only through the soul. And so we should believe that she was sanctified after the infusion of the soul.

But her sanctification was fuller than that of others sanctified in the womb. For others sanctified in the womb have been cleansed of original sin, but they did not receive the gift not to sin later, at least venially. But the blessed Virgin Mary was sanctified with such abundant grace that she was henceforth preserved free of all sin, both mortal and venial. And venial sin sometimes happens suddenly, namely, in that an inordinate movement of desire or of another emotion, a movement preceding reason, arises suddenly, and that is why we call such first movements sins. Therefore, since the blessed Virgin Mary never sinned venially, it follows that she did not experience inordinate emotional movements.

And such inordinate movements happen because the sense appetite, which is the subject of these emotions, is not so subject to reason that it is not sometimes moved to something outside the order of reason. And it is sometimes moved even to something contrary to reason, in which the movement of sin consists. Therefore, the sense appetite in the blessed Virgin Mary was so subject to reason by the power of the grace sanctifying her that the appetite was never moved contrary to reason. Nevertheless, the sense appetite was able to have some sudden movements not preordained by reason.

But there was something more ample in the Lord Jesus Christ. For the lower appetite in him was so subject to reason that it was moved to something only by the order of reason, namely, insofar as reason ordered or permitted the lower appetite to be moved by its own movement. And it seems to have belonged to the integrity of the original condition that lower powers were completely subject to reason. But the sin of Adam took away this subjection both in him and in others who contract original sin from him. And in the others, even after the sacramental grace cleanses them of original sin, the rebellion or lack of obedience of the lower powers to reason, which we call concupiscence, abides. Such concupiscence, however, in no way existed in Christ, as I have just said.

But the lower powers in the blessed Virgin Mary were not completely subject to reason, namely, that they would have no movement not preordained by reason, and yet they were so controlled by the power of grace that they would not be moved in any way contrary to reason. Therefore, we customarily say that concupiscence for sin remained substantially in the blessed Virgin Mary after her sanctification, but it was held in check.

◄¿ 225 ﺱ►

On the Perpetual Virginity of the Mother of God

And if the first sanctification thus fortified her against every sinful movement, much more did grace grow in her, and was concupiscence for sin weakened or even completely taken away when, according to the word of the angel, the Holy Spirit came upon her to form the body of Christ from her. And so, after she became a shrine of the Holy Spirit and the dwelling of the Son of God, it is impious to believe either that there was any sinful movement in her, or that she experienced the pleasure of carnal desire. And so we should despise the error of Helvidius, who, although he affirms that Christ was conceived and born of the Virgin, said that she later begot other offspring from Joseph.[71]

Nor does what Mt. 1:25 says, "Joseph did not know her," namely, Mary, "until she brought forth her first-born son," as if Joseph should have known her after she bore the son, support Helvidius' error. This is because *until* in this text signifies an unlimited span of time, not a limited one. For it is the custom of sacred Scripture to assert in a special way that something has or has not been done up to the point of time when it could come into question. For example, Ps. 110:1 says: "Sit at my right hand until I make your enemies your footstool." For there could be a question whether Christ sat at the right hand of God as long as his enemies do not seem to be subject to him, but no room for doubt will remain after this has been made known. Similarly, there could be a question whether Joseph knew Mary before the birth of the Son of God. And so the evangelist took care to remove the question, as if leaving beyond doubt that Joseph did not know Mary after the birth of Jesus.

Nor does the fact that the text calls Christ her first-born, as if she had other offspring after Christ, support Helvidius' error. For Scripture customarily calls the first-born the one before whom no one is begotten, even if no one should be begotten afterwards. For example, this is clearly the case regarding the first-born who were sanctified to the Lord according to the Law and offered to the priests.

Nor do the texts in the Gospels (Mt. 12:47 and Mk. 3:32) saying that Christ had brothers, as if his mother had other sons, support Helvidius' error. For Scripture customarily calls all of the same kin brothers, as Abraham called Lot his brother (Gen. 13:8), although Lot was his nephew. And accordingly, the texts call the nephews and other blood relatives of Mary, and also the blood relatives of Joseph, whom people considered the father of Christ, brothers of Christ.

And so the Creed says that Christ "was born of the Virgin Mary," calling her a virgin absolutely, since she remained a virgin before, in, and after the birth. And I have just sufficiently explained that nothing before or after the birth derogated from her virginity. But neither was her virginity broken in the birth, since Christ's body, which entered through closed doors to appear to the disciples (Jo. 20:19, 26), was able by the same power to exit from the closed womb of his mother. For it was not fitting that he who was born to restore corrupt things to their integrity would, by being born, take away integrity.

◄੨ 226 ੩►

On the Defects Assumed by Christ

And it was appropriate that the Son of God, assuming human nature for the salvation of human beings, manifested by his perfect grace and wisdom the end of human salvation. Just so, it was appropriate that there were in the human nature assumed by the Word of God some conditions that befitted the most worthy way of delivering the human race. And the most appropriate way was that human beings, who had perished through their injustice, were restored through justice.

The order of justice requires that one who by sinning became liable to a punishment should be freed by payment of the punishment due. But we seem in a way to do or suffer things that we do or suffer through friends, since love is the power uniting two lovers, making them somehow one. Therefore, there is no discordance from the order of justice if a friend frees someone by making satisfaction in that one's stead. And our first parent's sin brought perdition on the whole human race, nor was the punishment of any human being able to suffice to free the whole human race. For there was no condign or equivalent satisfaction whereby a mere human being making satisfaction absolved all human beings. Similarly, it did not suffice regarding justice that an angel, out of love for the human race, made satisfaction in the latter's stead. For an angel does not have infinite worth, and so satisfaction by the angel could not suffice for an unlimited number of people and their sins.

But only God is of infinite worth, and he, having assumed flesh, was adequately able to make satisfaction for human beings, as I have said before [I, 200]. Therefore, it was necessary that he assumed such a human nature in which he could suffer for human beings the things that they by sinning merited to suffer, in order to make satisfaction for them.

But not every punishment that human beings by sinning incurred is suitable for making satisfaction. For the sins of human beings come about because they turned away from God and toward transitory goods, and human beings are punished for sin in both respects. For human beings are deprived of grace and the other gifts by which they are united to God, and also deserve to suffer tribulation and defect in things for the sake of which they turned away from God.

Therefore, the order of satisfaction requires that the punishments that the sinner suffers in transitory goods recall the sinner to God. But the punishments that separate human beings from God are contrary to this recall. Therefore, no one makes satisfaction to God by being deprived of grace, not knowing God, or having a disordered soul, although these things are punishments of sin. Rather, one makes satisfaction by experiencing pain regarding oneself and loss regarding external things. Therefore, Christ ought not to have assumed the defects that separate human beings from God (e.g., privation of grace, ignorance, and the like), although they are punishments of sin. For this would render him less suitable to make satisfaction. On the contrary, in order for him to be the cause of our salvation, he needed to possess the fullness of grace and wisdom, as I have said before [I, 214–16].

But because human beings were punished for sin in that they necessarily had to die and could suffer in body and mind, Christ willed to assume such defects in order to redeem the human race by suffering death for human beings.

And yet we should note that such defects, although common to Christ and ourselves, are in him for one reason and in us for another. For such defects are the punishment of the first sin, as I have said [I, 193–95]. Therefore, since we contract original sin by our corrupted origin, we are consequently said to have contracted those defects. But Christ contracted no stain of sin by his origin, and he accepted those defects by his own will. And so we ought to say that he assumed rather than contracted those defects. For something is contracted that is necessarily brought in with something else. But Christ was able to assume human nature without such defects, just as he assumed it without sin, and the order of reason seemed to demand that he who was free of sin be free of punishment. And so it appears that such defects were in him by no necessity of corrupt origin or justice. And so we conclude that they were assumed voluntarily, not contracted.

But our body is subject to the aforementioned defects in punishment of sin, since we were free of them before sin. Therefore, we appropriately say that Christ, inasmuch as he assumed such defects in his flesh, bore the likeness of sin, as Paul says in Rom. 8:3: "God sent his Son in the likeness of sinful flesh." And so also Paul calls this capacity to suffer, or suffering, sin, adding: "And concerning sin, condemned sin in the flesh"; and says in Rom. 6:10: "The death he died for sin, he died once for all." And something more remarkable, Paul on this account even says in Gal. 3:13 that "he became cursed in our behalf." It is also said on this account that he assumed one element of our old condition, namely, punishments, in order to destroy both elements of our old condition, namely, sins and punishments.

And we should further consider that there are two kinds of penal defects in the body. Some are common to all (e.g., hunger, thirst, weariness after toil, pain, death, and the like), and some are proper to particular human beings, not common to all (e.g., blindness, leprosy, fever, maimed limbs, and the like). And the difference between these kinds of defects is that someone else, namely, our first parent, who incurred the common defects for his sin, transmitted them to us, while particular causes produce the proper defects in individual human beings.

But Christ had no cause of defect from himself, neither from his soul, which was full of grace and wisdom, and united to the Word of God, nor from his body, which was most excellently constituted by the almighty power of the Holy Spirit. Rather, he voluntarily assumed some defects in arranging to procure our salvation, as it were. Therefore, he ought to have assumed those defects that come from our first parent to other human beings, namely, the common defects, not the proper ones, which particular causes produce in individuals. Also, because he had come chiefly to restore human nature, he ought to have assumed those defects found in the whole nature.

Therefore, the aforementioned things make clear that Christ assumed our irreprehensible defects (i.e., defects that cannot detract from him), as Damascene says.[72] For if he were to have assumed defects of knowledge or grace, or even leprosy, blindness, or any like thing, this would seem to belong to derogation of the dignity of Christ and would be for human beings an occasion for detraction, while the defects of the whole nature give no such occasion.

4. Christ's Crucifixion and Resurrection

◄﹖ 227 ﹖►

Why Christ Willed to Die

Therefore, the aforementioned things make clear that Christ assumed some of our defects for an end, namely, our salvation, not out of necessity. But every potentiality, and habit or disposition, is ordered to actuality as its end. And so the capacity to suffer in order to make satisfaction or to merit does not suffice without actual suffering. For we call a person good or evil because of what the person does, not because the person can do good or evil things, and praise or blame is due for an action, not for a capacity to act. And so also Christ both assumed our capacity to suffer in order to save us and willed to suffer in order to make satisfaction for our sins. And he suffered for us the things that we by the sin of our first parent merited to suffer, the chief of which is death, to which all other human sufferings are related as the final thing, as Paul says in Rom. 6:23: "The wages of sin are death." And so also Christ willed to suffer death for our sins. As a result, when he without sin assumed the punishment due us, he delivered us from the penalty of death, as one is freed from the debt of punishment when another undergoes the punishment in one's stead.

He also willed to die in order that his death would be not only a remedial satisfaction for us but also a sacrament of our salvation, so that we, brought to life in the spirit, die to the life of the flesh in imitation of his death. Just so, 1 Pet. 3:18 says: "Christ died for our sins once for all, the just one for the unjust, so that he offered us to God, us who were put to death in the flesh but brought to life in the spirit."

He also willed to die in order that his death would be the model of perfect virtue for us. His death is the model of perfect virtue regarding charity, since "no one has greater love than that one lays down one's life for one's friends," as Jo. 15:13 says. For the more numerous and grievous things one does not avoid suffering for a friend, the more love one shows. But the most grievous of all human evils is death, which takes away human life. And so there can be no greater sign of love than that one exposes oneself to death for a friend.

His death is the model of perfect virtue regarding courage, which does not retreat from justice because of adverse things, since it seems most to belong to courage that one does not retreat from virtue even out of fear of death. And so Paul, speaking about Christ's passion, says in Heb. 2:14: "So that he through death might destroy the one who had the power of death, and free those who were throughout their life subject to bondage by the fear of death." For when he did not refuse to die for truth, he shut out fear of dying, because of which human beings are commonly subject to the slavery of sin.

His death is the model of perfect virtue regarding patience, which does not allow distress to overwhelm human beings in adverse things, since the greater the adverse things, the more resplendent is the virtue of patience in bearing them. And so the model of perfect patience is given in the greatest evil, death, if one should bear it without mental anguish. And the prophet predicted this about Christ, saying in Is. 53:7: "Like a lamb before a shearer, he will become dumb and will not open his mouth."

And his death is the model of perfect virtue regarding obedience, since the more one is obedient in more difficult things, the more praiseworthy the obedience is. But death is the most difficult thing. And so, to commend the perfect obedience of Christ, Paul says in Phil. 2:8 that "he became obedient to the Father even to death."

≺? 228 s≻

On the Death on the Cross

The same reasons also make clear why he willed to suffer death on the cross. First, he willed to do so because this is appropriate regarding the remedial satisfaction. For human beings are appropriately punished by means of the things in which they have sinned, as Wis. 11:17 says: "For one is also tormented by the thing in which one sins." And the first sin of a human being consisted of plucking the fruit of the wood of the tree of the knowledge of good and evil contrary to God's command. But instead of this, Christ permitted himself to be affixed to the wood of a tree in order to pay for things he did not steal, as Ps. 69:4 says of him.

Willing to suffer death on the cross is also appropriate regarding the sacrament. For Christ wished to show by his death that we should die to the life of the flesh so that our spirit would be lifted to higher things. And so also he himself said in Jo. 12:32: "When I have been lifted up from the earth, I shall draw all things to myself."

Willing to suffer death on the cross is also appropriate regarding the model of perfect virtue. For human beings sometimes avoid a shameful kind of death no less than the bitterness of death. And so it seems to belong to perfect virtue that one for the sake of virtue's goodness does not avoid suffering even a shameful death. And so, in order to commend the perfect obedience of Christ, Paul, when he said of Christ that "he became obedient even to death" (Phil. 2:8), added: "And death on the cross." And this seemed to be the most shameful death, as Wis. 2:20 says: "Let us condemn him with the most shameful death."

≺? 229 s≻

On the Death of Christ

And three substantial elements in Christ, namely, the body, the soul, and the divinity of the Word, were united in one person, and two of the three, namely, the soul and the body, were united in one nature. But the union of the body and the soul was dissolved in the death of Christ. For otherwise, the body would not have been truly dead, since the death of the body is nothing but the separation of the soul from it. Still, neither was separated from the Word of God regarding the union of the person.

But humanity results from the union of the soul and the body. And so we could not call the soul separated from the body of Christ by death a human being during the three days of his death. For I have said before that, because of the union of human nature and the Word of God in the person, we can properly predicate of the Son of God anything we predicate of Christ the human being [I, 203]. And so, since the personal union of the Son of God to both the soul and the body of Christ remained in death, we could predicate of the Son of God anything we predicate of either the body or the soul. And so also the Creed says of the Son of God that "he was buried," since the body united to him lay in the tomb, and that "he descended into hell," with the soul descending.

We should also consider that the masculine gender designates the person, and the neuter gender the nature. And so we say regarding the Trinity that the Son is another person than the Father, not another thing. Accordingly, therefore, during the three days of his death, the whole Christ was accordingly in the tomb, the whole Christ in hell, the whole Christ in heaven. This is because of the person, which was united both to the flesh lying in the tomb and to the soul despoiling hell, and was subsisting in the divine nature reigning in heaven. But we cannot say that the whole thing was in the tomb or hell, since the whole human nature was not. Rather, a part of the human nature was in the tomb or hell.

◄¿ 230 ȿ►

Christ's Death Was Voluntary

Therefore, the death of Christ was conformed to ours regarding what belongs to the nature of death (i.e., that the soul is separated from the body). But Christ's death was different from ours in one respect. For we die as if subject to death by a necessity of nature or of some violence inflicted on us, but Christ died by his own power and his own will, not by necessity. And so he himself said in Jo. 10:18: "I have the power to lay down my life and to take it up again."

And the reason for this difference is because natural things are not subject to our will. But the union of the soul and the body is natural. And so it is not subject to our will that the soul remains united to, or is separated from, the body. Rather, this needs to come from the power of something acting on us. But the whole of anything natural in Christ regarding his human nature was subject to his will because of the power of divinity, to which all of nature is subject. Therefore, it was in the power of Christ that his soul remained united to his body as long as he so willed, and was separated from it whenever he so willed.

And the centurion attending at the cross of Christ sensed a sign of this divine power when he saw Christ expire with a loud exclamation, which clearly showed him that Christ was not dying from a natural defect like other human beings. For human beings cannot give up their spirit with a loud cry, since they can at the moment of death scarcely even move their tongue perceptibly. And so the fact that Christ expired with a loud exclamation manifested divine power in him, and the centurion on that account said (Mt. 27:54): "Truly, this was the Son of God."

Still, we should not say that the Jews did not kill Christ, or that Christ killed himself, since we say that one who brings the cause of death to someone kills the other. But death results only if the cause of death should overcome nature, which preserves life, and it was in the power of Christ that nature yielded to or resisted the destructive cause as he himself willed. Thus Christ died voluntarily, and yet the Jews killed him.

◄₹ 231 §►

On Christ's Passion Regarding the Body

And Christ willed to suffer both death and other things that came from the sin of our first parent to his descendants, in order that, having entirely assumed the punishment for sin, he freed us from sin by making perfect satisfaction. And some of these things precede death, and others follow it. Both natural sufferings (e.g., hunger, thirst, weariness, and the like) and sufferings from violence (e.g., wounding, scourging, and the like) precede bodily death. Christ willed to suffer all of these things as things coming from sin. For, if human beings were not to have sinned, they would not have experienced the affliction of hunger, thirst, weariness, or cold, nor would they have endured violent suffering from external things.

Still, Christ endured these sufferings for a different reason than why other human beings do. For, in other human beings, there is nothing that can resist these sufferings, but there were in Christ sources to resist these sufferings: both uncreated divine power and the blessedness of his soul. And so much power belongs to the soul that its blessedness redounds in its own way to the body, as Augustine says.[73] And so, because the soul after the resurrection will be glorified by the clear vision and full enjoyment of God, the body united to the glorious soul will be rendered glorious, incapable of suffering, and immortal. Therefore, since the soul of Christ enjoyed the perfect vision of God, the overflow of glory from the soul to the body rendered the body incapable of suffering and immortal, insofar as this is from the power of the vision.

But it was disposed that, while the soul enjoyed the vision of God, the body at the same time suffered, with no overflow of glory from the soul produced in the body. For what was natural to Christ according to human nature was subject to his will, as I have said [I, 230]. And so he was able at will to prevent the natural overflow from his higher parts to his lower parts, so that he allowed each part to be acted upon or to do what was proper to it without hindrance by another part, which cannot be in other human beings. So also Christ sustained the greatest bodily pain in the passion, since the higher joy of reason did not mitigate his bodily pain in any way, as, conversely, the bodily pain did not prevent the joy of reason.

This also makes clear that only Christ was at the same time a wayfarer and one who comprehends. For he enjoyed the vision of God, which vision belongs to one who comprehends, but he enjoyed it in such a way that the body remained subject to sufferings, which subjection belongs to a wayfarer. And because it belongs to a wayfarer to merit by the good things the wayfarer does out of charity, whether for oneself or others, so it is that Christ, although he was one who comprehends, merited by the things he did and suffered, both for himself and for us. He did not merit for himself the glory of his soul, which he had had from the beginning of his conception, but did merit the glory of his body, which he achieved by his suffering. His individual sufferings and actions were also beneficial to salvation for us, both by way of example and by way of merit, inasmuch he could merit grace for us because of his abundant charity and grace, so that members received a share in the fullness of the head.

Indeed, any suffering of his, howsoever little, was sufficient to redeem the human race if one were to consider the dignity of the person. For the more worthy the person on whom a suffering is inflicted, the greater seems the injustice (e.g., if one should strike a ruler rather than one of the people). Therefore, since Christ is of infinite worth, any suffering of his has infinite value, so that it sufficed to wipe out an unlimited number of sins. Nonetheless, death, which, for the reasons cited before [I, 227], he willed to suffer in order to redeem the human race from sins, not any suffering of his, consummated the redemption of the human race. For, in any purchase, one needs to calculate both how much value the product has, and how much it costs to buy it.

◄₹ 232 ₴►

On the Capacity of Christ's Soul to Suffer

But because the soul is the form of the body, it follows that the soul also suffers in some way when the body suffers. And so, for the condition in which Christ had a body capable of suffering, his soul was also capable of suffering. We should consider that the soul has two kinds of suffering: one from the body, and the other from the object. We can consider this in any of the soul's powers, since the soul is related to the body in the same way that a part of the soul is related to a part of the body. And the power of sight suffers from the object (e.g., when strong light blinds sight), and from the bodily organ (e.g., when the injured pupil of an eye blinds sight).

Therefore, if we should consider the suffering of Christ's soul from the body, then the whole soul suffered when the body suffered. For the soul is essentially the form of the body, and all powers of the soul are rooted in the soul's essence. And so we conclude that every power of the soul suffered when the body suffered.

But if we should consider the soul's suffering from an object, not every power of the soul suffered, insofar as suffering in the proper sense signifies harm. For there could not be anything harmful from the object of any power, since I have already said before that Christ's soul enjoyed the perfect vision of God [I, 216]. Therefore, the higher reason of Christ's soul, which cleaves to the eternal things that should be contemplated and consulted, had nothing adverse or contrary whereby any suffering of harm would take place.

But sense powers, whose objects are material things, could suffer harm from injury to the body. And so there was sensibly perceptible pain in Christ when his body suffered. And as the external senses experience injury to the body as hurtful, so also internal imagination perceives it as harmful. And so internal distress results even when one does not experience bodily pain, and we say that Christ also suffered such distress. But both imagination and lower reason perceive things harmful to the body. And so also, from the apprehension of lower reason, which is engaged about temporal things, there could be suffering of distress in Christ, namely, inasmuch as his lower reason apprehended death and other injury to the body as hurtful and contrary to natural desire.

Moreover, out of the love that makes two human beings one, as it were, one may suffer distress not only from things that one apprehends by imagination or lower reason as harmful to oneself, but also from things that one apprehends as hurtful to others whom one loves. And so Christ suffered distress because he knew that the danger of sin or punishment threatened others whom he loved out of charity. And so he grieved both for himself and for others.

And love of neighbor belongs somehow to higher reason, inasmuch as one loves one's neighbor out of charity for God's sake. But the higher reason in Christ could not suffer distress about the defects of his fellow human beings, as the higher reason in us can. For Christ's higher reason, inasmuch as it enjoyed the full vision of God, understood whatever belongs to the defects of others as part of divine wisdom, which fittingly ordains both that one is free to sin, and that one is punished for sin. And so neither the soul of Christ, nor anyone of the blessed seeing God, can suffer distress over the defects of fellow human beings. But it is otherwise in wayfarers, who do not arrive at insight into the plan of divine wisdom. For wayfarers are distressed about the defects of others, even in their higher reason, when they think that it belongs to the honor of God and exaltation of the faith that some should be saved who are nevertheless damned.

Therefore, regarding the same things about which Christ suffered in his external senses, imagination, and lower reason, he rejoiced in his higher reason, inasmuch as he related those things to the order of divine wisdom. But relating something to something else is the proper work of reason. Therefore, we usually say that the reason of Christ shrank from death if we should consider his reason as nature does, namely, that death is by nature odious, but that he willed to suffer death if we should consider his reason as reason does.[74]

And as Christ had distress, so also there were the other emotions that arise from distress (e.g., fear, anger, and the like). For things whose presence brings distress cause fear in us when we think about them as future things, and when we are distressed by someone who hurts us, we become angry with the person. But Christ had these emotions in a different way than we do. For, in us, they commonly precede the judgment of reason and sometimes exceed the measure of reason. But in Christ, they never preceded the judgment of reason or exceeded the measure imposed by reason. Rather, the lower appetite, which is subject to emotions, was moved only as much as reason directed that it should be moved.

Therefore, it could happen that Christ's soul as to its lower part shrank from something that the soul as to its higher part desired. But there was no contrariety of appetites in him, or rebellion of the flesh against the spirit. This happens in us because the lower appetite exceeds the judgment and measure of reason. But in Christ, the lower appetite was moved according to the judgment of reason, inasmuch as he permitted each of the lower powers to be moved in its own way insofar as this befitted Christ.

Therefore, these considerations have made clear that Christ's whole higher reason was happy and joyful in relation to its object, since nothing in this regard could happen to higher reason to cause distress. But regarding the subject, even Christ's whole higher reason suffered, as I have said above. The enjoyment did not lessen the suffering, nor did the suffering prevent the enjoyment, since there was no overflow from one power to the other. Rather, each of the powers was permitted to do what was proper to it, as I have already said before [I, 231].

◀¿ 233 §▶

On Christ's Prayer

Since prayer manifests a desire, we can understand by different desires the nature of the prayer that Christ expressed in Mt. 26:39 when his passion was imminent: "Father, if it is possible, let this cup pass from me; still, not as I will, but as you will." For, in saying, "Let this cup pass from me," he signifies the movement of the lower and natural appetite by which one naturally shrinks from death and seeks life. But in saying, "Still, not as I will, but as you will," he expresses the movement of higher reason, which considers all things as included in the order of divine wisdom. And the phrase "if it is possible" also belongs to this, showing that only what proceeds according to the order of the divine will is possible.

And although the cup of suffering did not pass from him without him drinking it, we ought not to say that his prayer was not heard. For Paul says in Heb. 5:7: "He was heard" in all things "for his godly fear." For, inasmuch as prayer manifests a desire, as I said above, we pray absolutely for what we will absolutely. (So also, the desire of the prayer of the just has force with God, as Ps. 10:17 says: "The Lord heard the desire of the poor.") But we will absolutely what we desire by higher reason, to which alone belongs consenting to the act. And so Christ prayed absolutely that the will of the Father should be done, and not that the cup should pass from him, since he willed the latter by his lower part, not absolutely, as I said above.

◀¿ 234 §▶

On the Burial of Christ

And other defects, both regarding the body and regarding the soul, befall a human being from sin after their death. It is a defect regarding the body that the body is returned to the earth from which it was taken. We note this defect in us in two regards, namely, position and dissolution. There is defect regarding position inasmuch as the dead body is interred in the earth. And there is defect regarding dissolution inasmuch as the body is dissolved into the elements out of which it was constructed. Christ willed to suffer the first of these defects, namely, that his body was interred in the earth. But he did not suffer the other defect, namely, that his body was dissolved into dust. And so Ps. 16:10 says of him: "You will not allow your holy one to see corruption," that is, bodily putrefaction. And the reason for this is that Christ's body took its matter from human nature, but the power of the Holy Spirit, not human power, formed his body. And so, because of the material substance, he willed to suffer interment, which we customarily arrange for dead bodies, since the place for material substances should be according to the nature of their predominant element. But he did not will to suffer dissolution of the body constructed by the Holy Spirit, since he differed from other human beings in this respect.

◄₹ 235 s►

On the Descent of Christ into Hell

And regarding the soul, the consequence of sin in human beings after death is that they descend into hell, regarding both the place and the punishment. And as Christ's body was interred in the earth regarding place but not regarding the concomitant defect of dissolution, so also his soul descended into hell regarding the place but not to suffer punishment there. Rather, he descended into hell to free from punishment others, who were kept there because of the sin of our first parent, for which Christ had already made full satisfaction by suffering death. And so nothing after death remained for him to suffer, and he descended into the place of hell without any suffering of punishment in order to show himself the liberator of the living and the dead. And so also Peter Lombard says that "only he among the dead was free,"[75] since his soul in hell was not subject to punishment, nor his body in the tomb subject to dissolution. But although Christ on descending into hell freed those who were kept there for the sin of our first parent, he left there those who were obligated to punishments for their own sins. And so he is said to have bitten into hell rather than swallowed it,[76] namely, that he freed part and left part. Therefore, the Creed touches on these defects of Christ when it says: "He suffered under Pontius Pilate, was crucified, died, was buried, and descended into hell."

◄₹ 236 s►

On Christ's Resurrection and When It Happened

Christ freed the human race from the evils that had resulted from the sin of our first parent. Therefore, it was necessary that, as he bore our evils to free us from them, so also the first fruits of the human restoration accomplished by him should be evident in him. This was so that Christ should be proposed to us as a sign of salvation in two ways. By his passion, we consider what we incurred for sin, and what he suffered for us in order to free us from sin. And by his exaltation, we consider what he proposes to us to hope for through him. Therefore, with the death that had come from the sin of our first parent overcome, he was the first to rise to immortal life, so that, as mortal life first appeared in Adam sinning, so immortal life should first appear in Christ making satisfaction for sin. Others before Christ, whether raised by him or the prophets, had returned to life but were destined to die again. But "Christ risen from the dead never dies" (Rom. 6:9). And so, since he was the first to escape the necessity of dying, he is called the ruler of the dead and "the first fruits of those asleep" (1 Cor. 15:20), namely, that he is the first to have risen from the sleep of death, with the yoke of death broken.

And his resurrection should neither be delayed nor take place immediately after his death. For, if he were to have returned to life immediately after death, the truth of his death would not have been confirmed. And if his resurrection were to be long delayed, the sign of death overcome would not be evident in him, nor would hope be given to human beings that he freed them from death. And so he put off his resurrection until the third day, since this space of time seemed both long enough to confirm the truth of his death and not so long as to take away the hope of deliverance. For, if the resurrection were to have been delayed longer, the hope of the faithful would then be weakened. And so also some, with hope then lacking, as it were, said on the third day (Lk. 24:21): "We were hoping that he was about to redeem Israel."

Still, Christ did not remain dead for three whole days. But he is said to have been in the bowels of the earth for three days and three nights in that way of speaking whereby we are accustomed to posit the part for the whole. For, since day and night constitute a natural day, Christ is said to have been dead for the whole day by any part of the day or night in which he is counted as dead.

And Scripture customarily counts the night with the following day, since the Hebrews counted time by the course of the moon, which begins to appear in the evening. Christ was in the tomb on the latter part of Friday, which, if one should count this with the preceding night, the artificial day and night will be as if a natural day. And he was in the tomb on Friday night and the whole day Saturday, and so there are two days. He also lay dead in the tomb on Saturday night, which preceded Sunday, on which day he arose either in the middle of the night, as Gregory says,[77] or at dawn, as others say.[78] And so, if we should count either the whole night or part of the night with Sunday, there will be a third natural day.

Nor does it take away from mystery that he willed to rise on the third day to manifest thereby that he rose by the power of the whole Trinity. And so also it is sometimes said that the Father raised him up, and sometimes that he rose by his own power. This is not contradictory, since the same power belongs to the Father and the Son and the Holy Spirit. And he also willed to rise on the third day to show that restoration of life was not accomplished on the first day of the age (i.e., under the natural law) or on the second day (i.e., under the Mosaic Law) but on the third day (i.e., in the time of grace). It is also reasonable that Christ lay in the tomb for one whole day and two whole nights, since he by the one thing of our old condition that he assumed, namely, punishment, destroyed two things of our old condition, namely, sin and punishment, which the two nights signify.

◄ᶑ 237 ᶂ►

On the Property of the Risen Christ

And Christ recovered for the human race both what Adam had lost by sinning, and what Adam could have reached by meriting. For the efficacy of Christ for meriting was much greater than that of a human being before sin. Adam by sinning incurred the necessity of dying and so lost the capacity whereby he could not die had he not sinned. But Christ both eliminated the necessity of dying and acquired the necessity of not dying. And so the body of Christ after the resurrection became incapable of suffering and death, altogether incapable of dying, not like the capacity of the first human being not to die. We expect the same in the future in our own regard. And because the soul of Christ before his death was capable of suffering by the suffering of the body, it also follows that, with the body made incapable of suffering, the soul was likewise rendered incapable of suffering.

And the mystery of human redemption had now been fulfilled. To accomplish this mystery, the glory of enjoying the vision of God was by design restricted to the higher part of the soul, so that there was no overflow of the glory into the lower parts and the body itself, and each thing was permitted to do or suffer what was proper to it. Therefore, with the mystery of human redemption fulfilled, the overflow of glory from the higher part of the soul now completely glorified the body and the lower powers of the soul. And so, although Christ before the passion was both one who comprehends, since the soul enjoyed the vision of God, and a wayfarer, since the body was capable of suffering, he was now, after the resurrection, no longer a wayfarer but only one who comprehends.

◄ᶑ 238 ᶂ►

How Suitable Proofs Demonstrate Christ's Resurrection

And Christ anticipated our resurrection in order that his resurrection was the proof of hope for us, so that we also hoped to rise, as I have said [I, 236].

Therefore, in order to ground our hope of resurrection, fitting signs needed to manifest his resurrection and the property of his risen self. But he did not manifest his resurrection indiscriminately to all, as he manifested his humanity and passion, but only to witnesses preordained by God, namely, the disciples whom he had chosen to care for human salvation. For the condition of resurrection, as I have said before [I, 237], belongs to the glory of one who comprehends, and the knowledge of this glory is due only to those who render themselves worthy, not to all. And Christ manifested to those worthy both the truth of the resurrection and the glory of his risen self.

He manifested the truth of the resurrection by showing that the same one who had died rose, as regards both the nature and the existing subject. He showed the truth of the resurrection regarding the nature because he demonstrated that he has a real human body when he presented himself to his disciples to be touched and seen. And he said to his disciples in Lk. 24:39: "Touch and see, since a spirit does not have the flesh and bones that you see that I have." He also manifested the truth of the resurrection regarding the nature by performing acts that belong to human nature: eating and drinking with his disciples, and speaking and walking often with them, which are the acts of a living human being. But that eating was not necessary. For the indestructible bodies of the risen will have no further need of food, since there is no loss in such bodies that food needs to restore. And so also the food eaten by Christ did not go into nourishment of his body but was dissolved into the underlying matter. Still, because he ate and drank, he showed himself a real human being.

And regarding the existing subject, he showed himself to be the same one who had died by showing them the signs of his death in his body, namely, the scars of his wounds. And so he says to Thomas in Jo. 20:27: "Put your finger here and your hand into my side" and perceive the place of the nails. And he said to his disciples in Lk. 24:39: "See my hands and my feet, since it is I myself." But it was also by design that he preserved the scars of his wounds in his body, so that they proved the truth of his resurrection, since complete integrity is proper for the indestructible risen body. (We could say, however, that, even in the martyrs, some signs of their previous wounds will be evident, with proper decorum, in witness of the martyrs' virtue.) He also showed himself to be the same regarding the existing subject both by his way of speaking and by the other customary actions by which we recognize human beings. And so also the disciples recognized him in the breaking of the bread (Lk. 24:30–31), and he also announced to them that he would appear to them in Galilee, where he customarily conversed with them.

And he manifested the glory of the risen Christ when he entered their midst through closed doors (Jo. 20:19) and vanished from their eyes (Lk. 24:31).

198 COMPENDIUM OF THEOLOGY

For it belongs to the glory of the risen Christ that he have in his power to appear to ordinary mortals when he wishes, and not to appear when he should have so willed. Nonetheless, because faith had difficulty with the resurrection, he demonstrated by many signs the reality of the resurrection rather than the glory of his risen body. For, if he were to have completely demonstrated the unusual condition of his glorified body, he would have prejudiced faith in the resurrection, since the immensity of the glory would have excluded belief in it having the same nature. He also manifested all these things by both visible signs and intelligible proofs when he opened their senses to understand the Scriptures, and showed by the writings of the prophets that he was to rise.

◄¿ 239 ¡►

On the Power of the Lord's Resurrection

And as Christ by his death destroyed our death, so he by his resurrection restored our life. But two kinds of death and life belong to human beings. One death is of the body by its separation from the soul, and the other is of the soul by its separation from God. Therefore, Christ, in whom the second death had no part, by the first death that he underwent, namely, bodily death, destroyed both deaths in us, namely, bodily and spiritual deaths. Likewise, conversely, we understand two kinds of life: one of the body by the soul, which we call the natural life; the other of the soul by God, which we call the life of righteousness or the life of grace. And the latter life is by faith, whereby God dwells in us, as Heb. 10:38 says: "And my just one lives by faith."

There are accordingly also two resurrections: one a resurrection of the body, whereby the soul is reunited to the body; the other a spiritual resurrection, whereby the soul is reunited to God. But this second resurrection had no part in Christ, since sin never separated his soul from God. Therefore, by the resurrection of his body, he causes in us both resurrections, namely, resurrection of the body and spiritual resurrection.

But we should consider that, as Augustine says in his *Commentary on the Gospel of John,*[79] the Word of God revives souls, but the incarnate Word revivifies bodies, since it belongs only to God to vivify the soul. Still, since the flesh assumed by the Word of God is an instrument of divinity, and an instrument acts in the power of the chief cause, both of our resurrections, the spiritual and the corporeal, are related to the bodily resurrection of Christ as their cause. For all the things done in the flesh of Christ were salutary for us by the power of divinity united to it. And so also Paul, showing that the resurrection of Christ causes our spiritual resurrection, says in Rom. 4:25 that "he [Christ] was handed over for our sins and rose for our justification." And Paul shows in 1 Cor. 15:12 that the resurrection of Christ causes our resurrection: "If Christ rose, how do some say that the dead will not rise?"

And Paul beautifully attributes the forgiveness of our sins to the death of Christ, and our justification to his resurrection, so as to signify the conformity and likeness of the effect to the cause. For, as sin is put aside when it is remitted, so Christ by dying put aside the life capable of suffering, in which life there was the likeness of sin. But one gains a new life when one is justified. Similarly, Christ by rising obtained the new condition of glory. Therefore, the death of Christ causes the remission of our sin, both as an instrumental efficient cause, a sacramental exemplary cause, and a meritorious cause. And the resurrection of Christ was the instrumental efficient cause and the sacramental exemplary cause but not the meritorious cause of our resurrection. The resurrection of Christ was not the meritorious cause of our resurrection both because Christ was no longer a wayfarer, and so meriting was not proper for him, and because the brilliance of the resurrection was the reward for his passion, as Paul makes clear in Phil. 2:8–11.

Therefore, we clearly can call Christ "the first-born of those rising from the dead" (Col. 1:18). He is this both temporally, since he was the first to rise, as I have said before [I, 236]; causally, since his resurrection causes the resurrection of the others; and in the order of dignity, since he rose more glorious than all others. Therefore, the Creed includes this faith in the resurrection, saying: "On the third day, he rose from the dead."

◀? 240 ?▶

On the Two Rewards of His Abasement, Namely,
the Resurrection and the Ascension

And because, according to Paul (Phil. 2:8–9), the exaltation of Christ was the reward for his abasement, it was appropriate that a two-fold exaltation corresponded to his two-fold abasement. For, first, he humbled himself by suffering death in the flesh capable of suffering that he had assumed. Second, he humbled himself regarding place, when his body was buried in the tomb, and his soul descended into hell. Therefore, the glory of the resurrection, in which he returned from death to immortal life, corresponds to the first abasement, and the exaltation of the ascension corresponds to the second abasement.

And so Paul says in Eph. 4:10: "The one who descends is also the one who ascends over all the heavens." And as we say of the Son of God that he was conceived, was born, suffered, died and was buried, and rose according to his human nature, not his divine nature, so also we say of him that he ascended into heaven regarding his human nature, not his divine nature. For he never departed from heaven regarding his divine nature, always being everywhere. And so he himself says in Jo. 3:13: "No one ascended into heaven except the one who descended from heaven, the Son of Man who is in heaven." This gives us to understand that Christ is saying that he, by assuming an earthly nature, descended from heaven in such a way that he still always remained in heaven. And we should also consider from this that only Christ ascended to the heavens by his own power. For that place was due him who, by reason of his origin, had descended from heaven. But others, made his members, can ascend by his power, not their own.

And as it belongs to the Son of God to ascend into heaven regarding his human nature, so something else is added that belongs to him regarding his divine nature, namely, that he sits at the right hand of the Father. For we should not think that there is a right hand or a material sitting in this. But since the right side is the better part of an animal, this gives us to understand that the Son is with the Father, being in no way inferior to him regarding the divine nature but altogether his equal. Nevertheless, we can attribute even this to the Son of God regarding his human nature, so that we understand regarding the divine nature that the Son is in the Father himself by an essential unity, with whom he occupies one and the same royal throne, that is, the same power.

But some, namely, those to whom kings communicate some of their power, are accustomed to sit at the side of kings, and the one whom the king places at his right hand seems to be the most important in the kingdom. Therefore, we say that the Son of God, even regarding his human nature, meritoriously sits at the right hand of the Father, as one exalted, as it were, above every creature in the ranks of the heavenly kingdom.

Therefore, sitting at the right hand in both ways is proper to Christ. And so Paul says in Heb. 1:13: "And to which of the angels has he ever said: 'Sit at my right hand'?" Therefore, we profess this ascension of Christ in the Creed, saying: "He ascended into heaven and sits at the right hand of the Father."

5. The Last Judgment

◄ 241 ►

Christ Will Judge According to His Human Nature

Therefore, we clearly gather from the things said that we have been freed from sin and death by Christ's passion and death, his glorious resurrection and ascension, having obtained both righteousness and the glory of immortality. We have obtained righteousness in fact, the glory of immortality in hope. But the things we spoke of, namely, the passion, death, resurrection, and ascension, have been fulfilled in Christ according to his human nature. Therefore, we need to say that Christ by the things he suffered or did in his human nature, by freeing us from both spiritual and material evils, promoted us to spiritual and eternal goods. But it is appropriate that the one who acquires certain goods for certain people distribute the goods to them. And the distribution of goods to many people requires judgment, so that each one receives according to one's rank.

Therefore, God appropriately constituted Christ according to his human nature, by which he fulfilled the mystery of human salvation, judge over the human beings he saved. And so Jo. 5:27 says: "He gave power to him," namely, the Father to the Son, "to pass judgment, since he is the Son of Man." There is also another reason for this, since it was appropriate that those to be judged see their judge. But the authority to judge resides in God, and seeing him in his own nature is the reward that the judgment renders. Therefore, it was necessary that the human beings to be judged, both the good and the evil, see God as judge in the nature assumed, not in his proper nature. For, if the evil were to see God in his divine nature, they would then bring home the reward of which they rendered themselves unworthy.

The judging is also an appropriate reward of exaltation corresponding to the abasement of Christ, who willed to be even so abased that a human judge unjustly judged him. And so, in order to express this abasement, we explicitly profess in the Creed that he suffered under Pontius Pilate. Therefore, this reward of exaltation, so that God constituted him by his human nature judge of all human beings, living and dead, was owed him. Just so, Job 36:17 says: "Your case has been judged as the case of a wicked person, as it were. You will receive judgment, and your case judged."

And because judicial power belongs to the exaltation of Christ just as the glory of the resurrection does, Christ in judgment will appear in the glorious form proper to his reward, not in the abasement that belonged to his merit. And so Lk. 21:27 says: "They will see the Son of Man coming in a cloud with great power and majesty." And seeing his brilliance will cause joy for the elect, who loved him, and Is. 33:17 promises to the elect: "They will see the king in his beauty." But seeing his glory will cause confusion and mourning for the wicked, since the glory and power of the one judging bring sorrow and fear to those fearing damnation. And so Is. 26:11 says: "Let those jealous of my people see and be confounded, and let fire devour your enemies."

And although he shows himself in a glorious form, the signs of his passion will appear in him with beauty and glory, not with deformity. As a result,

202 COMPENDIUM OF THEOLOGY

when these signs are seen, both the elect, who recognize that Christ's passion freed them, will receive joy, and sinners, who only contemned the benefit, will receive sorrow. And so Rev. 1:7 says: "They will look on him whom they have pierced, and all the tribes of the earth will wail over him."

◄§ 242 §►

The Father Gave All Judgment to His Son, Who Knows Its Hour

But "the Father gave all judgment to the Son," as Jo. 5:22 says, and the just judgment of God now manages human life, since God "is the one who judges all flesh," as Abraham said in Gen. 18:25. Therefore, we should not doubt that the judgment that governs all human beings in this world also belongs to the judicial power of Christ. And so also the words of the Father addressed to him in Ps. 110:1 say: "Sit at my right hand until I shall make all your enemies your footstool." For Christ sits at God's right hand according to his human nature, inasmuch as he receives judicial power from God. And he now also exercises the power even before all his enemies seem manifestly subject at his feet. And so also he himself immediately after his resurrection said in Mt. 28:18: "All power in heaven and earth has been given to me."

And there is another judgment of God, in which he gives recompense to each individual at the moment of death regarding the soul insofar as the individual merited. For the just at their dissolution remain with Christ, as Paul desires to do (Phil. 1:23), but sinners at their death are buried in hell. And we should not think that this division was done without God's judgment, or that this judgment does not belong to the judicial power of Christ. For Christ especially says to his disciples in Jo. 14:3: "If I shall go away and prepare a place for you, I shall return and take you to myself, so that, where I am, you also may be." And to be taken is nothing other than to be dissolved so that we can be with Christ, since "we are away from the Lord as long as we are in the body" (2 Cor. 5:6).

But the recompense of a human being consists of both goods of the soul and goods of the body, which is to be resumed by the soul through the resurrection, and all recompense requires judgment. Therefore, it is necessary that there also be another judgment, which gives recompense to human beings according to the things they did regarding both their soul and their body. And this judgment is also proper for Christ. Consequently, as he, having died for us, rose in glory and ascended to the heavens, so also he by his power makes the bodies of our lowliness rise configured to the body of his brilliance and brings

them with him into heaven. In doing this, he precedes us, ascending and open-
ing the way in front of us, as Mic. 2:13 had predicted. But the resurrection of all
human beings will be accomplished at the same time and at the end of this age,
as I have already said before [I, 148 and 161]. And so there will be this general
and final judgment, and we believe that Christ will come a second time in glory
to do this.

But because Ps. 36:6 calls "the judgments of God a great abyss," and
Paul says in Rom.11:33 that God's "judgments are incomprehensible," there is
something deep and incomprehensible to human knowledge in particulars of
the aforementioned judgments. For, in the first judgment of God, which arranges the present life of human beings, the time of the judgment is manifest
to all, but the reason for the recompenses lies hidden, especially since, in this
world, both evil things often come to the good, and good things to the wicked.
But in the other two judgments of God, the reason for the recompenses will
be evident, but the time remains hidden. For human beings do not know the
time of their death, as Eccl. 9:12 says: "A human being knows not his end."
And no human being can foreknow the end of this age, since we foreknow
only those future things whose causes we understand. But the cause of the
end of the world is the will of God, which is unknown to us. And so only God,
not any creature, can foreknow the end of the world, as Mt. 24:36 says: "No
one knows about that day or hour, not even the angels of the heavens, but only
the Father."

But because we read "nor the Son" in Mk. 13:32, some took matter for error
from this, saying that the Son is less than the Father, since he does not know
things that the Father knows. And this could be avoided by saying that the Son
is ignorant of these things, regarding the human nature that he assumed, but
not regarding his divine nature, by which he has one and the same wisdom
with the Father or, to speak more plainly, is the very wisdom conceived in the
mind of the Father. But it also seems inappropriate that the Son, even by the
nature he assumed, does not know the day of judgment, since his soul, as
Jo. 1:14 testifies, is full of every grace and truth, as I have said before [I, 214–16].
Nor does it seem reasonable that, when Christ received the power to judge
because he is the Son of Man, he by his human nature should not know the
time for him to judge. For the Father would not have given him all power of
judgment if the judgment of determining the time of his coming were to be
taken away from him.

Therefore, we should understand this according to the usual way of speaking in Scripture, as it says that God knows something at the time when he
makes known knowledge of the thing. For example, God said to Abraham in
Gen. 22:12: "I know now that you fear the Lord." This means that God had

204 COMPENDIUM OF THEOLOGY

demonstrated Abraham's devotion by the deed, not that he who knows all things from eternity began to know it then. Therefore, Scripture also says that the Son does not know the day of judgment, since he did not give knowledge of it to his disciples but replied to their request in Acts 1:7: "It is not yours to know the times or moments that the Father in his power has appointed." But the Father is not ignorant in this way, since he gave knowledge of the matter at least to the Son by eternal generation. And some explain themselves more succinctly, saying that we should understand "nor the son" about an adopted son.

And so the Lord willed that the time of the future judgment will be hidden, so that human beings watch anxiously, lest they perhaps be found unprepared at the time of the judgment. On that account, he also wished the time of each one's death to be unknown. For each will appear in judgment in the same way as each departed from this world at death. And so the Lord said in Mt. 24:42: "Be watchful, since you do not know at what hour your Lord will come."

◄≀ 243 ≀►

Will All Human Beings Be Judged?

Therefore, the aforementioned things make clear that Christ has judicial power over the living and the dead, since he passes judgment on both those who are now living in this world and those who by dying leave it. And he will in the final judgment judge at the same time both the living and the dead. This will be so whether we understand the living to mean the just, who live by grace, and the dead to mean the sinners, who fell from grace, or the living to mean those who are found living at the Lord's coming, and the dead to mean those who died before.

But we should not understand this in such a way that some human beings living at that time are judged without ever experiencing bodily death, as some have held.[80] For Paul clearly says in 1 Cor. 15:51: "All of us will rise." And another line of the verse reads: "All of us will fall asleep" (i.e., die).[81] And if some texts should read, "Not all of us will fall asleep," as Jerome says in his *Letter to Minervius* on the resurrection of the flesh,[82] it does not take away the strength of aforementioned opinion. For Paul had said shortly before (v. 22): "As all die in Adam, so also all will be brought to life in Christ." And so the statement "not all of us will fall asleep" cannot refer to bodily death, which the sin of Adam transmitted to all, as Rom. 5:12 says. Rather, the statement would need to be interpreted as referring to the sleep of sin, about which Eph. 5:14 says: "Arise, sleeper, arise from the dead, and Christ will enlighten you." Therefore, those who are found alive at the coming of the Lord are not distinguished from those who died before because the former never die. Rather, they are distinguished in that the former will die and immediately rise in the very rapture that catches them up "in the clouds to meet Christ in the air" (1 Thess. 4:17), as Augustine says.[83]

But we should consider that three things seem to coalesce at a judgment: first, an individual is arraigned before a judge; second, the individual's merits are critically examined; and third, the individual receives a sentence.

Therefore, regarding the first, all the good and the wicked from the first human being up to the last will be subjected to the judgment of Christ, since "all of us are required to stand before the judgment-seat of Christ," as 2 Cor. 5:10 says. And even infants who died with or without baptism are not excluded from this universality, as a gloss on the same text says.[84]

Regarding the second, namely, critical examination of one's merits, not all will be judged, neither all the good nor all the wicked. For the critical examination of judgment is necessary where good and evil deeds are intermingled. But critical examination has no place where there is good without admixture of evil, or where there is evil without admixture of good. Therefore, there are some good who completely contemn temporal goods, having time only for God and the things of God. Therefore, since one commits sin by spurning the immutable good and adhering to transitory goods, there seems to be no notable mixture of good and evil in such persons. This is not to say that they live without sin, since 1 Jo. 1:8 says out of their mouth: "If we have said that we do not have sin, we deceive ourselves." But there are some slight sins in them that the fervor of their charity in some way consumes, so that the sins seem to be nothing. And so they will not be judged at the judgment by critical examination of their merits.

And there are those who, leading an earthly life and striving for worldly things, do not use such things contrary to God but unduly cling to them. These persons have to a notable extent some evil mixed with the good of faith and charity, so that what prevails in them cannot be easily perceived. And so such people will also be judged by critical examination of their merits.

Likewise, regarding the wicked, we should note that the beginning of approach to God is faith, as Heb. 11:6 says: "It is necessary that one approaching God believe." Therefore, in one who lacks faith, there is nothing good whose mixture with evil would make the person's damnation doubtful. And so that person will be damned without critical examination of the person's merits. But one who has faith without charity or good deeds has something whereby the person is united to God. And so a critical examination of the person's merits is necessary, so that it is quite clear what predominates in the person, whether good or evil. And so such a person will be condemned with critical examination of the person's merits, as an earthly king condemns a criminal citizen with a hearing but punishes an enemy without any.

And regarding the third, namely, pronouncement of the sentence, all will be judged, since they will bring home glory or punishment from the sentence of Christ. And so 2 Cor. 5:10 says: "So that each one receives recompense for each one's conduct in the body, whether good or evil."

◄៛ 244 ៛►

On the Process and Place of the Judgment

And we should not think that critical examination of the judgment is necessary in order that the judge should be informed, as happens in human judgments, since all things are "bare and open to his eyes," as Heb. 4:13 says. But the aforementioned critical examination is necessary in order that each one knows how both oneself and others are worthy of punishment or glory, so that the good rejoice over God's justice in all things, and the wicked grow angry with themselves. Nor should we think that such critical examination of merits is done word for word. For time beyond measure would be required to narrate the good or evil thoughts, words, and deeds of individuals. And so Lactantius was deceived to hold that the day of judgment will last for a thousand years.[85] But this period of time seems not to suffice, since several days would be required to complete the judgment of a single human being in the aforementioned way.

Therefore, it will be by divine power that each one is immediately conscious of all the good and wicked things that the person has done, for which the person is to be rewarded or punished, and not only about that person but also about each of the others. Therefore, where good deeds exceed evil deeds so much that the latter seem to be of no moment, or vice versa, there will seem by human evaluation to be no conflict between the good deeds and the evil deeds. And so we say that such persons are rewarded or punished without critical examination.

And although all attend Christ at this judgment, the good not only differ from the wicked by reason of their merits, but the former will also be separated spatially from the latter. For the wicked, who, loving earthly things, departed from Christ, will remain on earth. But the good, who clung to Christ, will meet him on the way when they are raised in the air to be conformed to him, both configured to his brilliant glory and spatially associated with him. Just so, Mt. 24:28 says: "Wherever the body will be, the eagles will also gather"; and the eagles signify the saints. And according to Jerome,[86] instead of the word *body*, the Hebrew designedly uses the word *ioathon*,[87] which means corpse, in order to recall Christ's passion, by which he also merited the power to judge. And human beings conformed[88] to his passion are raised by it into the company of his glory, as Paul says in 2 Tim. 2:12: "If we suffer with him, we shall also reign with him."

And so we believe that Christ will come down to judge near the place of his passion, as Joel 3:2 says: "I shall gather together all the peoples and settle with them in the valley of Jehoshaphat." This is at the foot of the Mount of Olives, from which Christ ascended. And so also the sign of the cross and other signs of his passion will be displayed when the Lord comes to judge, as Mt. 24:30 says: "The sign of the Son of Man will appear in the heavens." As a result, the wicked, looking on him whom they crucified, are sad and tormented, and those who are redeemed rejoice in the glory of the redeemer. Christ is said to sit at the right hand of the Father according to his human nature, inasmuch as that nature has been elevated to the most excellent good things of the Father. Just so, the just are said to stand at his right hand at the judgment, as if having the most honorable place with him.

◄ 245 ᔓ►

The Saints Will Judge

And not only Christ will judge at that judgment, but others also will. Some of these will judge only relatively, namely, that the good will judge the less good, or the wicked the more wicked, as Mt. 12:41 says: "The Ninivites will rise in judgment, and they will condemn this generation." Some will judge by approving the sentence, and all the just will judge in this way, as Wis. 3:8 says: "The saints will judge the nations." And some will judge, receiving judicial power from Christ, as it were, as Ps. 149:6 says: "Let there be two-edged swords in their hands." And the Lord promised the final judicial power to the Apostles in Mt. 19:28, saying: "In the new generation, when the Son of man will sit on the throne of his majesty, you who have followed me will also sit on twelve thrones judging the twelve tribes of Israel."

But we should not think that the Apostles judge only Jews, who belong to the twelve tribes of Israel. Rather, the twelve tribes of Israel signify all the faithful assumed into the faith of the Patriarchs. (Indeed, unbelievers are not judged but have already been judged.) Likewise, not only the twelve Apostles, who were at the time with Christ, will judge. (Indeed, Judas will not.) And Paul, who labored more than the others, will also not lack the honor of judging, especially since he himself says in 1 Cor. 6:3: "Do you not know that we shall judge the angels?"

And this honor properly belongs to those who, having left all things, followed Christ. For Peter in Mt. 19:27 had presupposed this when he asked:

"Behold, we have left all things and followed you. What, therefore, will there be for us?" And so Job 36:6 says: "He will give judgment to the poor." And this is reasonably so. For the critical examination of judgment concerns the acts of human beings who have used earthly things well or ill, as I have said before [I, 243]. But right judgment requires that the spirit of a judge should be impartial regarding things about which the judge has to judge. And so some, by completely taking their spirit away from earthly things, merit the honor to judge.

Proclaiming divine precepts also contributes to meriting this honor. And so Mt. 25:31 says that Christ will come with the angels to judge, and by angels we understand preachers, as Augustine says in his work on repentance.[89] For it is fitting that those who have proclaimed the precepts of life should critically examine the acts of human beings concerning observance of the divine precepts.

But the aforementioned persons will judge inasmuch as they will be engaged in making clear to each one the reason for the salvation or damnation of both each one and others, in the same way that we say higher angels enlighten lower angels or human beings.

Therefore, we profess this judicial power in Christ, saying in the Apostles' Creed: "Then he will come to judge the living and the dead."

SUMMARY

◄ 246 ►

On Distinguishing the Articles of Faith

Therefore, having considered the things that belong to the truth of the Christian faith, we should note that we trace all of the foregoing to definite articles, twelve according to some, and fourteen according to others.[90]

For, inasmuch as faith concerns things incomprehensible to reason, there needs to be a new article where some new thing incomprehensible to reason presents itself. Therefore, there is one article belonging to the unity of divinity. For, although reason proves that there is only one God, it is subject to faith that he directly governs all things such that he is to be worshiped in a particular way. Some posit three articles about the three persons, and three others about the three effects of God, namely: creation, which belongs to nature; justification, which belongs to grace; and reward, which belongs to glory. And so they posit seven articles in all about divinity. And they posit seven others about the humanity of Christ. The first is about his incarnation and conception. The second is about his birth, which has a special difficulty because of his coming forth from the closed womb of the Virgin. The third is about his passion, death, and burial. The fourth is about his descent into hell. The fifth is about his resurrection. The sixth is about his ascension. The seventh is about his coming at the judgment. And so there are fourteen articles in all.

But others, with equal reason, understand faith in the three persons in one article, since one cannot believe in the Father without believing in the Son and the love binding both (i.e., the Holy Spirit). But they distinguish the article on the resurrection from the article on the reward. And so there are two articles about God (his unity and the Trinity), four about the effects (creation, justification, the general resurrection, and the reward). Likewise, regarding faith in the humanity of Christ, they include his conception and birth in one article, as they include his passion and death in one article. Therefore, there are by this computation twelve articles in all.

And these things suffice regarding faith.

II

Hope

≈ 1 ≈

The Virtue of Hope Is Necessary for the Perfect
Christian Life

According to the opinion of the Prince of the Apostles, we are advised to render account both of our faith and of the things that are in us by hope (1 Pet. 3:15). Therefore, it remains for us, after the foregoing things in which we briefly treated of the belief of the Christian faith, to give you a full explanation of the things that belong to hope.

And we should consider that the desire of a human being can come to rest in some knowledge, since a human being by nature desires to know truth. And when one knows truth, one's desire is at rest. But the desire of a human being is not at rest in the knowledge of faith. For faith is imperfect knowledge, since belief is about things not seen. And so Paul in Heb. 11:1 calls faith "the assurance of things not evident." Therefore, with possession of faith, there still remains the movement of the soul toward something else, namely, to see perfectly the truth that one believes and to attain things that will be able to lead to such truth.

But because we have said that one of the examples of faith is belief that God has providence regarding human affairs [I, 130], a movement of hope arises from this in the spirit of the believer, namely, that the believer obtain by God's help the good things that the believer, taught by faith, by nature desires. And so, after faith, hope is necessary for perfect Christian life, as we have already said before [I, 1].

◄? 2 §►

The Prayer by Which Human Beings Obtain What They
Hope for from God Is Appropriately Indicated
to Them, and on the Difference between
Praying to God and Petitioning
a Human Being

The order of divine providence gives to each thing the means of reaching its end according to the means' suitability to the thing's nature. Therefore, divine providence also gave to human beings a fitting means to obtain things that one hopes for from God according to the way of the human condition. And the human condition has this character, that one brings a petition to obtain from someone, especially someone superior, what one hopes to obtain from the other. And so the prayer by which human beings obtain from God what they hope to obtain from him is made known to them.

But a petition to obtain something from a human being is necessarily different from a prayer to obtain something from God. First, one brings a petition to a human being in order to express the petitioner's desire and need. Second, one brings a petition to a human being in order that the spirit of the addressee should be inclined to grant the petition. But this has no place in a prayer poured out to God. For, in praying to God, we do not strive to manifest our needs or desires to him, who knows all of them. And so also Ps. 38:9 prays to him: "Lord, all my desire is before you"; and Mt. 6:32 says: "Your Father knows that you need these things." Nor do human words bend the divine will to will what it hitherto had not willed, since, as Num. 23:19 says: "God is not like a human being, that he should change his mind"; and as 1 Sam. 15:29 says: "And he does not change his mind by forgiving."

But prayer to obtain things from God is necessary for human beings for the sake of the very ones who pray, namely, that they consider their defects and incline their spirit to desire fervently and devoutly what they hope to obtain by praying. For this renders them suitable to receive what they pray for.

And we should consider another difference between a prayer made to God and a petition made to a human being. For the intimacy whereby one has access to petition a human being is a prerequisite for such a petition. But the very prayer we express to God makes us intimates of God, when we raise our mind to him and talk to him with a spiritual affection, adoring him in spirit and truth. And so intimate affection by praying prepares access to him to pray again more confidently. And so Ps. 17:6 says: "I have cried out," namely, by praying with confidence, "since you have heard me, O God." This is as if one, received into intimacy by the first prayer, should cry out more confidently with the second. And so perseverance or repetition of petition in prayer to God is suitable and deemed acceptable to him, as Lk. 18:1 says: "For it is necessary always to pray and never to weaken." And so also the Lord in Mt. 7:7 invites us to petition, saying: "Ask and you will receive, seek and you will find, knock and it will be opened to you." But in a petition made to a human being, persistent petitioning becomes annoying.

◄≀ 3 ≀►

It Was Appropriate for the Fulfillment of Hope That Christ Gave Us a Form of Praying

Therefore, because hope, after faith, is also required for our salvation, it was seemly that our savior moved us to a living hope, just as he initiated and perfected our faith by revealing the heavenly sacraments. And when he teaches us what to seek from him, he gives us a form of prayer that most directs our hope toward him. For he would not move us to petition unless he were to propose to listen favorably, and one seeks from another only regarding what one hopes for, and one petitions for the things that one hopes for. Therefore, when he teaches us to petition for things from God, he advises us to hope in God, and he shows us what we ought to hope for from God by the things that he indicates are to be requested.

Therefore, treating of the things included in the Lord's Prayer, we shall show whatever can belong to the hope of Christians, namely, in what we ought to place our hope, and for what reason, and what things we ought to hope for from him. Our hope should be in God, to whom we should also pray, as Ps. 62:8 says: "Hope in him," namely, God, "all the assembly of the people. Pour out your hearts in his presence," namely, by praying.

◄≀ 4 ≀►

The Reason We Should Seek from God in Prayer the Things We Hope for

And the chief reason why we should hope in God is because we belong to him as an effect to its cause. But everything acts for a fixed end, not in vain. Therefore, it belongs to each active thing to produce its effect in such a way that the effect does not lack the things by which it can reach its end. And so, in things produced by natural active things, nature is not found wanting in necessary things. Rather, nature gives to each thing produced the things necessary to constitute the thing's existing and to carry out the activity by which it reaches its end, unless, perhaps, the defect of a cause inadequate to produce such things prevents this.

And a thing acting through its intellect, in the very production of an effect, confers on it the things necessary for the intended end, and after the work has been completed, arranges for its use, which is the end of the work. For example, a blacksmith not only forges a knife but also arranges for its use in cutting. But God produced human beings as a craftsman produces an artifact. And so Is. 64:8 says: "And now, O Lord, you are our potter, and we your clay." And so, as an earthen jar, if it were to have the power to think, could hope in the potter, so also human beings ought to have confidence in God, that he govern them rightly, and so Jer. 18:6 says: "As clay in the hands of the potter."

And the confidence that a human being has in God ought to be most certain. For I have said above that a cause fails in the right disposition of its work only because of a defect in it. But God can have no defect. He cannot lack knowledge because "all things are bare and open to his eyes," as Heb. 4:13 says. He cannot lack power because "his hand is not so short that he cannot save," as Is. 59:1 says. And he cannot lack a good will because he is "the Lord, good to the soul hoping in him," as Lam. 3:25 says. And so the hope by which one has confidence in God does not confound one who hopes in him, as Rom. 5:5 says.

We should further consider that, although providence arranging things watches carefully regarding all creatures, it has care of rational creatures in a special way. That is to say, rational creatures are marked with the dignity of his image, they can attain to knowing and loving him, and they, having discernment of good and evil, have mastery of their actions. And so it is proper to them to have confidence in God, both that he preserves them in their existing in accord with the condition of their nature, which is true of other creatures, and that they, by keeping away from evil and doing good, merit something from him. And so Ps. 36:6 says: "You, O Lord, will save human beings and beasts," namely, inasmuch as he confers on human beings along with irrational creatures things that pertain to supporting life. And v. 7 adds: "And the children of human beings will hope in the cover of your wings," as if protected by his special care.

And we need to consider further that the capacity to do or obtain something is added when any perfection is acquired. For example, air illuminated by the sun has the capacity to be the medium of vision, and water heated by fire has the ability to cook food. And a thing could hope for this if it were to have the power to think. But the perfection of grace, by which "we are made sharers in the divine nature," as 2 Pet. 1:4 says, is added to human beings above their nature. And so also we are accordingly said to be reborn as children of God, as Jo. 1:12 says: "He gave them the power to become children of God." But adopted sons can properly hope for an inheritance, as Rom. 8:17 says: "If sons, then also heirs." And so it belongs to human beings by reason of this spiritual rebirth to have a higher hope in God, namely, of gaining eternal life, as 1 Pet. 1:3–4 says: "He gave us a rebirth into a living hope, an imperishable inheritance," etc.

And because we who have received the spirit of adoption cry, "Abba, Father," as Rom. 8:15 says, so the Lord, to show us that we should pray with this hope, began his prayer by invoking the Father, saying (Mt. 6:9–13; Lk. 11:2–4), "Father," etc. Likewise, the fact that one says, "Father," prepares one's disposition to pray in a pure way and obtain what one hopes for. Moreover children should imitate their parents. And so those who profess God as Father ought to attempt to imitate God, namely, by avoiding things that render them unlike God and by sticking to things that make them like him. And so Jer. 3:19 says: "You will call me Father, and you will not fail to follow after me." Therefore, "if," as Gregory of Nyssa says,[1] "you direct your gaze on worldly things or ambition human glory or the filth of emotional desire, how do you, who are living a corrupt life, call the begetter of incorruptibility Father?"

◄⅋ 5 ⅋►

We Should Invoke God, from Whom We Seek the Things We Hope for, by Praying "Our Father," Not "My Father"

And among other things, those who recognize themselves as children of God should especially imitate him in love, as Eph. 5:1–2 says: "Imitate God as his dearly beloved children, and walk in love," etc. And God's love is universally for all human beings, not restricted to some. Just so, Wis. 11:25 says: "For he loves all things that exist"; and especially human beings, as Dt. 33:3 says: "He loved the peoples." And so Cyprian says: "Prayer is for us public and common, and when we pray, we pray for the whole people, not for one person alone, since we, the whole people, are one."[2] And Chrysostom says: "Necessity compels praying for oneself, but fraternal charity urges praying for another."[3] And so we say, "our Father," not "my Father."

Likewise, we should consider that, although our hope chiefly relies on God's help, we help one another to obtain more easily what we seek. And so 2 Cor. 1:10–11 says: "He will deliver us ... with you helping on our behalf in prayer, so that, by so many persons praying for us, many give thanks to God on our behalf for what belongs to his gift in us." And so also Jas. 5:16 says: "Pray for one another that you should be saved." For, as Ambrose says: "Many little people, when assembled together, become great, and it is impossible that the prayers of many are not heard."[4] Just so, Mt. 18:19 says: "If two of you should agree on earth about anything that they should seek, my Father in heaven will do it for you." And so we do not offer our prayer as individuals but say, "our Father," as if by unanimous consent.

We should also consider that our hope is in relation to God through Christ. Just so, Rom. 5:1–2 says: "Justified by faith, let us continue in peace with God through our Lord Jesus Christ, by whom we have access through faith to the grace in which we are. And let us glory in the hope of the children of God." For he who is the only-begotten, natural Son of God has made us adopted sons, since "God sent his Son that we receive adoption as sons," as Gal. 4:4–5 says. Therefore, we ought to profess God as Father in such a way as not to derogate from the privilege of the only-begotten one. And so Augustine says: "Do not claim anything specially for yourself. The Father is special only to Christ and is common to all of us, since the Father begot Christ alone but created us."[5] And so we say, "our Father."

⊰ 6 ⊱

The Phrase *Who Art in Heaven* Shows the Power of God, Our Father, to Whom We Pray, to Grant the Things We Hope for

It usually happens that one loses hope because of the powerlessness of the one from whom help was to be expected. For it is not enough for confident hope that the one on whom the hope relies has the will to help unless such a one has the power to do so. And we express the sufficient readiness of the divine will to help us by professing God as Father, but, lest there should be doubt about the excellence of his power, we add (Mt. 6:9): "Who art in heaven." For we say, "art in heaven," to mean that God circumscribes the heavens by his power, not that the heavens contain him, as Sir. 24:5 says: "I [wisdom] alone have circled the ring of heaven." Indeed, his power has been raised even above the whole expanse of the heavens. Just so, Ps. 8:1 says: "Your majesty has been raised above the heavens, O God." And so we profess his power, which sustains and transcends the heavens, in order to confirm the confidence of our hope.

This also excludes an impediment to prayer. For some subject human affairs to a fate necessitated by the stars,[6] as Jer. 10:2 says: "Do not be afraid of the heavenly signs that the pagans fear." Such an error takes away the efficacy of prayer, since, if our life is subject to the necessity of the stars, we can change nothing about it. Therefore, we would in prayer vainly petition for things, whether to obtain particular goods or to be delivered from evils. Therefore, in order that this should not be an obstacle to the confidence of those petitioning, we say: "Who art in heaven," that is, to the one who moves and regulates the heavens. And so the power of the heavenly bodies cannot prevent the help that we hope for from God.

It is also necessary for prayer to be efficacious with God that a human being seek things that are worthy to expect from God. For Jas. 4:3 says to certain persons: "You seek and do not receive because you seek wrongly." But they wrongly seek things that earthly, not heavenly, wisdom suggests. And so, as Chrysostom says,[7] "When we say, 'who art in heaven,' we do not confine God there, but the spirit of the one praying is led from earth and linked to the highest regions."

And there is another impediment to prayer or the confidence that the one praying has in God, namely, if one should think that human life has been removed from divine providence. Just so, Job 22:14 says of God in the person of the wicked: "The clouds are his cover, nor does he consider our affairs, and he walks around the poles of the heavens." And Ez. 9:9 says: "The Lord abandoned the earth; the Lord does not see." But the Apostle Paul, preaching to the Athenians, showed the contrary, saying (Acts 17:27–28): "He is not far from each of us, since we live, move, and exist in him," namely, because he preserves our existing, governs our life, and directs our movement. Just so, Wis. 14:3 says: "And you, Father, govern all things by your providence," insofar as not even the least animals are withdrawn from his providence. And Mt. 10:29 says: "Are not two sparrows sold for a penny? And not one of these will fall to the ground without your Father's approval."

But human beings obtain divine care in so much more excellent a way that Paul in 1 Cor. 9:9 says in comparison to animals: "God does not have concern for oxen." This is not to say that he has no care of them at all, but that he does not have such care of them as he has of human beings, whom he punishes or rewards for good or evil things, and he preordains them for eternity. And so also the Lord in Mt. 10:30 adds to the previously cited words: "But even all the hairs of your head are numbered," as if all that belongs to a human being is to be restored in the resurrection. And this ought to remove all lack of confidence from us. And so also v. 31 adds: "Therefore, do not be afraid; you are worth more than many sparrows." And so, as I have said before [II, 4], Ps. 36:7 says: "The children of men will hope in the cover of your wings."

Because of God's special care for all human beings, we say that he is close to them. But we say that he is especially close to the good, who strive to be close to him by faith and love, as Jas. 4:8 says: "Come close to God, and he will come close to you." And so also Ps. 145:18 says: "The Lord is near to all who call upon him in truth." Not only is he close to them, but he also dwells in them by grace, as Jer. 14:9 says: "You, O Lord, are in our midst," etc.

And so, in order to increase the hope of the saints, we say, "who art in heaven," "that is, in the saints," as Augustine explains.[8] "For," as he says, "there seems to be spiritually as much distance between the just and sinners as there is materially between the heavens and the earth. And to signify this, we turn in prayer toward the east, from where the dawn rises."[9] And both the saints' closeness to God and the dignity that they have obtained from God, who through Christ made them heavens, increase their hope and their confidence in prayer. Just so, Is. 61:16 says: "That you may fix the heavens and make the earth firm," since he who made them heavens will not deny heavenly goods to them.

◄≀ 7 ≀►

What Kind of Things We Should Hope for from God, and on the Nature of Hope

Therefore, having set forth the things by which human beings conceive hope regarding God [II, 4–6], we need to consider what are the things that we should hope for from him.

First, we should consider in this matter that hope presupposes desire. And so, in order to hope for something, it is first necessary that we should desire it, since we say that one fears or even despises things that one does not desire, not that one hopes for such things.

Second, one needs to think that it is possible to obtain what one hopes for, and hope adds to desire in this respect. For one can desire even things that one does not think that one can obtain, but one cannot hope for them.

Third, what is hoped for is necessarily something difficult. For we despise slight things rather than hope for them, or if we do desire them, as if having them close at hand, we seem to possess them as present things, not to hope for them as future things.

Fourth, we should consider that one hopes to obtain by another some of the difficult things that one hopes to obtain, and to obtain other of the things by oneself. And there seems to be this difference between these things, that one uses the effort of one's own power to obtain the things that one hopes to obtain by oneself, but one petitions to obtain the things that one hopes to obtain from another. And if one hopes to obtain something from a human being, we call this a petition in an absolute sense, but if one should hope to obtain it from God, we call this a prayer, which is "a petition of fitting things from God," as Damascene says.[10]

And only the hope that one has from God, not from oneself or even another human being, belongs to the virtue of hope. And so Jer. 17:5 says: "Cursed be anyone who trusts in a human being and thinks flesh one's support." And v. 7 adds: "Blessed be the one who trusts in the Lord, and the Lord will be that one's assurance." Therefore, the things the Lord taught us to seek in our prayer are shown to be things to be desired by us, possible, and so difficult that we obtain them by divine, not human, power.

◄ℰ 8 ℱ►

On the First Petition, in Which We Are Taught to Desire That the Incomplete Knowledge of God in Us Be Perfected, and This Is Possible

Therefore, we need to consider the order of desire proceeding from charity, so that we can understand the order of things that we should both hope for and seek from God. And the order of charity has this character, that one love God above all things, and so, first, charity moves our desire for the things that belong to God. But desire regards a future good, and nothing comes in the future to God insofar as we consider him in himself. Rather, he is eternally disposed in the same way. Therefore, our desire cannot be brought to things that, as considered in themselves, belong to God, namely, that he obtain some goods that he does not have. And our love is brought to these very things so that we love them as they are.

But we can desire that God, who in himself is always great, should be magnified in the opinion and reverence of all. And we should not think of this as something impossible. For, inasmuch as human beings were made to know God's greatness, they would seem to have been made in vain if they could not attain to perceiving it. This would be contrary to what Ps. 89:47 says: "Have you made the children of human beings in vain?" And the desire whereby all naturally desire to know something about divine things would be in vain. And so there is no one who is completely deprived of knowledge of God, as Job 36:25 says: "All human beings see him."

But this is so difficult that it surpasses all human capacity, as Job 36:26 says: "Behold how great God is, surpassing our knowledge." And so knowledge of God's greatness and goodness can come to human beings only through the favor of divine revelation. Just so, Mt. 11:27 says: "No on knows the Son except the Father, nor does anyone know the Father except the Son and the one to whom the Son wished to reveal him." And so Augustine says in his *Commentary on the Gospel of John:* "No one knows God unless the one who knows him makes him known."[11]

God made himself known to human beings to a degree by natural knowledge, since he poured the light of reason into them, and made visible creatures, in which traces of his goodness and wisdom are in some way reflected. Just so, Rom. 1:19 says: "What is knowable about God," that is, knowable by natural

222 COMPENDIUM OF THEOLOGY

reason, "has been manifested to them," namely, to the pagans, "since he has revealed it to them," namely, by the light of reason and by the creatures that he made. And so v. 20 adds: "For, by the created world, the invisible things of God are clearly perceived in the things he has made, when we understand them." But this knowledge is imperfect. For human beings cannot perfectly perceive the created world, and the created world fails to represent God perfectly, since the power of this cause infinitely surpasses its effect. And so Job 11:7 says: "Do you, perhaps, understand the traces of God, and do you completely discover the almighty?" And Job 36:25, after saying, "all human beings see him," adds: "Each sees from afar."

And from the imperfection of this knowledge, it followed that human beings, departing from truth, erred about knowledge of God in various ways. They erred to such an extent that some "became vain in their thoughts, their foolish mind was darkened, and they changed the glory of the indestructible God into the likeness of destructible images of human beings, birds, four-legged animals, and reptiles," as Rom. 1:21, 23 says. And so, in order to recall human beings from this error, God more plainly gave them knowledge of him in the Old Law, which recalls human beings to the worship of one God, as Dt. 6:4 says: "Hear, O Israel. The Lord your God is one God." But this knowledge of God was both wrapped in the obscurities of figures of speech and confined within the borders of one people, the Jews, as Ps. 76:1 says: "God is known in Judea; his name is great in Israel."

Therefore, in order that true knowledge of God should reach the whole human race, God the Father sent the only-begotten Word of his truth into the world so that through him the whole world should come to a true knowledge of the divine name. And the Lord began to do this with his disciples, as Jo. 17:6 says: "I have manifested your name to the human beings you gave me from the world." Nor did his intention end with only them having knowledge of divinity. Rather, his intention was that they spread the knowledge throughout the world, and so he adds in v. 21: "That the world may believe that you sent me." And the Apostles and their successors continually do this when they lead human beings to knowledge of God, until the name of God is considered holy and honored throughout the world. Just so, Mal. 1:11 said: "My name is great among the peoples, from the rising of the sun to its setting." Therefore, in order that what he began should reach its consummation, we say in petition (Mt. 6:9; Lk. 11:2): "Hallowed be thy name." "And we do not seek this as if his name should not be holy, but so that all consider the name holy, that is, that God should become so known that nothing would be considered holier," as Augustine says.[12]

And among other signs that manifest the holiness of God to human beings, the most evident is the holiness of the human beings that the divine indwelling sanctifies. For Gregory of Nyssa says: "Who is so bestial who, looking at the pure life in believers, does not glorify the name invoked in such a life?"[13] Just so, Paul says in 1 Cor. 14:24: "If all [in a church assembly] should be prophesying, and an unbeliever or simpleton should enter, all reprove him"; and v. 25 then adds: "And so he, falling on his face, will adore God, proclaiming that God is truly in our midst." And so Chrysostom says about the petition "hallowed be thy name": "He also commands us to ask in prayer that our lives glorify him, as if to say: 'Make us live in such a way that all glorify you through us.'"[14]

And then God is sanctified in the minds of others through us insofar as we are sanctified through him. And so, by saying, "hallowed be thy name," as Cyprian says: "We desire that his name should be sanctified in us. For he himself said (Lev. 11:44): 'Be holy because I am holy.' Therefore, we seek that we who have been sanctified in baptism persevere in what we have begun to be. And we also pray daily to be sanctified so that we who daily fail may wipe away our sins by constant sanctification."[15] And so we make this the first petition because, as Chrysostom says, "the fitting prayer of one beseeching God is to seek nothing more than the glory of the Father and to hold all things secondary to praise of him."[16]

◄§ 9 §►

The Second Petition: That He Make Us Sharers in Glory

And after desiring and petitioning that God be glorified, human beings then desire and need to become sharers of that glory. And so we make the second petition (Mt. 6:10; Lk. 11:6): "Thy kingdom come." Regarding this petition, just as in the first petition [II, 7–8], we first need to consider that we appropriately desire the kingdom of God. Second, we need to consider that human beings can come to obtain it. Third, we need to consider that one can attain this only by the help of divine grace, not by one's own power. And then, fourth, we will need to consider how we seek the coming of the kingdom of God.

Therefore, we should first consider that, for each thing, its proper good is naturally desirable. And so also good is appropriately defined as "that which all things desire."[17] And the proper good of each thing is what perfects that thing, since we call each thing good because it reaches its own perfection. But a thing lacks goodness inasmuch as it falls short of its proper perfection. And so it follows that each thing desires its perfection. And so also a human being by nature desires to be perfected, and although there are many grades of human perfection, the good that regards the final perfection of human beings falls by nature especially and chiefly within their desire. We know this good by the sign that the natural desire of a human being comes to rest in it. For the natural desire of human beings tends only toward their proper good, which consists of some perfection. Therefore, it follows that human beings have not yet reached their final perfection as long as there remains something for them to desire.

Something still remains to be desired in two ways. Something remains to be desired in one way when the thing desired is sought for the sake of something else. And so, when the thing has been obtained, desire still is not at rest but is carried over to the other thing. Something remains to be desired in the second way when something does not suffice to obtain what a human being desires. For example, a morsel of food does not suffice to sustain nature and so does not satisfy the natural appetite.

Therefore, the good that human beings first and chiefly desire ought to be such that they do not seek it for the sake of something else, and that it satisfies them. And we generally call this good happiness inasmuch as it is the chief good of human beings. For we call some human beings happy because we believe that all is well with them. We also call this good blessedness inasmuch as the good denotes an excellence. We can also call this good peace inasmuch as the good satisfies desire, since there seems to be internal peace when desire is at rest. And so Ps. 147:14 says: "He who maintained your borders in peace."

Therefore, it is clear that the happiness or blessedness of human beings cannot be in material goods. First, it cannot because we by nature desire material goods for the sake of something else, not for their own sake. For material goods are appropriate for human beings because of their body. And the body of a human being is ordered to the soul as its end. It is so ordered because the body is the instrument of the soul, which moves it, and every instrument is for the sake of the skill that makes use of it. It is also so ordered because the body is related to the soul as matter to form, and form is the end of matter, just as actuality is the end of potentiality. And so the final happiness of human beings does not consist of riches, honors, health, beauty, or any such things.

Second, the happiness or blessedness of human beings cannot be in material things because material goods cannot suffice for human beings. This is clear in many ways. It is clear in one way because there are two kinds of appetitive power, namely, the intellectual and the sense, and so two kinds of desire. Therefore, the desire of the intellectual appetite strives chiefly for intellectual goods, which do not concern material goods. It is clear in a second way because material goods, as the lowest in the order of things, receive a particular goodness, not universal goodness. That is to say, material things receive goodness in such a way that this material good (e.g., pleasure) has a particular aspect of goodness, that material good (e.g., bodily health) has another particular aspect of goodness, and so forth. And so the human appetite, which by nature tends toward universal good, cannot find sufficiency in any of these goods, or in many of them, however many, since they fall short of the infinity of universal good. And so Eccl. 5:10 says: "A miser is not satisfied with money."

Third, the happiness or blessedness of human beings cannot be in material goods because human beings intellectually understand universal good, which is not locally or temporally circumscribed. Therefore, it follows that the human appetite desires good by its suitability to the intellect's understanding, which is not temporally circumscribed. And so human beings naturally desire everlasting durability, but such durability cannot be found in material things, which are subject to passing away and many changes. And so it follows that the human appetite does not find in material things the sufficiency that it requires. Therefore, the final happiness of human beings cannot be in them.

And sense powers, as they act through bodily organs, have bodily activities and operate regarding material things. Therefore, it follows that the final happiness of a human being does not consist of the actions of the sensory part (e.g., any pleasures of the flesh). And the human intellect also has some activity regarding material things when a human being knows material substances with the theoretical intellect and manages material things with the practical intellect. And so it follows that we also cannot posit the final happiness and perfection of human beings in the activity of the theoretical or practical intellect focusing on material things.

Likewise, we cannot posit our final happiness in the activity of the human intellect by which the intellectual soul reflects on itself, for two reasons. The first reason is because the soul as such is not blessed. Otherwise, it would not be necessary for it to act to acquire blessedness. Therefore, the soul does not acquire blessedness by the mere fact that it focuses on itself. The second reason is because happiness is the final perfection of human beings, as I have said above. And since the perfection of the soul consists of its proper activity, it follows that we note its final perfection by its best activity, and this regards its best object, since actions are specified by their objects. But the best object for which the soul's activity can strive does not belong to the soul, since the soul understands that there is something better than itself. And so the final blessedness of human beings cannot consist of the activity whereby the soul focuses on itself.

By like reasoning, the final blessedness cannot consist of the activity whereby the soul focuses on any other higher substances, provided that they have something better toward which the activity of the human soul can tend. But the activity of human beings tends toward any good, since the intellect apprehends universal good, and so human beings desire that good. And so the activity of the human intellect, and consequently of the will, extends in some way to whatever grade good extends.

But good in the highest degree is found in God, who is good essentially and the source of all goodness. And so it follows that the final perfection of human beings and their final good consists of adhering to God, as Ps. 73:28 says: "It is good for me to cling to God." This is also very clear if one should look at the sharing in other things. For example, all individual human beings receive the true predicate *human being* by sharing in the specific essence. And we call each of them a human being only because each shares in the specific essence, not because one human being shares in the likeness of another. One human being brings another to share in the specific essence by way of generation, namely, by a father begetting a child. But blessedness or happiness is simply the perfect good. Therefore, all sharers in blessedness are necessarily blessed only by sharing in the blessedness of God, who is essential goodness itself, although one human being helps another to tend toward, and arrive at, blessedness. And so also Augustine says in his work *On True Religion:* "We are not blessed by seeing angels but by seeing the truth by which we love them and wish joy to them."[18]

And the human mind may be brought to God in two ways: in one way by God himself; in the second way by something else. God himself brings the human mind to himself, for example, when it sees him in himself and loves him because of himself. And something else brings the human mind to God, for example, when his creatures raise the spirit of human beings to him. Just so, Rom. 1:20 says: "We see the invisible things of God by the things he made, when we understand them."

And perfect blessedness cannot consist of tending toward God by something else. First, it cannot because blessedness signifies the end of all human acts, and so true and perfect blessedness cannot consist of something that has the nature of a change toward the end rather than the nature of the end. But a movement of the human mind causes us to know and love God by something else inasmuch as the mind is brought by one thing to another. Therefore, true and perfect blessedness does not consist of this.

Second, if the blessedness of a human being consists of the human mind adhering to God, it follows that perfect happiness requires perfect adherence to him. But the mind cannot by knowledge or love perfectly adhere to God through any creature, since any created form falls infinitely short of representing the divine essence. One cannot know something of a higher rank of creatures by the form of a lower rank (e.g., a spiritual substance by a material substance, or a heavenly body by an elementary material substance). Therefore, just so, far less can one know the essence of God by a created form.

But we negatively perceive the nature of higher material substances by considering lower material substances (e.g., that higher material substances are neither heavy nor light). And we acquire negative knowledge about angels by considering material things (e.g., that angels are spiritual and incorporeal). Just so, we know about God through creatures what he is not rather than what he is. Likewise, the goodness of each creature is minimal in relation to the divine goodness, which is infinite. And so the manifold goodness in things, which comes from God and is his benefaction, does not raise the mind up to perfect love of God. Therefore, true and perfect blessedness cannot consist of the mind adhering to God by something else.

Third, according to right order, we know less known things through things that are more known, and we likewise love less good things through things that are more good. Therefore, since God is the prime truth and the highest goodness, he as such is supremely knowable and lovable. Therefore, the natural order is such that one knows and loves all things through him. Therefore, if one's mind needs to be brought to the knowledge and love of God by creatures, this happens due to the mind's imperfection. Therefore, such a one has not yet attained perfect happiness, which excludes all imperfection. Therefore, we conclude that perfect blessedness consists of the mind adhering to God in himself by knowing and loving.

And because it belongs to a king to dispose and govern subjects, we say that something reigns in human beings insofar as it disposes other things. And so Paul in Rom. 6:12 warns: "Let sin not reign in your mortal body." Therefore, since perfect blessedness requires that one know and love God himself as such, so that he brings the human spirit to other things, God reigns truly and perfectly in the blessed. And so Is. 49:10 says: "He who has pity on them will govern them and give them springs of water to drink," namely, that he will renew them with the most excellent goods of every kind.

We should also consider that the intellect understands by a likeness or form everything that it knows, just as the external sense of sight sees a stone by the form of a stone. Therefore, the intellect cannot see God essentially through a created likeness or form representing his essence, as it were, since we perceive that the likeness of a lower order of things cannot represent something of a higher order regarding its essence. And so it happens that we cannot understand a spiritual substance regarding its essence through any material likeness. Therefore, since God surpasses the whole order of creatures, much more than a spiritual substance surpasses the order of material things, it is impossible for us to see God essentially through any material likeness.

And this is very clear if one should consider what it is to perceive a thing essentially. For one who does not understand one of the things that belong essentially to human being does not perceive the essence of human being (e.g., one who knows animal without knowing rational does not know the essence of human being). And whatever we predicate of God belongs to him essentially. No created likeness can represent God as to all the things that we predicate of him. For there are different likenesses in the created intellect through which we understand the life, wisdom, justice, and all other such things that belong to God's essence. Therefore, no one likeness representing the divine essence can inform the created intellect in such a way that we can see God essentially in it. And if many likenesses could, the oneness identical with his essence will be lacking. Therefore, no one created likeness or even many can raise the created intellect to see God in himself essentially.

Therefore, we conclude that, in order for a created intellect to see God essentially, it is necessary that the divine essence be seen in itself, not by one or another form, and this by a union of the created intellect to God. And so also Dionysius says in his work *On the Divine Names* that when "we acquire our most blessed end by seeing God," a superior intellectual knowledge of God will fill us.[19] And it is unique to the divine essence that the created intellect can be united to it without any intermediate likeness, since the essence of God is its existing, which is proper to no other form.

And so, if an intrinsically existing form cannot inform an intellect (e.g., if the substance of one angel ought to be known by the intellect of another angel), a likeness of the form, a likeness informing the intellect, needs to accomplish this. But this is not necessary in the case of the divine essence, which is its existing. Therefore, the very vision of God makes the blessed mind one with God in understanding. But the subject understanding and the object understood are necessarily in some respect united. And so, with God reigning in the midst of the saints, they will also reign with God. And so Rev. 5:10 says out of their mouth: "You have made us a kingdom and priests to our God, and we shall reign over the earth."

We also call this kingdom, where God reigns in the midst of the saints, and the saints with God, the kingdom of heaven. Just so, Mt. 4:17 says: "Repent, for the kingdom of heaven is close at hand," in the way of speaking by which we attribute being in heaven to God. We attribute being in heaven to God, not because he is confined to the heavenly bodies, but in order to signify the eminence of God above every creature, like the eminence of the heavens above other material substances. Just so, Ps. 113:4 says: "High above all peoples is the Lord, and his glory is above the heavens." Therefore, we also call the blessedness of the saints the kingdom of heaven, not because their reward is in the material heaven, but because it consists of contemplating a nature above the heavens. And so also Mt. 18:10 says about [children's] angels: "Their angels in heaven always see the face of my Father, who is in heaven." And so also Augustine explains what Mt. 5:12 says, "Your reward is rich in heaven." He says in his work *On the Lord's Sermon on the Mount*: "I do not think that heaven here means the upper parts of this visible world, since our reward is not to be placed in revolving things. Rather, I think the words 'in heaven' refer to the spiritual firmaments, where everlasting justice dwells."[20]

We also even call this final good, which consists of God, eternal life in the way of speaking by which we call the soul's vivifying action life. And so we distinguish as many ways of vivification as there are kinds of activity by the soul. The highest activity of the soul is intellectual, and Aristotle says that intellectual activity "is life."[21] And because acts take their species and name from their object, we call the vision of divine eternity eternal life, as Jo. 17:3 says: "This is eternal life, that they know you, the true God," etc.

We also call this final good comprehension, as Phil. 3:12 says: "And I press on so that I may somehow comprehend," and this is not said in the way of speaking by which comprehension signifies enclosure. For what is enclosed by something else is entirely and completely contained by it. But a created intellect cannot completely see the essence of God, namely, so that it arrives at the complete and perfect way of seeing God, which is to see God as much as he can be seen. For God is visible by the brilliance of his reality, and his reality is infinite. And so he is infinitely visible, and this cannot be suitable to a created intellect, whose power in understanding is finite. Therefore, only God, infinitely understanding himself by the infinite power of his intellect, completely comprehends himself by understanding himself.

But comprehension is promised to the saints as the word *comprehension* signifies a laying hold. For example, if one man is pursuing another, we say that he grasps the other when he could hold the other in his hands. Therefore, "as long as we are in the body," as 2 Cor. 5:6–7 says, "we are far from the Lord, since we walk by faith and not by sight." And so we strive for him as if from afar. But when we shall see him essentially, we shall have him in us by his presence. And so, in the Song of Songs 3:4, the bride seeking the groom that her soul loves, at last finding him, says: "I held him, and I did not let him go."

The aforementioned final good contains everlasting and complete joy. And so also the Lord says in Jo. 16:24: "Seek, and you will receive, that your joy may be complete." But there can be full joy only regarding God, in whom the entire fullness of goodness resides, not regarding any creature. And so also the Lord says about the faithful servant in Mt. 25:21: "Enter into the joy of your Lord," namely, rejoice about your Lord. Just so, Job 22:26 says: "You will then abound with delights in the Almighty." And because God rejoices most about himself, the faithful servant is also said to enter into the joy of his Lord, inasmuch as he enters into the joy that his Lord enjoys. Just so, the Lord also promises to his disciples elsewhere (Lk. 22:29–30): "As my Father appointed the kingdom to me, I appoint that you eat and drink at my table in my kingdom." This does not mean that, regarding the final good, the saints, now made indestructible, consume material foods. Rather, the table signifies the refreshment of the joy that God has about himself, and the saints about God.

We also need to note fullness of joy not only by the object rejoiced in, but also by the disposition of the subject rejoicing. That is to say, the one rejoicing has the object rejoiced in present, and love relates the whole affection of the one rejoicing to the reason for the joy. And I have already shown above that the created mind, by seeing the essence of God, has him present to it.

The vision of God also completely inflames the desire for divine love. For, if each thing is lovable inasmuch as it is beautiful and good, as Dionysius says in his work *On the Divine Names,*[22] one cannot see God, who is the very essence of beauty and goodness, without love. And so perfect love results from the perfect vision of him. And so also Gregory the Great says in a homily on Ezekiel: "The fire of love, which begins to burn here, burns more brightly in the love of the beloved when one will see him."[23] And the more something is loved, the greater is the joy of having it present. And so the joy is complete, regarding both the object rejoiced in, and the subject rejoicing, and this joy makes human blessedness perfect. And so also Augustine says in his *Confessions* that blessedness is "joy about truth."[24]

And we should further consider that, since God is the very essence of goodness, he is consequently the goodness of every good. And so we see every good when we see him, as the Lord says to Moses in Ex. 33:19: "I shall show you every good." Therefore, we possess every good when we possess him, as Wis. 7:11 says: "All goods came to me along with wisdom." Therefore, by seeing God, we shall possess in that final good the complete sufficiency of all goods. And so also the Lord in Mt. 24:47 promises the faithful servant that the Lord "will place him in charge of all his goods."

And because evil is contrary to good, it is necessary that evil be universally excluded when every good is present. For there is no "sharing of righteousness with iniquity," nor "fellowship of light with darkness," as 2 Cor. 6:14 says. Therefore, there will be in that final good not only complete sufficiency for those possessing every good, but also full rest and security by freedom from every evil. Just so, Prov. 1:33 says: "Whoever will listen to me will rest without fear and enjoy abundance with fear of evils taken away."

It further follows from this that there will be complete peace in heaven. For only the disquiet of internal desires, when human beings desire to have what they do not yet have, or the trouble of some evils that they either are suffering or fear to suffer, prevents their peace. In heaven, the disquiet of desire will cease because of the fullness of every good, and every external trouble will also cease because of the absence of every evil. And so we conclude that there is in heaven the perfect tranquility of peace. Hence Is. 32:18 says: "My people will sit in the beauty of peace," and this designates the perfection of peace. And to show the reason for the peace, Isaiah adds: "And in secure dwellings," namely, without fear of evils, "and in rich leisure," which belongs to the abundance of every good.

And the perfection of the final good will last forever. For it will not be able to fail through lack of the goods that a human being will enjoy, since such goods are eternal and indestructible. And so Is. 33:20 says: "Your eyes will see Jerusalem, the rich city, the dwelling that will in no way be able to be removed." And v. 21 gives the reason: "Because only there is the great Lord, our God," since the whole perfection of that condition consists of enjoying divine eternity.

Likewise, that condition will not be able to fail through destruction of the things existing there, since they are either by nature indestructible, as in the case of angels, or will be transposed into indestructibility, as in the case of human beings. "For this destructible thing needs to put on indestructibility," as 1 Cor. 15:53 says. And so also Rev. 3:12 says: "I shall make the one who will conquer, a column in the temple of my God, and such a one will never leave it."

Nor will that condition be able to fail because the will of a human being turns away in disgust, since the more one sees God, who is the essence of goodness, the more necessary it is to love him, and so also the more one will desire to enjoy him. Just so, Sir. 24:20 says: "Those who eat me [wisdom] will hunger for more, and those who drink me will thirst for more." Therefore, 1 Pet. 1:12 also says about the angels seeing God: "On whom the angels desire to gaze."

Likewise, that condition will not fail through an enemy's attack, since every troublesome evil will cease in heaven. Just so, Is. 35:9 says: "No lion," that is, attacking devil, "will be there, and no evil beast," that is, evil human being, "will climb on to it [the way of holiness] or be found there." And so also the Lord says in Jo. 10:28 that his sheep "will never perish," and that "no one will snatch them out of my hand."

And that condition cannot be ended because God excludes some people from it. For no one will be banished from that condition because of sin, which will be altogether absent from a place where there will be no evil. And so Is. 60:13 says: "All of your people will be just." Nor will anyone be banished to promote a greater good, as God in this world sometimes withdraws spiritual consolations and other benefits of his from the just so that they more eagerly seek those things and recognize their defect. They will not because the condition then is one of final perfection, not one of emendation or progress. And so the Lord says in Jo. 6:37: "I shall not cast out one who comes to me."

Therefore, the condition will have all the aforementioned goods in perpetuity, as Ps. 5:11–12 says: "They will exult forever, and you will dwell with them."

Therefore, the aforementioned kingdom is perfect blessedness, having, for example, the immutable sufficiency of every good. And because all by nature desire blessedness, it follows that all appropriately desire the kingdom of God.

◄ॐ 10 ॐ►

Human Beings Can Obtain the Kingdom of God

And we need further to show that a human being can reach that kingdom. Otherwise, they would hope for and seek it in vain.

First, it is clear that this is possible for a human being because of God's promise. For the Lord says in Lk. 12:32: "Do not be afraid, little flock, since it has pleased my Father to give you the kingdom." And the divine good pleasure is efficacious to implement everything that it disposes, as Is. 46:10 says: "My plan will stay in place, and every will of mine will be done." And Rom. 9:19 says: "For who will resist his will?"

Second, an evident example shows this to be possible. For it was far more difficult . . . [25]

Notes

1. On Augustine generally, see Henry Chadwick, *Augustine* (New York: Oxford University Press, 1986). On Neo-Platonism in the Latin tradition, see S. Gersh, *Middle-Platonism and Neo-Platonism: The Latin Tradition* (Notre Dame: University of Notre Dame Press, 1986).

2. For an older but useful survey of the reception of Aristotle before A.D. 1277, see Fernand van Steenberghen, *Aristotle in the West: The Origins of Latin Averroism*, translated by L. Johnson (Louvain: E. Nauwalaerts, 1955). For a recent survey and annotated bibliography, see Mark D. Jordan, "Aristotelianism, Medieval," *Routledge Encyclopedia of Philosophy*, general editor Edward Craig (London: Routledge, 1998).

3. See n. 2, supra.

4. On Aristotle generally, see J. L. Ackrill, *Aristotle the Philosopher* (Oxford: Oxford University Press, 1981), and J. Barnes, *Aristotle* (Oxford: Oxford University Press, 1982).

5. On Averroes generally, see M. R. Heyoun and A. de Libera, *Averroes et l'averroisme* (Paris: Presses Universitaires, 1991), and O. Leaman, *Averroes and His Philosophy*, 2nd edition (Richmond, England: Curzon, 1997). On Averroes and the intellect, see H. A. Davidson, *Alfarabi, Avicenna, and Averroes on Intellect* (New York: Oxford University Press, 1992).

6. Aquinas so interpreted Aristotle (ST I, Q. 46, A. 1).

7. Aquinas, partially on the basis of a faulty Latin translation, so interpreted Aristotle (*Commentary on the De anima* of Aristotle, Lecture 10, nn. 742–45). Aristotle himself seems to hold that the human soul as such perishes with the dissolution of the composite. He explicitly holds that the active intellect, and only the active intellect, is immortal (*De anima* III, 5, 430a 17–25), but he is ambiguous about whether that intellect is a faculty of each human being or a separate substance operative in human beings only during their lifetime. If he means the former, which is unlikely, the individual human

soul as such would presumably not be immortal, although part of it would be. If he means the latter, which is likely, there would evidently be no immortality of any part of the individual human soul.

8. On medieval universities generally, see Hilda De Ridder-Symoens, editor, *A History of the University in Europe, Volume I: Universities in the Middle Ages* (Cambridge, England: Cambridge University Press, 1991).

9. *Bulletin Thomiste* 10 (1957–1959):78.

10. On Augustine and the soul as substance, see *City of God* XIII, 1. His position on the creation of the human soul with that of the angels before generation of the human body also presupposes that the soul is a complete substance. See *On the Literal Meaning of Genesis* VII, 24–28 (PL 34:368–72).

11. Albert wrote a treatise on the soul (*De anima*). On Albert generally, see A. de Libera, *Albert le Grand et la philosophie* (Paris: Vrin, 1990).

PART I

1. Thomas here means not only temporal happiness but also heavenly blessedness.

2. *Enchiridion* 3 (PL 40:232; CCL 46:49).

3. Motion in the narrowest sense refers to locomotion, but it may also refer to any movement from potentiality to actuality (i.e., change). In the next chapter, for example, Thomas affirms that God is immoveable (i.e., unchangeable).

4. *On the Consolation of Philosophy* V, prose 6 (PL 67:838; CSEL 67:122).

5. The four material elements of medieval cosmology were earth, fire, air, and water.

6. Aristotle, *De anima* III, 1 (429a19).

7. I, 15, 9, 21, 18, 28, and 32, respectively.

8. The Nicene-Constantinopolitan Creed.

9. Cf. John Damascene, *On Orthodox Faith* I, 9 (PG 94:837A).

10. *On Interpretation* II, 14 (24b1–2).

11. *De anima* III, 7 (431b29).

12. Ibid. II, 24 (424a18).

13. On *the Literal Meaning of Genesis* XII, 6 (PL 34:458; CSEL 28–1:388).

14. Thomas seems to mean to say that there is no need to assign a property by which the *Father alone* is distinguished from the Holy Spirit.

15. Thomas seems to mean to say that there is no need to assign a property by which the *Son alone* is distinguished from the Holy Spirit.

16. Cf. Gilbert de la Porrée, *Exposition on the De Trinitate of Boethius* I, 5, n. 43.

17. Cf. Averroes, *Commentary on the De anima* III, comm. 5.

18. E.g., *De anima* III, 1 (429a16–18); 4 (430a15–16).

19. Principally, Avicenna, *De anima*, part 5, chap. 5.

20. An active thing is an efficient cause.

21. Cf. *On the Literal Meaning of Genesis* VII, 2 (PL 34:356–57; CSEL28–1:201–202).

22. The activity considered here is transitive, that is, causal.

23. *Metaphysics* V, 14 (1019b21–23).

24. E.g., Avicenna, *Metaphysics*, tr. 9, chap. 4. Cf. ST I, Q. 47, A. 1.

25. The Latin words *beatitudo* and *felicitas* both mean happiness, but Thomas uses the former for the complete happiness of the blessed enjoying the vision of God, and the latter generally for the incomplete happiness of the virtuous in this life. (*Felicitas* in chap. 1 is an exception. See n. 1.) Accordingly, I translate *beatitudo* as *blessedness*.

26. E.g., Bonaventure, *Commentary on the Sentences* II, d. 41, a. 1, q. 1 fund. 1.

27. *Categories* 11 (14a23–25).

28. Aristotle, *Metaphysics* I, 5 (986a26). Cf. Thomas, SCG III, 9.

29. *Homilies on the Gospels*, hom. 34 (PL 76:1249D).

30. *On the Heavenly Hierarchy* 8, n. 1 (PG 3:237D; Dion. 873).

31. See n. 29, supra.

32. *On the Heavenly Hierarchy* 9, n. 1 (PG 3:257B; Dion. 893).

33. Ibid. 7, n. 3 (PG 3:209C; Dion. 858).

34. Augustine, *The City of God* V, 9 (PL 41:148), attributes this opinion to Cicero. Cf. Cicero, *On Divination* II, 5.

35. E.g., Possidonius the Stoic, cited by Augustine, *The City of God* V, 2 (PL 41:142; CCL 47:129).

36. Ibid. V, 1 (PL41:141; CCL 47:128).

37. Thomas refers here to the fact that the Latin noun *fatum* derives from the verb *fari*.

38. *On the Consolation of Philosophy* IV, prose 6 (PL 63:815A; CSEL 67:96). Thomas has added the word *immutable*.

39. *The City of God* V, 1 (PL 41:141; CCL 47:128).

40. See n. 38, supra.

41. Gregory the Great ascribes this view to a certain Eutychius. See *Morals* XIV, 56 (PL 75:1077D).

42. In SCG IV, 82, Thomas attributes this view to some pagans, citing Augustine, *The City of God* XII, 13 (PL 41:360–61; CCL 48:368).

43. Cf. Averroes, *Metaphysics* VII, comm. 34.

44. E.g., Avicenna, *Metaphysics* V, 5.

45. Cf. Augustine, *The City of God* XXII, 20 (PL 41:782; CCL 48:840).

46. E.g., Aristotle, *On the Generation of Animals* I, 18 (725a11).

47. Augustine, *Confessions* VII, 16 (PL 32:744; CCL 33:161).

48. Aristotle, *Physics* II, 4 (194b13).

49. For this view, Thomas cites Avicenna in CS IV, d. 44, q. 3, a. 2, q. 1, and cites Algazel in SCG III, 145.

50. Gregory the Great, *Dialogues* IV, 29 (PL 77:368A).

51. Ibid.

52. E.g., Albert the Great, *On the Resurrection*, tr. II, a. 5.

53. *Isagoge*, translated by Boethius. See *Aristoteles latinus* I, nn. 6–7, ed. L. Minio-Paluello (Bruges-Paris: 1966).

54. For summaries of the Christological errors discussed by Thomas in I, 202–208, see E. A. Livingstone, ed., *The Oxford Dictionary of the Christian Church*, 3rd ed. (Oxford: Oxford University Press, 1997).

55. Thomas here conflates two texts: Mk. 12:33 and Mt. 26:37.

56. The text here is corrupt. I follow the reading of the Leonine editors (i.e., leave a lacuna in the text).

57. Cf. Peter Lombard, *Sentences* III, d. 6, chaps. 4–6.

58. Pope Alexander III, *Letter to William, Archbishop of Rheims*, February 18, 1177 (PL 200:685).

59. See Peter Lombard, *Sentences* III, d. 6, chap. 2.

60. E.g., William of Auxerre, *Golden Summary*, part 3, tr. 1, q. 3.

61. See ST III, Q. 19, A. 1.

62. *Letter 4, to Gaius* (PG 3:1072C; Dion. 619).

63. E.g., Bonaventure, *Commentary on the Sentences* III, d. 8, a. 2, q. 2; and Albert the Great, *Commentary on the Sentences* III, d. 8, a. 2.

64. Cf. I, 210.

65. Thomas introduces the topic of this chapter with the two ways people call grace a favor: as the enjoyment of someone's favor, and the favor that someone bestows on another.

66. *On the Divine Names* 7 (PG 3:868B; Dion. 388).

67. Cf. Jerome, *Letter 124, to Avitus,* chap. 4 (PL 22:1070; CSEL 56:114).

68. Cf. Augustine, *On Heresies* 9 (PL 42:27; CCL 46:294).

69. Cf. Augustine, *On the Literal Meaning of Genesis* X, passim.

70. Aristotle, *On the Generation of Animals* II, 4 (738b20; 740b24).

71. Cf. Jerome, *Against Helvetius* (PL 23:185–206).

72. *On Orthodox Faith* III, 20 (PG 94:1081A).

73. *Letter 118,* n. 14 (PL 33:439; CSEL 34–2:679).

74. E.g., Bonaventure, *Commentary on the Sentences* III, d. 16, a. 2, q. 1.

75. *Sentences* III, d. 21, chap. 1.

76. Cf. Gregory the Great, *Homilies on the Gospels,* hom. 22, n. 6 (PL 76:1177C).

77. Ibid., hom. 21, n. 7 (PL 76:1173C).

78. E.g., Augustine, *On the Trinity* IV, 6 (PL 42:894; CCL 50:174).

79. *Commentary on the Gospel of John,* tr. 19, n. 15 (PL 35:1552–53; CCL 36:198).

80. Cf. Augustine, *The City of God* XX, 20 (PL 41:688; CCL 48:734).

81. This is the reading of the Vulgate. Most scholars reject the reading.

82. *Letter 119,* n. 2 (PL 22:967; CSEL 55:447).

83. See n. 80, supra.

84. Peter Lombard, *Glossa* (PL 192:40B).

85. Scholars have not found the source of this reference in the known works of Lactantius.

86. Cf. *Commentary on Matthew,* on 24:28 (PL 26:179C; CCL 77:229).

87. There is no known word *ioathon* in Hebrew, and Jerome did not cite the word.

88. I have corrected a typographical error in the Leonine text. The text should have *conformati*, not *conformari*.

89. In the same sense, see *Sermon 351,* n. 8 (PL 39:1544).

90. These two divisions of the articles of faith are found in Philip the Chancellor (ca. A.D. 1220), *Summary of the Good.*

PART II

1. *On the Lord's Prayer* II, (PG 44:1141D–44A).

2. *On the Lord's Prayer* 8 (PL 4:524A; CSEL 3–1:271)

3. Pseudo-Chrysostom, *Incomplete Work on Matthew*, hom. 14 (PG 156:711).

4. Pseudo-Ambrose, *Commentary on the Letters of Paul*, on Rom. 15:31 (PL 17:177D; CSEL 81:474–75).

5. Pseudo-Augustine, *Sermon 84* (PL 35:1908).

6. Cf. SCG III, 85.

7. *Homilies on Matthew*, hom. 19 (PG 57:278).

8. *On the Lord's Sermon on the Mount* II, 5 (PL 34:1276; CCL 35:107).

9. Ibid. (PL 34:1277; CCL 35:107–108).

10. *On Orthodox Faith* III, 24 (PG 94:1089C).

11. *Commentary on the Gospel of John*, tr. 58, n. 3 (PL 35:1793; CCL 36:475).

12. *On the Lord's Sermon on the Mount* II, 5 (PL 34:1277; CCL 35:109).

13. *On the Lord's Prayer* II (PG 44:1153C-55A).

14. *Homilies on Matthew*, hom. 19 (PG 57:279).

15. *On the Lord's Prayer* 12 (PL 4:526C-27A; CSEL 3–1:274–75).

16. See n. 14, supra.

17. Aristotle, *Ethics* I, 1 (1094a3).

18. *On True Religion* 55 (PL 34:170; CCL 32:258).

19. *On the Divine Names* 1, n. 4 (PG 3:592BC).

20. *On the Lord's Sermon on the Mount* I, 5 (PL 34:1236–37; CCL 35:15).

21. Aristotle, *Metaphysics* XII, 8 (1072b26–27).

22. *On the Divine Names* 4, n. 10 (PG 3:708A).

23. *Homilies on Ezekiel* II, hom. 2 (PL 76:954A; CCL 142:231).

24. *Confessions* X, 23 (PL 32:793; CSEL 33:252).

25. This chapter and the *Compendium* end abruptly in this incomplete sentence.

Glossary

Accident: *an attribute that inheres in another. See* Substance.

Action: *activity.* There are two basic kinds of action. Transitive activity produces an effect in something other than the active cause (*see* Cause). Immanent action, which is the activity of living things, perfects the being that acts. This includes the vegetative activities of nutrition, growth, and reproduction, the animal activities of sense perception and sense appetites, and the immaterial activities of intellection and willing. Only God has perfectly immanent activity.

Actuality: *the perfection of a being.* Existing is the primary actuality of every being. A specific substantial form actualizes finite beings and distinguishes one kind of being from another. Particular accidental forms further actualize finite beings. *See* Accident, Form (Substantial), Matter (Prime), Potentiality, Substance.

Angel: *a purely spiritual (intellectual) creature.*

Appetite: *the desire or striving of finite beings to actualize potentialities.* Material things have so-called natural appetites. Plants have, in addition, the vegetative appetites of nutrition, growth, and reproduction. Animals have, in addition, sense appetites. Human beings have, in addition, an intellectual or rational appetite, the will. *See* Will.

Cause: *something that contributes to the being or coming-to-be of something else.* The term refers primarily to an efficient cause, that is, a cause that by its activity produces an effect. A final cause is the end for the sake of which an efficient cause acts. An exemplary cause is the idea or model of a desired effect in the mind of an intellectual efficient cause preconceiving the effect. There are two intrinsic causes: form, which makes an effect to be what it is, and matter, which receives the form. *See* Action, End, Form (Substantial), Intention, Matter (Prime).

Charity: *the supernatural virtue whereby one is characteristically disposed to love God above all things, and other things for his sake. See* Virtue.

Coming to Be, Passing Away: *the process of substantial change.* In substantial change, prime matter gains a new substantial form. *See* Form (Substantial), Matter (Prime).

Concupiscence: *the inclination of human sense appetites toward actions contrary to reason.* The inclination is not completely subject to reason *See* Appetite, Emotions.

Creation: *the activity that causes things to exist from no preexisting matter.*

Emotions: *movements of sense appetites.* They involve either desire for something pleasant or repugnance regarding something difficult. They may be ordinate (in accord with right reason) or inordinate (contrary to right reason). *See* Concupiscence, Moral Virtues.

End: *the object for the sake of which something acts.* The end is intrinsic if it is built into the nature of an active thing. It is extrinsic if it is the conscious object of a rational being's action. *See* Cause, Intention.

Essence: *that which makes something what it is substantially. See* Nature.

Existing Subject: *the individual thing that underlies something else.* In Christ, the incarnate Son of God, there is only one existing subject of both his divine and human natures. *See* Subject.

Faith: *the supernatural virtue whereby one is characteristically disposed to believe what God has revealed about himself and his plan of salvation for human beings. See* Virtue.

Fatherhood: *the notion or property of the Father generating the Son.*

Form (Substantial): *what makes something to be the kind of thing it is. See* Accident, Cause, Matter (Prime), Substance.

Generation: *the procession of the Son from the Father.*

Genus: *the essence of a material thing in a way not completely determined.* For example, *animal* is the genus of *human being.* See Species.

Grace: *a supernatural aid or gift from God to human beings.*

Habit: *the characteristic disposition or inclination to be or act in a certain way.* Habits belong chiefly to the intellect or the will. They may be innate or acquired, natural or supernatural, good or bad. *See* Virtue.

Happiness: *the state of perfection of human beings.* Human beings attain incomplete happiness in this life by engaging in activities of reason and acting in accord with right reason. They attain perfect happiness in the next life when they behold God as he is in himself.

Hope: *the supernatural virtue whereby one is characteristically disposed to expect the reward of eternal life if one lives virtuously in this life. See* Virtue.

Hypostasis: *existing subject, especially of a rational nature; Greek theological name for the persons of the Trinity.*

Intellect: *the power to understand.* In human beings, the active intellect causes the potential intellect to understand the essences of material things, form judgments, and reason deductively. *See* Reason.

Intention: *the act whereby rational beings strive for ends. See* Cause.

Matter (Prime): *the intrinsic cause of material things underlying their substantial form. See* Cause, Form (Substantial), Rational Soul, Soul.

Miracle: *things God causes outside the natural order of secondary causes.*

Moral Virtues: *virtues consisting of the right characteristic disposition of the will toward requisite ends (e.g., just, courageous, moderate deeds). See* Emotions, Prudence.

Nature: *the essence of a thing considered as the source of its activities. See* Essence.

Notion: *a property by which we note the distinction of persons in the Trinity, namely, the Father being without a source, the Father's fatherhood, the Son's sonship, the Father and the Son's origination of the Holy Spirit, and the Holy Spirit's procession from the Father and the Son.*

Original Justice: *the original state of righteousness, immortality, and complete subjection of lower sense powers to reason that Adam and Eve enjoyed before they sinned.* *See* Original Sin.

Original Sin: *the sin of Adam in which he lost righteousness, immortality, and complete subjection of his lower sense powers to reason. His seed transmits the sin and its effects to his descendants.* *See* Original Justice.

Person: *subsistent thing in an intellectual nature.* *See* Existing Subject, Hypostasis.

Potentiality: *the capacity to be or become something.* Potentiality limits actuality. Active potentiality is the same as power. *See* Accident, Actuality, Power, Substance.

Power: *the active capacity to perform a certain kind of activity.* For example, the intellect and will of human beings are powers. *See* Potentiality.

Principle: *the universal premise of an argument.* First principles are those that presuppose no other principle, or at least no other principle than the principle of contradiction. There are theoretical and practical first principles.

Prudence: *the intellectual virtue consisting of the right characteristic disposition to reason correctly about what human beings should or should not do.* *See* Habit, Moral Virtues, Virtue.

Procession: *the derivation of one thing from another.* In the Trinity, the Son proceeds from the Father by generation, and the Holy Spirit proceeds from the Father and the Son but is not generated by them.

Property: *See* Notion.

Providence: *God's disposition of created things and their activities for the good of the universe in general and the good of human beings in particular.*

Purgatory: *abode where repentant sinners after death discharge the temporal punishment due for sin.*

Rational Soul: *the substantial form of human beings and the ultimate source of their powers and activities. See* Form (Substantial), Soul.

Reason: *(1) the process of drawing conclusions from principles; (2) the power to draw conclusions from principles; (3) the power of the intellect in general. See* Form (Substantial), Rational Soul.

Relations in the Trinity: *the relation of the Father to the Son (fatherhood), of the Son to the Father (sonship), of the Father and the Son to the Holy Spirit (origination of the Holy Spirit), and of the Holy Spirit to the Father and the Son (procession of the Holy Spirit).*

Science (Aristotelian): *Knowledge about things through knowledge of their causes. See* Cause, Intellect.

Senses: *powers of perception through bodily organs.* The senses are external (e.g., sight) and internal (e.g., imagination). *See* Power.

Sin: *offense against God's laws or commands.* A sin is mortal if a human being turns away from his or her ultimate end, namely, God, and venial if a human being turns aside from the way to the end.

Sonship: *the property or notion of the Son being begotten by the Father.*

Soul: *the substantial form of a living material thing. See* Form (Substantial), Rational Soul.

Species: *the substantial identity of material things insofar as the identity is common to many things.* Species are composed of a genus (an incompletely determined essence) and a specific difference that completely determines the essence. *See* Genus.

Subject: *something underlying something else. See* Existing Subject.

Substance: *what subsists in itself and not in another. See* Accident, Subject.

Virtue: *human excellence.* Virtue is an enduring quality and so a characteristic disposition. Intellectual virtues have intellectual activities as their object. Theoretical intellectual virtues comprise understanding first principles, scientific knowledge, and theoretical wisdom. Practical intellectual virtues comprise prudence (practical wisdom) and skills. Moral virtues consist of characteristic readiness to act according to the dictates of prudence. Prudence and moral virtues may be acquired or infused. Faith, hope, and charity are infused theological virtues. *See* Charity, Faith, Habit, Hope, Moral Virtues, Principle, Prudence, Science (Aristotelian).

Will: *the intellectual (rational) human appetite; the intellectual faculty of desire.* The will necessarily desires the ultimate human perfection, namely, happiness, but freely desires particular goods, since the latter are only partially good. *See* Appetite, Happiness, Power.

Bibliography

For a comprehensive bibliography on the works of Aquinas and commentaries on his life and thought, see Brian Davies, *Aquinas* (London: Continuum, 2002), pp. xi–xxii. Among more recent books, the following are noteworthy:

Thomas Aquinas, *The Cardinal Virtues*, translated and edited by Richard J. Regan (Indianapolis: Hackett Publishing Company, 2005).

———, *A Summary of Philosophy*, translated and edited by Richard J. Regan (Indianapolis: Hackett Publishing Company, 2003).

Etienne Gilson, *Thomism: The Philosophy of Thomas Aquinas*, 6th final and substantially revised edition (Toronto: Pontifical Institute of Medieval Studies, 2002).

Fergus Kerr, editor, *Contemplating Aquinas* (London: SCM Press, 2003).

Herbert McCabe, *Aquinas* (London: Continuum, 2005).

Rik van Nieuwenhove and Joseph Wawrykow, editors, *The Theology of Thomas Aquinas* (Notre Dame: University of Notre Dame, 2005).

The SCM Press A to Z of Thomas Aquinas (London: SCM Press, 2005).

Eleanore Stump, *Aquinas* (London: Routledge, 2003).

Rudi A. te Velde, *Aquinas on God* (Aldershot, England: Ashgate, 2007).

Index of Persons

General Index

CPSIA information can be obtained
at www.ICGtesting.com
Printed in the USA
BVHW042240150922
646942BV00003B/6

9 780195 385311